FILL ALL THINGS:

The Dynamics of Spirituality in the Parish Church

by
Robert A. Gallagher

Parishes —
"United in love
and forming people
for 'real' life."

Robert Gallagher

ASCENSION PRESS
The Episcopal Resource Center
P.O. Box 1190
Fayetteville, AR 72702

ISBN 0-9820-3950-2

Fill All Things:
The Dynamics of Spirituality in the Parish Church

The Core Frameworks of Parish Life

Robert A. Gallagher
Ascension Press, 2008

Forewords

I asked two friends to write forewords. My thought was that each would bring a unique perspective to the task. Scott Benhase is the Rector of Saint Alban's, Washington, D.C. Scott and I have been members of the Order of the Ascension together for over twenty years. He brings a rich and deep experience in urban parish ministry. Michelle Heyne is the chief compliance officer for a Seattle-based company. She has served as treasurer and on the vestry at Saint Paul's Church, Seattle, and is currently a member of Trinity Parish, Seattle. She has co-authored a short paper with me on aligning the role of a vestry with the needs and realities of parish churches.

From Scott Benhase

Bob Gallagher's gifts have benefited the church's mission and ministry for nearly four decades. With *Fill All Things: The Dynamics of Spirituality in the Parish Church*, Bob has brought to bear his many gifts for understanding the comprehensiveness and complexity of parish life. This is a work that is long overdue in the church. I believe it was Woody Allen who said that "Ninety percent of life is just showing up." Well, ninety percent of parish leadership is having a clear understanding of the dynamics of parish life; to know how change occurs in organizations like the church, and how leaders function effectively and faithfully in the real world of the parish.

In these pages, Bob offers no cheap prescriptions for developing a vital, healthy parish life. He promotes no programs that will magically transform the church's mission and ministry. There are no quick fix remedies contained herein. There are no gimmicks found in this book that one can insert into the parish's life to make all things well. The church is awash in such prescriptions and programs and, while they may do some good in a particular context, they are disastrous in others because they do not take into account the complex dynamics of human community in the life of the church. What Bob offers in this book is a descriptive lens through which church leaders can begin to comprehend how parish communities function in healthy and unhealthy ways. The core frameworks presented here will help the reader analyze and understand church communities function, not in theory, but in real life practice. That alone is worth a lot for church leaders.

But other works have done similar, excellent analysis and have offered cogent ways of understanding the dynamics of parish life. What differentiates this book from others is that it provides not just analysis and comprehension, but frameworks, models, and real world examples that will help church leaders move a parish community toward healthy patterns, habits, and standards in their common life and mission. It is one thing to know how a parish community really functions. It is quite another thing entirely to know how to help that same parish community get unstuck and move forward toward transformation.

Along with Bob and other members of the Order of the Ascension, I have used and applied the core frameworks and the other assessment and reflection tools in this book. I can attest to how helpful they have been for me and the clergy and lay leaders with whom I have served. For example, I have used the Renewal-Apostolate Cycle in every adult catechesis class I have led in the last twenty years. That framework helps participants understand their need to live into the fullness of the baptismal life through both their inward and outward journey. I have watched participants nod their heads and maybe for the first time see how their whole life in Christ comes together as individuals in the fellowship of the church community. I have also used the same framework with vestries as a way for us to analyze whether or not we were corporately paying attention to the essentials of our common life.

All church leaders will keep this volume within reach on their bookshelf. They will find that long after they have read it through, they will reach for it often and use it as an effective lens to understand and respond to the complex dynamics of parish life.

From Michelle Heyne

Fill All Things: The Dynamics of Spirituality in the Parish Church is a book structured around a set of frameworks through which to approach church development issues. Because I naturally avoid formal models and techniques, I was perhaps less than eager to delve into it. In both my professional life and my lay leadership positions my tendency is to figure things out on the fly and assume that everything will work out, whether through talent, toil, or the mysteries of the Holy Spirit. This springs from an appreciation of complexity and a comfort with things being open-ended. Unfortunately, it also may lead to my being bogged down, working too hard on things I can't control, and sometimes driving other people crazy with my independence and desire for spontaneity.

This book invited me to consider parish life and my vocation as a Christian in a structured, systematic way. It helped me see the rich interaction of the parish community as something to be carefully considered and nurtured through leadership that values the whole in all its intricacy but does not allow the central mission of the Church to be subsumed by ego, busy-ness, or factions. Perhaps most important, it underscored the importance of a knowledgeable and committed laity, a laity that understands its critical and active role in the Body of Christ and does not see itself as a spectator in someone else's version of God's drama.

This book combines a deep appreciation for parish life in all its myriad unfoldings, along with a practical approach about how to actually deal with that life and make it better. And through it all, Bob keeps his focus on the Holy One and on the supernatural and quotidian impact of the sacraments. It is a tall order to care about both the holiness of the Church and the real-life interaction of sinners. It is a tall order to talk about Glory and "frameworks" in the same paragraph. Ultimately, though, this book helps us see the futility of dividing these matters. It is a truly useful and illuminating response to incarnational life and I hope it will be used widely by all manner of Christians, lay and ordained alike.

Preface

Even as an undergrad I had this strange way of coming at writing assignments. I'd do my research, explore ideas with others, make notes for myself, incorporate what I was thinking and learning into various programs – and having done all that, having thoroughly enjoyed all the thinking and exchange – I was done. Writing it out for someone else to read and grade seemed like an odd thing to do.

This is a book I've wanted to complete. I've wanted to complete it for at least 20 years. Other projects always seemed more pressing. My friends in the Order of the Ascension (OA) have been asking me to finish this book since the mid 1990s. They have gently stayed on my case all this time and I appreciate the support.

The four models in this book were developed out of my own struggle to understand and put words to the distinctive dynamics and issues I saw in parish life. The organization development (OD) training I had received helped me become more sensitive to the forces at play in any organization and to appreciate the value of theory and models in efforts to improve organizational life and productivity. But the more I came to understand the concept of organizational culture, the more I longed for ways to express the organic spiritual processes of Episcopal parishes. The standard OD models and methods were very useful in understanding and responding to much that went on in the parishes with which I was working. But they didn't get at the unique and interesting dynamics and purpose of the parish.

My writing process has been partly an introvert's going within and expressing what I had seen and come to know as Christ's way with his Body the Church. It has also been a dialogue and exchange with many others, for example – the pastoral theology of Martin Thornton, the organization development work of Edgar Schein, Margaret Wheatley and Chris Argyris, the learning process of participants in 30 years of congregational development training programs, especially the participants in the Church Development Institute and the many parish and organizational leaders I have worked with as a consultant.

A number of people have given their time and skills in reading, editing and offering advice. Special thanks to Rebecca DeBow and Michelle Heyne. I also want to thank my friends in the Order of the Ascension. For 25 years we have gathered each year for a week of retreat and mutual spiritual guidance in our role as leaders and consultants to parish churches. The thoughtfulness and competence of those conversations has stimulated my imagination, kept me focused vocationally, and supported me personally. The yearly OA gathering has contributed to this piece of work by the expectation that I would finally get to it and in the rich, honest reflections about the parishes we were serving.

Introduction

Images and Frameworks

Parish leaders all face the issue of how to give their attention, time and energy in ways that truly serve the well being of the parish. They all carry mental images, usually unconscious, that help them do that. Some may think about the parish as though it is some form of social service agency. They are likely to evaluate the parish based on what it does in ministries to help those in need. Others may complain that the parish needs to be "run more like a business." They may look for signs of what they understand to be a business culture, possibly efficiency or effectiveness or productivity. Other images that people may hold include: club, social change movement, historical society, and mental health clinic.

We all carry around these ideas about what the parish exists to accomplish and how it is to go about accomplishing it. We are usually not completely clear about this. We may vaguely hold several conflicting ideas at the same time. For some of us it's not so much an idea we have as a feeling we seek. Some look for friendliness and warmth, others for quietness and piety, and some for bold affirmations of faith. I've heard people judge parishes based on how often people say "Jesus" or use the word "diversity." All this influences how leaders use their time and energy. They are all rooted in mental frameworks we have that give order and meaning to what we are experiencing. The process is inevitable and necessary. It can also illuminate or distort our understanding of the identity, primary task, and activities of parish churches.

See Resource section: "The Church: Analogies & Images"

The four frameworks offered in this book have been used by thousands of Episcopal Church parish leaders and consultants to better understand and address some of the central dynamics of parish life. I've seen them used by parish vestries, support groups of clergy, and diocesan leaders. I've also read hundreds of congregational development project reports that made use of the frameworks, along with other organization development resources, to design and implement interventions that have made a positive difference in many parishes.

The Christian Life Model was developed in the mid 1970s and used in a variety of training programs for leaders and consultants. In 1983 I wrote about the model in *Power from on High*. The other three frameworks were "in process" from the early 1980s and by 1986 were being used in the Church Development Institute as "core" models to help participants better see some of the unique dynamics and issues of Episcopal parishes. I and others have also used the models, with appropriate modification, with people in other religious traditions and leaders of non-profit organizations. In the 1980s, when teaching in Hartford Seminary's D. Min program I used them with groups of clergy from many denominations. Students were invited to create their own models that fit the tradition they came from. In all cases the central dynamics were affirmed while language and theological assumptions would be modified to fit the person's heritage and denominational culture.

From 1990 to 2006 two-thirds of my clients were non-profit organizations (NPOs) engaged in affordable housing, domestic abuse, education, and social services. The models that I used with parishes also were helping me serve these NPOs. An example was what I came to see about the

Benedictine Promise. The Benedictine Promise was a model (stability, conversion of life, and obedience) that I found working in the back of my head with these secular organizations. I didn't use Benedict's language in communicating with those clients but I did use his wisdom.

The polarity of organizational stability and organizational change is a standard understanding in organization development work. All systems need to find a way to manage that polarity and many executive directors see that as a major part of their role. What the Benedictine Promise added to the conversation was "obedience." For my NPO clients I translated that into organizational listening. Many NPO leaders found this extremely helpful as a way of conceptualizing their work. There was simply more reality and more richness to the idea that what they were doing was managing the dynamics among three elements: stability, change and listening. Some experienced a significant improvement in their management when they found that focusing attention on creating process, structures and a climate for listening helped in managing the change/stability polarity.

About Models

Four frameworks are presented in the book: The Renewal – Apostolate Cycle; the Christian Life Model; The Benedictine Promise; and the Shape of the Parish. These frameworks are offered so leaders can see more clearly what is happening in the deeper and more hidden places of parish life and act to improve that life. The frameworks are models. In this context a model is a simplified version of something more complex. In efforts to transform and improve organizations they are used to see and explore both the obvious and the more hidden aspects of a parish. We use them to do analysis, explore relationships, and as a starting place in solving problems, developing capacities, and shaping the future life of the organization.

Conceptual models simplify the complex dynamics and forces present in a situation, and at the same time, help us perceive more complexity than we usually notice.

Models are limited. They focus our attention on some elements of a situation. There is no one model that will serve all situations. Therefore, one of the competencies of a congregational development practitioner is the ability to select which model or models will best help us understand and intervene in a specific situation.

Models are like a map, "a great help on the journey, yet not the same as the journey itself. The journey is full of smells and sights, of wonder and awe, of fear and excitement; the map is only lines on a paper. Still, maps help us move forward on a purposeful journey." (From *Power from on High*, Ascension Press, 1983)

Many models, including the four in this book, overlap with one another. They bleed into and can inform one another. As we use them to look at a particular parish we may find ourselves starting with one model and gradually drifting to some element of another.

How about the models in this book? Do they work?

Almost all organizational models will tell you something about an organization. They all "work" to some extent. The trick is for leaders or consultants to select a model that will illuminate the particular situation in front of them.

That means that we, leaders and consultants, do the work. Parish leaders, consultants, and diocesan officials are always engaged in the process of maintaining and advancing the health and faithfulness of parishes. We all have mental models that guide us in that work. If the models are used by people with some level of leadership skill, and adequate emotional and spiritual maturity, then there's a good chance that the models will help them in the process of understanding the parish's dynamics and planning action to improve things.

Of course, some models are in themselves more useful than others. What I look for in a model is whether it:

- Is easy enough to recall. If I can't reconstruct the elements in my head then it's not likely to come to me when I need it. Models with many elements may be useful if there is some integrating thread I can use in recalling the model. Otherwise, models with too many pieces are often useless.
- Has a mix of complexity and simplicity. It offers me a starting place into the complexity of some dynamic in the parish system. In itself the model is easy enough to understand and the more I work with it the more it helps me in seeing what is happening in the situation.

Parish leaders have used the models in this book over the past 25 years. Overwhelmingly people have reported that they have found them extremely helpful. The responses I've heard have affirmed the usability of the frameworks in terms of the criteria I noted above. People have also reported that they value the way in which these models point to possibilities and spiritual dynamics unique to a parish community. So, I know they have "worked" for some people.

Will they help you?

A way to decide on their usefulness for you is to use them and assess your experience. Use the models in trying to understand your own parish. Be curious and wonder aloud. Draw each model on a pad of paper and then make notes about how each element is expressed in your parish. Allow your mind to wander and notice where you go. Use the models to explore the ways in which the parish church is a "wonderful and sacred mystery."

The Parish Church

The parish church is a "wonderful and sacred mystery." Now that's coming from someone who has been part of Episcopal parishes for 63 years, who has been the vicar of parishes, consulted with hundreds of them, and worked with thousands of parish leaders. I've seen the pettiness, the fear, the bickering and the abuse. In fact I've participated in all of it at one time or another. For me the parish church is still a "wonderful and sacred mystery."

We can use the behavioral sciences to better understand the workings of the parish church. The work of Peter Serge on organizational learning, Edgar Schein on organizational culture, and Ed Friedman on self-differentiation and triangulation, all applies to our work with parishes. But there's more.

In the day-by-day life of most parishes people are loved and learn to love. They are nurtured in hope. They are accepted as they are and offered a glimpse of themselves in glory. In the messy and sometimes difficult interactions and exchanges of being in community, people are offered their true selves; again and again we are offered real life. That's what I've seen and experienced.

Here's the faith part: This all happens because of the real presence of Christ in the Eucharistic community; this strange society in which we encounter the presence of Christ in the Blessed Sacrament and in one another. The parish is a microcosm of the larger church. It shares in the nature and mission of the whole church. It's not just that the church in some eternal and larger sense is one, holy, catholic and apostolic; the parish is also one, holy, catholic and apostolic. It is the Body of Christ. It is the People of God. And it has as its mission "to restore all people to unity with God and each other in Christ."

Parish & Congregation

In this book I'll frequently use "parish" and "congregation" in an interchangeable manner. This is primarily as an acknowledgment of what has become common usage in parts of the Episcopal Church. "Parish," though, is the better word. It's part of our tradition. It also suggests the mix of congregation(s), institutional life, and relationship with a geography or community of interest beyond itself. Most Episcopal parishes have at least two very distinct congregations with different spiritualities; we call them the 8:00 and 10:00 services.

Note: To those who get obsessed with things like categories of churches in the diocesan canons (parishes, aided parishes, missions, congregations), the solution is to simply call them all parishes. Deal with the differences by mission strategy agreements as fits each case. Dioceses need the authority to intervene if a parish is unable to adequately maintain its life because of conflict, lack of imagination or energy, or insufficient income.

Mission

My assumption is that every parish church starts with the same mission. The Prayer Book puts it this way: "The mission of the church is to restore all people to unity with God and each other in Christ." So, the mission of my parish is to join in God's work of restoring people to unity; especially to do that within its own life and in the communities it engages. There is no need to write something called a "mission statement." It actually may help us get the right orientation for ministry if we see the mission as something we receive and participate in rather than make up in a committee.

The mission of holy unity is carried within the life and ministry of the parish, in its worship, study, and action, in the social life of the community and in all the work done around spiritual growth. It also helps if the leadership and a critical mass of members consciously and intentionally carry the mission in themselves, their life and work. The organic life of the Body will carry that mission forward even if the people of a congregation are unaware. But it allows for a partnership and fuller life when there is some degree of awareness. I think that's why some leaders try to engage parishes in creating a mission statement. They hope that the process will internalize the mission; that it will help place the mission onto their hearts and minds. There may also be a hope that the process will increase a sense of ownership and therefore commitment to the mission. There's some truth to that—involvement in the creation process is part of what increases ownership. Two problems with it are 1) seeing mission as something we create can also undercut people's engagement with and understanding of the church's mission; and 2) a parish's sense of direction is either there or not there; most parishes with mission statements still lack any real direction. Many without statements are clear about who they are, where they are going, and what they are doing.

Ways of approaching this that may help are:

1. Assume that the parish already has a mission and is to some extent living that mission.
2. Concentrate on shaping a healthy parish culture with great liturgy, a strong social life, and an effective adult formation strategy. This hard and long-term work creates a mission-focused parish by its being and doing, by its identity, integrity and direction, rather than by statements or plans. If you have a plan but do not have the stuff of mission in the very ways of the parish, there is the danger that you will live an illusion.
3. Teach the church's mission in a manner that internalizes it in people's awareness and living. Make the Prayer Book's statement the starting place for the parish's understanding of its purpose. Have people memorize it. Repeat it frequently. Also, work with people in educational settings in ways that help them connect the words to the day-by-day substance of their lives. Help them explore how God's work of Holy Unity touches and is expressed in their lives.
4. If you want a mission statement that has the fingerprints of members on it try a process that makes the Prayer Book's statement a "given." Make that the first sentence of your statement. Then have people identify the particular emphasis and character by which this parish lives that mission in its life and in its world. That may turn the process into a truly strategic exercise that will help guide the parish's use of resources.

Having said all the above I want to add a caution about how the church has decided to express the mission. I wonder if it is based in an excessive concern for harmony; whether it ends up having unforeseen consequences such as conflict avoidance, excessive homogenization in parish life, and the punishment of differences. Have we taken what is a polarity and suppressed one of the poles? Of course, it's not that the catechism definition of mission caused these things. Rather it's that we drafted the statement out of a culture that doesn't handle power and conflict well, that doesn't understand that trust is something to develop and not just something to notice in its absence, and that God's will is about both individual growth and community life.

John Macquarrie wrote, "…our belief is that the whole process only makes sense in so far as, in the risk and the struggle of creation, that which *is* is advancing into fuller potentialities of being and is overcoming the forces that tend toward dissolution; and that continually a richer and more fully diversified unity is built up. …The end, we have seen reason to believe, would be a commonwealth of free, responsible beings united in love; and this great end is possible only if finite existents are preserved in some kind of individual identity. Here again, we may emphasize that the highest love is not the drive toward union, but rather letting-be."

Primary Task

Now I want to use a term from organization development – "primary task." The primary task is the most important and essential process an organization uses in fulfilling its mission. For example, for years Loren Mead and others have been proposing that the primary task of a diocese is congregational development. I think that's correct. I think the diocese also has at least two important secondary tasks: 1) engaging the society and culture of the geographic region that makes up the diocese, including issues of justice, compassion and evangelization that are regional in nature; and 2) participation in the wider church by its connection with other dioceses, the national church, the Anglican Communion and ecumenical bodies.

A diocese may do many worthwhile things, but it has failed if it doesn't nurture the health and faithfulness of its parishes.

Being clear about the organization's primary task is essential if we are to focus resources in the service of mission. Some people in the business community talk about "stacking resources toward success." That has to do with placing your human, material and financial resources in service of the primary things you are trying to accomplish. Primary task clarity allows us to stack our resources.

What is the primary thing that a parish church does toward fulfilling the mission? What is it that a parish is especially suited for, organically created for? My view is that the parish church's primary task is the renewal of baptismal identity and purpose in those related to the parish. The baptismal and Eucharistic community is about Glory, giving glory to God in liturgy and in human lives that are "real lives," fully alive lives. The parish is a community and a place in which people share in the Glory of God. All of which is to say that the primary task of a parish is worship – it is adoration, reverence, devotion, and love.

The primary process is what I'm describing as the Renewal – Apostolate Cycle, the first model in this book. In Eucharist and Office, in equipping and education, in the routine exchanges of parish life, the task is to renew people in their baptismal identity and purpose, so that they have "real lives," so that they worship in all that they are and do. A parish may also have a number of secondary tasks. They could be seen as parallel tasks to those of a diocese (being part of something larger than itself and engagement and ministry with a community or communities outside itself).

Questions: Practice and Theory

If the mission and the primary task are in some sense "given," then what else is needed as the parish establishes its own way of being and doing? What else is needed to provide direction and focus to energies and resources?

I believe it's useful to begin with questions that center our attention on a few significant areas of work. For example:

1. What three things will we do this year to improve how we manage the routine business of parish life?
2. What three things will we do this year to improve how we form people, offer ourselves in worship, incorporate new members, or live together as a community?
3. Given our current circumstances, what will make the most difference if we pay attention to it now?

It can even be more useful when we root that practical starting place in a broader model. The next step is both discernment and action planning. For example:

- What three things can we do this year to enhance the way this parish helps people in the Renewal – Apostolate Cycle?
- In what area of the Christian Life are we strongest (worship- - doctrine – action)? How might we develop that further, build upon it, grow in it?
- Where in our life together can we be more stable? What needs to change, be done differently? How might we better listen to one another? Who do we need to listen to that we have failed to listen to?

I'd urge parishes to stay with these practical and more immediate questions instead of spending time creating mission statements. The process of developing mission statements can serve as a learning tool. It can be a way of having people look at what the church, especially this parish, exists for. It's the kind of discussion that for many people would be too abstract if they weren't going to produce something (in this case the statement). The problem is that we usually end up with a very broad statement that mirrors what's in the Prayer Book catechism (as it should) and isn't specific enough to be used in focusing resources. It also takes up all the time and energy people are usually willing to give to such thinking. Mission statement processes are often just a poor stewardship of our time together.

Concentrate on the practical and immediate needs and possibilities. To the extent a parish is already a healthy, apostolic community, it will arrive at faithful answers. To the extent the parish is less than healthy and apostolic, the activity of creating a mission statement is not likely to have much impact on that condition.

Mission, Primary Task, Ways of Being and Doing

In summary, it may be useful for a parish to see a distinction among, and the interdependence of, three elements: 1) mission, 2) primary task, and 3) the ways of being and doing that take shape in parish culture and direction. The mission is "given" and is the whole church's participation in God's mission to restore all things to unity. Most parishes carry out that mission in relationship to their members and the extended community that the members, or the parish as a community, touch in daily life. The primary task is the parish's participation in people's movement between renewal in baptismal identity and purpose and apostolic living in daily life. A parish's sacramental and social life is the foundation for that cycle. It is the unique way in which a parish enters into and expresses the church's mission.

The most important and basic way in which parishes incarnate the mission and primary task is in the parish's culture. In organization development language, culture is the mix of "ways of doing and being," espoused values, and deeper underlying assumptions about why things work as they do in life and about the nature of things about God, humanity, the church, and so on. Culture includes all the practices of liturgy, community life and decision-making. It also includes formal and informal statements the parish draws upon to say what it cares about, what it values.

At the deepest level of organizational culture is the parish's grounding in the assumptions of orthodox faith and practice. This isn't dealt with by bold proclamations of orthodoxy (beware of such parishes). These deeper assumptions are shaped by, and expressed in, the parish's ways of liturgy, social exchange, and apostolic practice – is the parish known as a community of prayer, mutual listening and love, hospitality and compassion; in this community do men and women grow in Christ?

Congregational Development

Congregational development as a field of study and category of strategic action emerged in the late 1960s and early 1970s. The major contributor to its appearance was the work of Loren Mead and Project Test Pattern (PTP), which later developed into the Alban Institute. PTP was an initiative of the national church generally concerned with evangelization but more specifically with how to best revitalize parishes. What Loren Mead quickly discovered was that the emerging discipline of organization development had application to church systems. PTP's work builds on what the church had been doing since the 1950s in the field of group dynamics and experiential education. The Episcopal Church was among the first religious organizations to involve itself in the learning and application about groups and organizations happening in universities, the military, and other organizations.

In the 1970s and early 80s there were large ecumenical training programs that equipped church leaders and consultants in "organization development in religious systems." The training often involved a minimum of three years, 300 hours of experiential workshop training, reading in the field, application projects, work with mentors, and a supervised internship. Today that approach continues in the work of the Church Development Institute (CDI).

The Church Development Institute created a training program that includes organization development but has integrated ecclesiology, pastoral theology, and ascetical theology. In recent years CDI has reintegrated in its training more experiential work that helps participants in the "use of self" and group dynamics and development. CDI now offers the most complete program available in congregational development.

Three interrelated streams of thought have emerged about how to define congregational development.

For some it is about starting new parish churches. That may involve special training or not. If there is any training it may focus on a short-term, entrepreneurial approach to development or it may include consideration of longer-term development dynamics and how to start the new parish with clarity about the primary task of formation.

Others seem to think of congregational development primarily as a division of work that includes anything related to revitalizing congregations or starting new parishes. In such cases people may have been appointed as diocesan congregational development officers with little or no training in the field.

The approach I'm taking in this book is to understand parish development (or congregational development) in a manner consistent with its roots. In that sense it is a field of competency with trained practitioners who serve the church in many roles. The level of competency may range from graduate level work with CDI or a university program in organization development, to having done a few days of workshops with a national or diocesan program office.

As an approach and discipline, congregational development has something to offer just about all aspects of parish and diocesan life. Everything that impacts the parish's health and its ability to form people in Christ is related to the field – the recruiting and training of lay and clergy leadership, ways of encouraging and supporting parish leaders, how we begin new parishes, issues of the parish's financial health, and so on.

So, a search process is understood as a major intervention in a parish's life, and the methods used to carry out the search require considerable skill on the part of consultants. This isn't a place to be running volunteers through a few days of training, handing them a manual, and dropping them into a parish's life.

Another example would be using competencies of congregational development in beginning a new parish. Leaders might be helped by the field's knowledge about creating healthy organizational cultures from the beginning and its understanding of the management of narcissism in entrepreneurial work. Connecting congregational development with new start-ups might point to the need for explicit agreements about denominational loyalty and the need in the earliest stages to integrate spiritual life and growth alongside the emphases on growth in numbers.

A Short Definition of Parish Development

Parish development is an effort to increase a parish's ability to improve its:

- Health as a community and organization
- Capacity to be productive in its primary task of worship and formation
- Ability to both define itself in relation to its heritage and to adapt to new challenges and opportunities that emerge in the church and society
- Strategic, problem-solving and renewal process

By making use of the theory and methods of pastoral and ascetical theology and of applied behavioral science, usually with the assistance of a leader or consultant trained in the field, and carried out in as collaborative and inclusive a manner as possible given the parish's current capacities and requirements.

A Longer Definition of Parish Development

- The development of the parish as a community of faith with a unique identity, purpose and dynamics.
- The development of the parish as an organization that can be understood, assessed, and improved using the knowledge and methods of pastoral and ascetical theology and organization behavior and development.

The goals of congregational development include:

A. Developing the community of faith by enabling a pattern and culture of congregational life that is:

- Rooted in our tradition
- Adapted to the local context
- Appropriate for the particular group(s) of people drawn to the congregation
- Reflective of the unity, holiness, catholicity and apostolicity of the Church.

And that:

1. Renews people in their baptismal identity and purpose and sends them, in Christ, for an apostolate in family, with friends, in work, civic life and church.
2. Nurtures the Christian life of people at all phases of maturity; gives special attention to guiding and equipping those of Apostolic Faith; encourages all toward a more prayerful, disciplined, and compassionate Christian life.
3. Fosters a strong life and ministry of worship, doctrine, action and oversight.
4. Enables people to seek the presence of Jesus Christ in the people, things and circumstances of life, through stability, conversion of life and obedience.

B. Developing the congregation as an organization that:

1. Has established structures, processes and a climate that allow it to effectively manage its important and pressing business (e.g., projects, problems, crises, etc.) while giving adequate attention to strategic issues (e.g., long-term development and renewal, people development, planning and envisioning, relationship building, engaging new opportunities, crisis prevention)
2. Has increased its ability to adapt to new conditions, solve problems and learn from experience.
3. Has an increased ability to engage formation issues such as:
   - A vision that is sacramentally actualized in the parish's culture. That vision includes the defining of identity, purpose, values, organizational culture and related programs and activities
   - Attracting new people (as staff and/or members) who join in living within a healthy culture.
   - Increased competence and commitment in liturgy, spiritual life and discipline, and emotional intelligence.
   - Creating an alignment, an adequate "fit," among the various aspects of the organization's life such as income/expenses, space/program needs and possibilities, vision/resources of leadership, energy and money
   - Establishing relationships with external "public" or constituencies that have a stake in the organization.

The Layout of the Book

There are four main sections, one on each of the four core frameworks used in the Church Development Institute. The four frameworks are followed by a section of resources.

Each section includes this basic outline:
1. An exercise – If you complete the exercise before going on you are likely to get more out of your reading[1].
2. A diagram of the framework – This is a one page overview of the framework.
3. An explanation of the framework
4. Notes on other comparable models

There will be some repetition of illustrations, strategies and methods because the models overlap in what they illuminate and suggest.

The Vision

> Hold onto your breath
> Hold onto your heart
> Hold onto your hope
> March up that gate
> And bid it open
> > *Optimistic Voices*, in The Wizard of Oz

Two of my readers suggested that the book would be helped by an early statement of my vision for parish churches. I had two thoughts in response. One was that the vision was scattered here and there throughout the book. The other was that while what I was offering certainly had implications for what a parish could be at its best, it was less about what we could do to accomplish our vision and more about the organic and inherent dynamics present in all parishes. In that sense it is about my perspective on what God does in and through all parishes.

I believe that the parish church is an instrument of God's mission. In and through parishes the process of sanctification takes place. Its existence is a sacramental pathway into real life for many people. Parishes all touch upon a mystery that they have not created, that holds them in love, and takes them along that way of continued growth in love and service.

This process is largely and most powerfully advanced in two aspects of parish life – liturgy and the social life of the parish community. Other things are important; education, pastoral care, and spiritual guidance all play significant roles. The centrality of liturgy and social life seems most apparent to me at Advent and Christmas. It's a time when many parishes reduce their busyness with programs and meetings and our attention turns to spending time with God and each other. It's easy to dismiss what we experience as being mere sentimentality, and I'm sure there's some truth to that. But it's also a focused period of time in which many of us have experienced a taste of real life.

---

[1] The one page overview and exercises are available for purchase as handouts at www.CongregationalDevelopment.com.

Something I learned as a parish priest and as a consultant to religious and secular organizations is that real vision always begins with something already true in the organization. Vision isn't about blue sky dreaming. It's about building upon, expanding, and growing what is already true in the life of the organization. And what is possibly the truest thing about a parish church is that it is a microcosm of the whole church. The mission of the whole church is its mission. The marks of the whole church are its marks—one, holy, catholic, apostolic. The other thing we might say about the ground to build a vision upon is that the parish has unique dynamics that to some extent we can understand. That allows us to engage in activities that work with those dynamics.

My vision for a parish church is grounded in the above definition of congregational development.

A healthy and faithful parish continues to develop its capacity to:

- Renew people in their baptismal identity and purpose and send them, in Christ, for an apostolate with friends and family, at work, in civic life and in the church.
- Foster a strong life and ministry of worship, doctrine, action and oversight.
- Enable people to seek the presence of Jesus Christ in the people, things and circumstances of life, through stability, conversion of life and obedience.
- Nurture the Christian life of people at all phases of maturity; give special attention to guiding and equipping those of apostolic faith; and encourage all toward a more prayerful disciplined and compassionate Christian life.

I. THE RENEWAL - APOSTOLATE CYCLE

The Renewal – Apostolate Cycle: An Exercise

Renewal

1. How are you renewed emotionally and physically?

2. How are you renewed spiritually?

3. What role does participation in the parish play in your renewal? How does it help? In what ways has it hindered?

Apostolate

1. Where is it that you find yourself making a contribution to the welfare of humanity? Where are you aware of being an instrument of God's love?

- In my family
- With friends
- In the work I do
- In my relationship with co-workers
- In volunteer work I do
- In working with a civic group or community organization
- Other?

2. How has being part of the parish helped or hindered this?

Share – If you are reading this with others each might spend a few minutes sharing something in the above responses. A useful norm is to only share what you want to share.

The Renewal – Apostolate Cycle: A Diagram Overview

The Renewal - Apostolate Cycle is a way of describing a central dynamic of Christian life. The Cycle focuses our attention on the Christian's movement between being renewed in baptismal identity and purpose and living as instruments of God's love and grace in daily life. The Cycle is interested in both the individual's movement and in the ways in which the parish church supports and facilitates that movement. This is the primary task of any parish church.

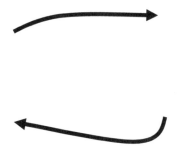

RENEWAL
**Renewal in baptismal
identity and purpose
in worship, study, the
parish's social life, and
being equipped for
Christian action**

APOSTOLATE
**Participation in the work
of Christ in service,
evangelization and
stewardship
In areas of:**
- **Workplace**
- **Family & Friends**
- **Civic Life**
- **Church**

A Cycle

The cycle is between a conscious and intentional attention to God, prayer life, our relationships, Christian formation **and** a subconscious reliance upon God as members of the Body of Christ, in the workplace, family, friendship, civic life and congregational life.

In that Cycle:

We need:	Which is helped by:	Which the parish helps by:
To accept our dependence on God	Openness to spiritual guidance	An emphasis in its life on worship; nothing comes before the Eucharist and Daily Office. Also, more attention to formation and spiritual growth than other programs or ministries.
To accept responsibility for ordering our spiritual life	Establishing a rule of life	Offering programs and guidance in creating, experimenting with, and revising a spiritual discipline.
To accept our interdependence with others in the Church	Life in Christian community, a parish church	Being a healthy and faithful parish church and by helping people relate to the parish community in ways appropriate to their personality and the parish's capacities. Having opportunities for social life and the development of friendships.

The Renewal – Apostolate Cycle: An Exploration

For the real saint is neither a special creation nor a spiritual freak. He is just a human being in whom has been fulfilled the great aspiration of St. Augustine – "My life shall be a real life, being wholly full of Thee." And as that real life, the interior union with God grows, so too does the saints' self-identification with humanity grow. They do not stand aside wrapped in delightful prayers and feeling pure and agreeable to God. They go right down into the mess; and there, right down in the mess, they are able to radiate God because they possess Him. – Evelyn Underhill in *Concerning the Inner Life*

The Renewal-Apostolate Cycle is a way of describing the Christian's movement between being formed in Christ and the apostolate of daily life. It is also a way of describing the work of the parish church.

In Renewal

In renewal we intentionally engage in disciplines and patterns of behavior that ground us more deeply in our identity and purpose as baptized members of the church. We grow up into Christ -- by living with others in a parish community that is healthy and faithful; by worship and prayer; and by learning so we might have increased self awareness and responsibility. It is the process of becoming light, salt, leaven; of developing "an inquiring and discerning heart;" and of becoming what Evelyn Underhill calls "instruments of love."

I've worked with hundreds of parishes over the years in a variety of roles – parish priest, diocesan staff, and as a consultant. In the course of that work I've interviewed and surveyed thousands of people as individuals and in groups.

In the interview process used by CDI participants, and in some parishes, when people are asked about how they are emotionally and physically renewed they talk about things like exercise, music, rest, sexual intimacy, being with friends, being hugged, walking city streets or country roads, having a pet, and dancing. When they are asked about what contributes to their renewal as baptismal people they speak of a priest's spiritual guidance, educational programs, the beauty of the worship space, a parish climate in which they don't have to always meet the expectations of others, being part of a special support group, intercessory prayer groups, a discipline of daily prayer and spiritual reading, helping and serving others, and being exposed to other people's spirituality.

The activity that has most frequently been mentioned as renewing baptismal life is the Sunday Eucharist, the gathering of the community to be reconstituted in what it already is. It's the week-by-week coming together of the community, in Eucharist and coffee hour, in which the eucharistic community engages itself. That's what people return to when describing the mystery of how they are renewed in the Christian life. They talk about being with people they love and who love them; how the ritual is always there; old and new friendships within the parish; a breakfast group after the early Mass; and how the Sunday gathering of the Eucharistic community brings them in contact with people of different temperaments, views, ages, sexual orientations, expressions of intelligence, economic well-being, and on occasion people of other races. They speak of hymns and personalities, of beauty and grace, of ancient things that are also contemporary, and about the odd way in which it all seeps in and changes them.

When asked, some see a relationship between their emotional and physical renewal and the renewal of their baptismal identity and purpose. Some make no distinction, seeing them as one thing; others see physical/emotional renewal as a base for the other; and still others express it as a kind of fabric into which baptismal renewal and physical/emotional renewal are woven together in the fabric of their life.

In working out an approach to our own renewal we will want to take into account the realities of our personality, the options available in the tradition, and consultation with other Christians. We may find some way of thinking about it that seems especially useful. Graham Greene saw three ways for people to be open to spirituality: we need moments of solitude, the ability to suffer with another, and the ability to pay attention to the restlessness of our soul. The Benedictine tradition sees a dynamic engagement among obedience, conversion of life and stability. Henri Nouwen, in *Reaching Out*, offers a dynamic among the three poles of loneliness and solitude; hostility and hospitality; and illusion and prayer.

In Apostolate

In our apostolate we join Christ in the transformation of the world. The starting point is the place we are with family and friends, in our workplace, in civic life, and as we participate in the church's oversight and collective apostolate.

Most of us, most of the time, have a primary vocation in the arenas of our daily life. We are instruments of compassion and justice in our workplace, with family and friends, and in civic involvement. This is a process that is largely organic and subconscious. We are light and salt to the extent we have become light and salt. We are invited to love and serve in the places we find ourselves. The process isn't at its core a matter of our planning and awareness; rather it is dependent on our status as people incorporated by baptism into the Body of Christ. It is living as an extension of the sacrament that is the Church in which God's compassion and justice is offered through us in the routine and ordinary places of life.

In addition to this primary, organic, apostolic vocation, some of us may have a vocation that involves participation in the church's collective work. So, we may serve on the vestry, become a catechist, assist in the Eucharist, clean the bathrooms, or participate in the parish's service ministries or its evangelistic program.

Many people experience within their apostolic activity a type of renewal. It's as though there is an interior movement that in the midst of action brings a sense of calmness, of peace and deep joy. It's more than satisfaction in doing the work well. It's a form of recollection, an awareness of the presence of God, a sharing in the Divine Life. This comes as a gift. It's grounded in a person's baptism and nurtured by the habits of prayer and reflection. These moments are times of both renewal and apostolate.

Some find the idea of apostolic living and witness confusing and at times distasteful. They may have picked up the idea that being a servant, evangelist and steward in daily life is an overtly religious activity. It's almost as though for it to "count" others need to understand that you are a Christian and that you do these things because you are a Christian. There's a kind of "in your face" quality to it. Many experience that way of thinking as aggressive and intrusive. For most Episcopalians such behavior is offensive.

There are two ways of thinking about this that I've found useful. The first, as I noted above, is that usually the process is organic and unseen – to the extent that in the working of grace upon us, we have become salt and light, we will simply be salt and light in the relationships and situations of our daily life. Second, in those cases where there is a more intentional and conscious expression of faith we may find it useful to recall that part of the apostolic life is to be concerned about the dignity of others. A certain apostolic humility is called for.

Using the Cycle in Congregational Development

The model is used in two ways:

1. By individuals in reflecting on, and shaping, a pattern of spirituality.

Many of us have had the experience of participating in a group exercise in which you draw and share your spiritual lifeline. Each person draws a line that represents their relationship with God and the church from birth to the present. Then each is invited to share their line, and in doing that, to tell the group of their experience with God and the church. On occasion we are asked to reflect on the exercise and say what we have learned or taken away from it. In stating what has been learned a common theme is often how God has worked with each person in different ways.

That's not a new insight for most people at the intellectual level but it is often new at the operational level. We know in our heads that the journey is different for different people. At the same time we may hold onto a formula about how it happens, or should happen, or we vaguely assume that our own way into faith is that of others.

The various ways of God's movement in our lives is also seen in how people live the Renewal – Apostolate Cycle. Each person will have a unique way of living in the Cycle. Some have an inclination toward renewal, others to apostolic action; some are nurtured more by contemplation, others in the Eucharist; many are called to an apostolate in the family, others in civic life. People have different starting places. We are inclined to distinct ways of being fed for the journey. We express the faith that is in us in a variety of ways. So, each will have his or her own way of living this rhythm. How God works with me on the journey may be very different from how God works with my friend. The practices and disciplines of the Christian life that feed one may not feed another.

Over time, and in relationship with the parish community, most people also come to share in the common patterns of Christian life. As they mature, the desire for a balanced spiritual discipline may become stronger. And in God's mysterious way with us we may find ourselves becoming both more unique and more connected with others. Is that part of what Augustine meant by having a "real life"?

In every congregation there are people with a vocation to serve the church as a community of faith. They serve on the vestry and parish committees, they organize service projects and attend to the incorporation of new members. But most members have another calling. Their lives, and therefore their ministry, are more about family and friendships, the work they do, or their participation in civic life.

People also have levels of competence in managing the rhythm of the Cycle. Some easily accept adult responsibility for their spiritual life; others are inclined to an immature dependency. Some carry images of the church and its mission that are distorted and will in turn distort the parish's life and action. The distortion may arise because they transfer inapt ways of thinking and acting from businesses or social service agencies or political movements onto the parish church. It also comes from having taken some true, but narrow expression on the mission, and made it the whole thing. So, some speak of the Great Commission and quote Matthew, others look to the command to love, and still others to the call to proclaim release to captives and liberty to the oppressed. Each is a true and partial expression of the mission, not a statement of the whole mission.

2. The cycle can also be used by parish leaders in exploring and improving the parish's ministry of formation.

The parish offers a common life. The quality of that life and its capacity to transform individual lives varies widely among parishes. Dietrich Bonhoeffer was struck by how even the most miserable of parish churches could produce faithful Christians. I've often taken comfort in his insight as I've consulted with some parishes. The Episcopal Church also has parishes that are marked by the ability to competently nurture people, as they are, with whatever spiritual maturity they currently possess, while at the same time inviting them into a deeper and richer life.

Each parish has its way of being and doing. It's this parish culture that often has the most significant formative impact on people. An environment is created that influences and changes people. That cultural environment includes the parish's collective behavior, its stated values and its deeper, often unconscious or unarticulated, assumptions about matters like leadership, participation, influence, inclusion, acceptance, and information flow, along with even larger issues such as the nature and purposes of human beings, God, and the church. The parish's culture may be one of deep prayer and compassionate action; or of responsibility, participation and attention to effectiveness in the formation of members; or anxious and turf-focused; or driven and obsessed by some standard of success; or relatively superficial in the way people relate with one another and God. Whatever its shape that culture becomes the soil that feeds us and the air we breathe.

Because parish culture is so close to us it is something about which most leaders have no awareness. We live in it but aren't aware of it or engaged in thoughtfully shaping it. Using an external consultant with training in organizational culture is one method parishes have to develop "eyes to see" what is usually hidden. There are also experiential training programs available that can help leaders develop an ability to work with organizational culture. A related issue is that in too many places leaders find themselves so caught up in program development and implementation, or in responding to the most difficult members, or in administrative matters around property and finances, that they have little time for truly developmental and formative work. The ability of leaders to get their heads above water is central to a parish's development as a community of formation.

The ability of parish leaders to improve the Renewal–Apostolate Cycle is directly related to:

- Seeing the more hidden aspects of the parish's culture in relationship to the Cycle.
- Giving adequate time and energy to shaping a culture that is more supportive of the Cycle.

There are five broad organizational activities that can help the improvement process:

1. Engage in regular reflection, assessment and discernment about its way of being and doing.
2. Use a trained external consultant to assist with that process
3. Shape the parish so it offers the environment and activities that will best contribute to the formation of its members.
4. Provide a climate that *accepts* people where they are now in their living of the Cycle and *invites* them to go deeper
5. Clear away the barriers and distortions present in its common life that interfere with the Cycle

The parish can provide opportunities for people to assist them to accept responsibility for, and to manage, the Cycle. That might include helping them to:

1. Understand the Renewal – Apostolate Cycle. Many people need a way of articulating the broad pattern in which they participate. The Cycle offers such a model.
2. Take responsibility for how they live in that pattern by shaping a spiritual discipline in a process of reflection, self-disclosure, feedback and spiritual guidance. Reflect on how they live it now and explore ways they might experiment with and more faithfully, effectively and efficiently live the Cycle.
3. Increase their appreciation for the diversity of ways people live the Cycle. By hearing the stories and feelings of others, members may learn that the way they live in the Cycle is but one-way. That may serve them in their own experimentation and make them wiser as they support others.

In the church we are understandably cautious in any discussion about the end result we seek in formation. I think the caution is a mix of our wanting to be very respectful toward one another and of the work of the Holy Spirit; a general tendency, especially among priests, to not be very specific about such things; and a bias against what we see as the tools of business in seeking results and specific outcomes. Yet a parish, and each member, needs ways of talking about what the "new person" in Christ looks like. Discussing the Prayer Book's baptismal covenant has become a popular way of doing that. I find a prayer that follows the covenant even more useful:

> Give them an inquiring and discerning heart, the courage to will
> and to persevere, a spirit to know and to love you, and the gift of
> joy and wonder in all your works.

For me, focusing too much on the baptismal convent language comes close to living by law. I experience the prayer as more graceful. And it works as a form of "measurement." I know it when I see it.

Having two or three ways of describing the kind of person being formed can help a parish offer language that may speak to different people while avoiding a tendency to literalism.

See Resource section: "Renewal: What Kind of Person is Being Formed?"

Apostolate – Being instruments of his love with family and friends, in the workplace, in civic life, and in the church

At the end of the Eucharist we are dismissed from the assembly to engage the stuff of our daily lives. We have fed on Christ so we may be food for others. We return to work, civic life, family and friends as instruments of God's love. These relationships are both the place of our apostolate and active ministry while also playing a role in our renewal as people and as Christians.

Much of the discussion about lay ministry, or the ministry of the baptized, has in recent years focused on the lay Christian's role in the ministries and governance of the church. That's certainly been a significant development that has both strengthened the church and enhanced human dignity. But all too often this movement and discussion have eclipsed the more central ministry of the baptized in the places in which they live out daily life. A useful correction in language that some are using is to use the word "ministry" to refer to activities with or through the church, and to use "apostolate" when referring to our engagement as Christians and people in our daily life. But whatever language we use the distinction is important. A parish's obsession with its own needs can diminish the life and vocation of most Christians and end up alienating members from either the church or from their daily life.

In each area of apostolic life and action we have the opportunity to be fully present as we now are; to be concerned for the well being of others; and to enact in our lives the Eucharistic pattern of taking, blessing, breaking, and sharing. John Gardner wrote about how the society needed people who would be loving-critics of the institutions in which they worked. I think his idea applies not just to the places where we work but also to our families, friends, town and nation, and church. The stances of unloving-critic or the uncritical-lover are really ways of avoiding one another and ourselves.

Apostolate within the Family

In *Hunting for Hope: A Father's Journeys,* Scott Russell Sanders writes about the values of family life: "The family values that I embrace are the habits of the heart and mind essential for creating and maintaining such a community, and among these are generosity and fidelity and mercy, a sympathetic imagination, a deep and abiding concern for others, a passion for justice, a sense of restraint and a sense of humor, a relish for skillful work, a willingness to negotiate differences, a readiness for cooperation and affection…. While the family is not the only place where we might acquire such habits, it is the primary one. And above all it is the place where we are most likely to learn the meaning of love."

Here's another way of describing what is involved in the stewardship of our families.

- Nurture the relationships – Work at connecting to each individual as well as the family as a group.
- Give thanks – Again and again bring your mind and heart to a place of thankfulness for your life, one another, your home and the food you eat.
- Break the destructive patterns, the ways of living and being that seem to get passed down from generation to generation.
- Make space to acknowledge and resolve wounds and unfinished business.

- Share your spirituality with one another. Express what you are able to express, as a family and as individuals.
- Understand your role in the family as a vocation. Through you the incarnate Christ loves and serves in the family. In raising children, caring for the sick, enjoying life, having sex, getting old, and dealing with all that life brings – in and through the baptized person Christ is present. Desmond Tutu pointed toward that vocation. "You don't choose your family. They are God's gift to you, as you are to them."

Maureen Dowd reported on the "Whom Not to Marry" lecture that Father Pat Conner would deliver to high school seniors, mostly girls. "Never marry a man who has no friends," he starts. "This usually means that he will be incapable of the intimacy that marriage demands … "Does he use money responsibly? Is he stingy? Most marriages that founder do so because of money … "Steer clear of someone whose life you can run, who never makes demands counter to yours … "Does he have a sense of humor? … "A therapist friend insists that 'more marriages are killed by silence than by violence.' … Does he possess those character traits that add up to a good human being — the willingness to forgive, praise, be courteous? Or is he inclined to be a fibber, to fits of rage, to be a control freak, to be envious of you, to be secretive?" (NY Times July 7, 2008). As a letter to the editor noted on the following day Fr. Conner's lecture applies to both men and women.

A part of the family's vocation is to act for a society in which families are supported and protected. During the Second World War William Temple wrote *Christianity and Social Order*, in which he took the position that the nation needed to shape itself in a way that families had adequate housing, some leisure in which to spend time together, and salaries that ensure the good upbringing of children. Temple's understanding was that government was to nurture a family life that flowed from a view of "the decency and dignity proper to human beings who are the children of God." One of the prayers offered in the Sacrament of Marriage is "that they may reach out in love and concern for others." Marriage has a vocation beyond the joy and well being of the couple. A good starting point might be helping to create a society in which all sorts of families are helped to develop and thrive.

Possibly the most important understanding we can bring to our family life is our sacramental view of life. There is spiritual grace in all the struggles and pleasures of family life.

The family. We were a strange little band of characters trudging through life sharing diseases and toothpaste, coveting one another's desserts, hiding shampoo, borrowing money, locking each other out of our rooms, inflicting pain and kissing to heal it in the same instant, loving, laughing, defending, and trying to figure out the common thread that bound us all together.
Erma Bombeck

Apostolate with Friends

We are called to be friends with God. "No longer do I call you servants, for the servant doesn't know what his lord does. But I have called you friends, for everything that I heard from my Father, I have made known to you." (*John 15:15*) But it's not just being friends with God that is part of a full spiritual life. Friendship with other people is both apostolate and renewal.

Particular friendships are part of what helps us mature in Christ. Saint Anselm wrote a "Prayer for Friends" that expresses the importance of close friends.

I love all men, in and for your sake,
    though not as much as I ought or as I desire.
I pray your mercy upon all men,
yet there are many whom I hold more dear
Since your love has impressed them upon my heart
    with a closer and more intimate love,
    so that I desire their love more eagerly –
I would pray more ardently for these.
        The Prayers and Meditations of Saint Anselm, Penguin Classics

In *The Four Loves* C.S. Lewis sees our friendships as being part of how God shapes our lives and deepens our capacity for love and Glory. Lewis notes that the development of friendships can appear to be a matter of chance - "a few years difference in the dates of our births, a few more miles between certain houses …the accident of a topic being raised or not raised at a first meeting – any of these chances might have kept us apart." He continues, "But for a Christian, there are, strictly speaking, no chances. A secret Master of Ceremonies has been at work. Christ, who said to the disciples, 'Ye have not chosen me, but I have chosen you,' can truly say to every group of Christian friends, 'You have not chosen one another but I have chosen you for one another.' The friendship is not a reward for our discrimination and good taste in finding one another out. It is the instrument by which God reveals to each the beauties of all the others."

The parish may have a special role to play in a society in which people are increasingly isolated. In the past twenty years there has been an increase in the percentage of people who have no close friends. In 1985 just 10% of Americans said they had no close friends, but by 2004 the percentage increased to 24.6%. There was a corresponding increase in the percentage of people who only confided in family members (from 57% to 80%). The research done by the National Opinion Research Center at the University of Chicago had only guesses about why this was occurring, mentioning things like more people living in the suburbs, a longer commute, more time being spent at work, and more stay-at-home entertainment taking place.

In *Habits of the Heart: Individualism and Commitment in American Life,* Robert Bellah offered an understanding of friendship grounded in Aristotle, suggesting that friendship has three components: "Friends must enjoy each other's company, they must be useful to one another, and they must share a common commitment to the good." In *Fierce Tenderness*, Mary Hunt defines friendship as "voluntary human relationships that are entered into by people who intend one another's well-being and who intend that their love relationship is part of a justice-seeking community." It appears that at the moment our society is having a more and more difficult time nurturing or even understanding friendship in the way described by Bellah and Hunt. The parish church may offer a setting for both thinking about and experiencing friendship.

C.S. Lewis explored the relationship between companionship and friendship by suggesting that both had value and that friendship might emerge out of companionship. "Friendship arises out of mere Companionship when two or more of the companions discover that they have in common some insight or interest or even taste which the others do not share and which, till that moment, each believed to be his own unique treasure (or burden). The typical expression of opening Friendship would be something like, 'What? You too? I thought I was the only one.'" Lewis then notes that companionship is based in some shared activity or interest, "a common religion, common studies, a common profession, even a common recreation." He goes on to describe a movement from companionship into friendship. "All who share it will be our companions, but one or two or three who share something more will be our Friends. In this kind of love, as Emerson said, *Do you love me?* means *Do you see the same truth?* - Or at least, 'Do you *care about* the same truth?' The man who agrees with us that some question, little regarded by others, is of great importance, can be our Friend. He need not agree with us about the answer." (*The Four Loves*)

Parish churches are for many people a place of friendship. Some people are first attracted to a parish in the hope of meeting people and developing friendships. The connections begun in liturgy, classes and parish social gatherings are frequently extended into dinner together, time in a coffee shop or tavern, or brunch after the Sunday Eucharist. We might pick up on Aelred's thinking about how a Christian community can be a "school of love." For him the monastic community was not only Benedict's "school for the Lord's service," it was also a "school of love."

In community people establish spiritual friendships, and in and through those friendships are brought to friendship with God. Aelred's view was that human beings long for God because God has placed that desire in their heart. In loving Christ as a dear friend we can realize our longing. For Aelred, "God himself is friendship," and "he who dwells in friendship, dwells in God and God in him." John Henry Newman pointed to the same natural operation that expanded the range of our loving. "The love of our private friends is the only preparatory exercise for the love of all men."

Parish-based friendships can develop into spiritual friendships, and both can be a pathway into friendship with God and compassion for others. These friendships make us a friend of God. In sacramental reality the two are intertwined – friendship with people leads to friendship with God, and being God's friend will find expression in friendship with other people.

Charles Williams had two expressions that capture what happens in the "school of love" we experience with friends. There are the "acts of the City," the acts of sacrifice, forgiveness, reconciliation and substitution that are the sacramental activities of spiritual friendship. And there are the exchanges of daily life, the "habits of heaven" – of forgiving and letting ourselves be forgiven, in helping one another and allowing ourselves to be helped.

Much of the work I do involves helping leaders and parishes claim who they are as people and as communities. This journey to "self" is a struggle I've felt honored to share with others. In my training and consulting one of my highest values has been around this solitary struggle toward having a sense of self, knowing yourself, and being able to effectively use who you are. Alongside that reality is another. That the discovery and growing into "self" is done in communion – in and with Christ, in the community of the Blessed Trinity, in a parish, and most especially with our friends. Charles Williams expressed it this way, "This abides - that the everlasting house the soul discovers is always another; we must lose our own ends - we must live in the habitation of our lovers, my friend's shelter for me, mine for him."

We connect to our deepest longings in and through our friends. There is something in our friend that allows us to see our own desires and to experience what we like about ourselves. "In each friendship we are brought face to face with ourselves, with one another, and with a larger world in which the forces of attraction work beyond our ultimate control." (Mary Hunt in *Fierce Tenderness*)

Our sharing in the life of God, this participation in Glory is, of course, about everyone, including everyone we know and everyone we will never know. It is a proclamation of something that is universal or as the baptismal promise expresses it, "to respect the dignity of every person." That's one outcome of understanding the Glory. C.S. Lewis wrote, "the dullest and most uninteresting person you can talk to may one day be a creature which, if you saw it now, you would be strongly tempted to worship."

But, in our experience we know it's not just about "all people." One paradox of the gospel is that we are not just to love those we know, we are to love all people *and* also what may seem like the opposite—it does us no good to love everyone if we don't love those who are closest to us. But it's more than that—those closest to us play this special role in our salvation, in our full and true life in the City of God.

We need to allow it all to be personal and particular. We don't want to fall for the idea that there is something more Christian about loving the masses more than loving your friends, those who walk with you in life. In some sense the beginning and the end is to see and honor the glory in our friends, our lovers, our spouse, and our partners. It's not chance, it's grace - *your love has impressed them upon my heart.*

Rowan Williams saw the relationship of particular friendship with the stewardship of the whole world. "A priest is someone who in his or her friendship reveals to me the face of God. … To be a kingdom of priests then, is to be a people through whose friendship God can be seen. Are we friends to God's world? We shall be so if we learn to be friends of Jesus Christ and friends with one another." (At St Patrick's Cathedral, Armagh, 22 February 2005). We need to take great care about the impact of those parishes in which the priest fears close friendships because of how they might confuse or set loose jealousy. A priest who will not risk real and deep friendship within the parish steals from that parish the depth of Christian life.

Our friends, lovers, partners and spouses – they are in our life and we are in their life – as part of God's Glory. In raising his friend Jesus says, "Did I not tell you that if you believed, you would see the glory of God?"

Thomas Merton wrote, "I will remind us of what we know; that our living and dying and serving is risky; that we are to 'serve him wittily'; and that we are to serve him in companionship with others, living and dead, friends and enemies, but most especially, in companionship with those we know and love best."

We need to hear the saints, to hear the Word from Anselm, Aelred, Merton, Williams, and Lewis. We need to hear Jesus' love for Lazarus, Mary and John. We need to hear about how in what seems so ordinary in life, God manifests Glory; and how that Glory is present even if there is at times a stench.

Our friends see more of us than others. As with most people they at times are only aware of what is most visible. But there are also times when they see what is invisible, the unseen – they may see right through our flaws to the image of God, to the Glory.
They are not blind to our selfishness and imperfection;

but in the ways of the City,
they have been chosen for us,
they are companions in serving
they are our shelter, and
they discern the true being, who,
when perfected in heaven,
"you would be strongly tempted to worship."

Apostolate in the Workplace

"If you want to produce Christian work, be a Christian, and try to make a work of beauty into which you have put your heart; do not adopt a Christian pose." -Jacques Maritain

A parish's efforts to support people in a workplace apostolate can begin with listening. The connection between faith and work is not an area with which many parish churches have much experience. But it is an area that is organically related to the parish. Parishioners are involved in the working world. They are employed, own a business or volunteer in all the sectors of organizational life of society. Their work is a source of joy and pain. It is an opportunity for compassion, service and justice. In most parishes we know relatively little about this central aspect of people's lives. Start with listening.

Here are two examples of such listening.

- The priest and parish deacons, possibly along with others, can engage in a systematic interviewing process to better understand people's spiritual life, including the role of work in that life. This might be seen as an early pastoral contact with a person new to the parish. It could be revisited every so often. Here are some of the questions that could be used.

    1) What are the major sources of pressures, demands and expectations in your life? (If not mentioned ask about this in relation to work).
    2) How do you feel about them? (such as joy, empty, angry, pleased, afraid, unhappy, excited, guilt, alive) Could you say more about those feelings?
    3) How do you manage these expectations, demands and pressures? (How does work factor in that?)
    4) How do you renew yourself emotionally and physically? How does that relate to your work?
    5) How do you renew yourself spiritually? How does that relate to your work?
    6) How does your practice of Christian faith and/or the congregation's life help or hinder the processes of spiritual, emotional and physical renewal? Do you feel within yourself some pressure to as Maritain said, "adopt a Christian pose."
    7) How do you connect with Maritain's idea about work, "try to make a work of beauty into which you have put your heart?"

- In the parish's foundations course[2] and other educational programs create opportunities for faith sharing that touch on the work place. For example, begin a gathering by having small

---

[2] A foundations course is a substantial educational and training program that is repeated over the years and is used to incorporate people into the parish and the spirituality of the Episcopal Church. There's

groups of people share what their work is and what they find most rewarding about it. Or if you have people do a spiritual lifeline exercise ask them to include their work life as part of what they offer.

The places in which we work are all environments that are morally ambiguous. That's simply the nature of things. That ambiguity is usually not obvious to us. The ways of the organization for which we work can become like the air we breathe. The practices of the organization become such a normal way of doing business that employees hardly recognize ethical and moral problems and opportunities. We can become so accustomed to the way things are that we can't see ways of improving the impact the organization has on the society or its own employees.

In that situation the baptized person's call is to self-awareness and self-control, an understanding of what is "good," wisdom, and all the other virtues. We will each be as much "in Christ" as we have become up to that moment when organizational decisions are being made and action taken. The parish's work is to be the soil for the slow process of sanctification; that means by which people are formed to "see" what is happening within and around them. In *True Prayer*, Kenneth Leech suggests that the ability to see clearly was linked to solitude and solidarity. It is Michael Ramsey's priestly image of standing before God with the people on your heart. That stance of the priest in and for the parish community is also the stance of the whole priestly people of God in relationship to the world, including the places in which we work.

The parish's task is not moralistic judgment or exhortation to more compassion but the slow process of sanctification in which women and men are brought into relationship with the eyes and heart of Christ.

In the parish's exploration of workplace issues in education, preaching and spiritual guidance we need to avoid oversimplifying things. For example, when we hear about managers maximizing profits and focusing on the return to the shareholder there may be an impulse to react negatively because it often comes at a cost for employees and communities. What we can overlook is that the shareholder benefiting from that return increasingly includes working people, pension plans, universities, social service agencies, and churches, and not just faceless corporations and "the rich." There are real complexities and competing values to be addressed. It may help to consider such cases as polarities that we are called to engage and manage; sometimes deciding in one direction, sometimes in the other.

This listening to understand the workplace can also include a priest's daily reading of a news website or newspaper, before or after having said the morning office.

In 2004 The *Wall Street Journal* had an article by Ellen E. Schultz and Theo Francis on "How Cuts in Retiree Benefits Fatten Companies' Bottom Lines." (3/16/04) The report makes the case that the argument made by many companies blaming surging health care costs for the practice of cutting retiree health care benefits or having them cover more of the cost, is at best a half truth. The article says, "In fact, no matter how high health care costs go, well over half of large American corporations face only a limited impact from the increases...."

---

more on foundations course in the chapter on the Christian Life Model, in the "Weaving the Threads into a Fabric" section, and in the Resources section.

The reporters suggest that a possible factor in play is that when companies cut benefits they create income and/or accounting gains. "In some case it flows straight to the bottom line," i.e., it helps the company meet goals for its earnings and the focus on *how much* profit the company will book rather than whether the company can truly "afford" the premiums.

So, is what we have here another story of corporate greed? That wouldn't be very shocking in a year which was filled with stories of corporate executives being sentenced to prison. Was this just legal greed as opposed to illegal greed?

Or is what we are looking at in this case the balancing of a business's legitimate interest in making a profit for its owners with the legitimate needs of employees?

On other occasions the news offers examples of confusion among religious people about how as Christians we engage the workplace.

In "Thou Shalt Not Call in Sick: Movement Brings Religious Ethic to the Workplace," the *New York Times* looked at how some people are approaching faith-at-work issues. The article included a picture of a Bible sitting on top of business files on someone's desk.

The piece offers some insight into a very limited version of the apostolate in the workplace. It may be so limited and partial that the thinking behind it would qualify for a heresy award. The focus is on personal piety and in particular on making the workplace more like a church by having prayer groups and bible study. It's also about personal ethics, especially about controlling our personal competitiveness. And it's about seeing the workplace as an opportunity for personal forms of evangelism. It all reflects a particular form of American evangelical religious practice. It's not my own tradition so maybe it's partly a matter of taste.

However, this approach also tends to fit neatly into the economic and political desires of conservative organizational leaders. A woman who works at the Centers for Disease Control and Prevention saw the role of her Christian Fellowship at the Center in these terms – "It's a tremendous benefit to management. We teach biblical principles like rendering yourself as a servant." Usually missing in approaches like this are understandings of corporate stewardship with room for the place of organized labor as a counter balancing force; or companies with values directed towards employee well-being and broader social responsibility, alongside economic gain; or the role of employees as having responsibility for promoting changes in organizational life that enhance human dignity. The danger is that by focusing on biblical principles like being a servant, without including the biblical witness to compassion and justice, we end up using religion as a means of promoting submission to the status quo and we discourage the development of individual conscience.

A significant problem with many of these activities is the confusion they suggest about apostolic activity. It seems that some Christians think it's desirable to turn all sectors of their life into places of religion. It's as though they aren't quite comfortable unless everything feels like "church."

There's a difference in demanding company space and time for a bible study group and using your break to say the Office. There's a difference between demanding time for a prayer group in the company's meeting room and asking for 20 extra minutes at lunch to go to a noon Eucharist. There's a difference between acts of public prayer that impose your spirituality on others and silently offering brief acts of recollection and intercession. There's a difference between leaving tracts on your co-workers desk and wearing a cross or having a Bible or Prayer Book among the items on your desk. There's a difference between proselytizing and a genuine conversation among co-workers about faith and values. There's a difference between an aggressive imposing of yourself and your ways on others and the Gospel's way of kindness, gentleness, and patience. To respect the dignity of others requires sensitivity about whether the other person is comfortable having the conversation and respect for the viewpoint and feelings of others.

Many people have a longing for integration. They want life to have a unity and wholeness. That longing is addressed by bringing together work and faith in our renewal activities as well as in workplace practices. In our striving for integrated lives some are more drawn to spiritual disciplines that ground their work in an awareness of the presence of God. Others are attracted to an ethical orientation seeking direction and boundaries.

Sometimes the starting place is listening to what is happening to parishioners. When the rector of a church in one of the wealthier areas of New Jersey realized that an increasing number of men in the parish had been laid off from executive positions in Manhattan-based corporations, he started a support group. They met weekly for prayer, conversation and something to eat.

Another example might be when I joined with a group of clergy who invited a top executive of a major oil company to meet with us so we could better understand his work and the choices he faced. He was an Episcopalian active in a Connecticut parish. This was a sophisticated and thoughtful person. The clergy were surprised when he turned from a description of the difficult decisions he and others faced around environmental issues and corporate survival and success to his feelings about the church. What he shared went something like this, "I find it personally painful when the bishops and many parish clergy begin with the assumption that those of us who work in the corporate world are involved in something that is inherently evil or wrong. I look to my church for understanding and support and I find condemnation." He went on to express his deep frustration with what he experienced as judgments being made by people who seemed to have little awareness of how our economic system worked and the kind of complex decisions he and others had to make every day. What he wanted from the church was not agreement but dialogue, basic principles, and a wiliness to listen as well as preach. A friend who has spent most of her adult life working in the business world said, "Aside from a legal technicality, corporations don't exist apart from the people that run them." We need to remember that some of those people are members of the Body of Christ.

While it may be true, as Harold Lewis puts it in *Christian Social Witness*, that the church institutionally needs to have "a preference for the poor," it is also true that we need to have a pastoral commitment to our members who have more wealth and power. It may help if our starting place is to see the two as part of the same mission. If on the one hand the church strives to influence the world toward a more equal distribution of resources, we may also want to better understand how the economic system functions and the choices facing our members who work in business and government.

It helps for clergy and lay leaders to have a broad awareness of how faith and work meet. All too often we have narrowed down our understanding so much that all activity in the world seems questionable. The church shows its confusion in many ways. One is what, in some places, we have done with the vocational diaconate. In some dioceses the operational definition of a servant ministry seems to only include things such as nursing and social work. Deacons are then seen as religious social workers that exist to run the parish's service ministries. It's a narrow vision that is disrespectful of many people's vocations. We might consider a broad view of the diaconate that includes the service ministry orientation but also adds two other roles: the deacon as administrator and the deacon as an interpreter of the needs, concerns, and hopes of the world to the church. In that last role we need to see among our deacons more corporate executives, labor union leaders, and politicians.

Here are some of the possible connections between the laity's experience in the workplace and their apostolate. These are ways in which people participate in Christ's service, evangelization and stewardship of the world.

- **Being.** By being people that have become more and more "in Christ," light, salt, leaven. Christians serve, evangelize and act as stewards just by being present in the workplace. There is an organic influence from people who are in the process of falling and rising and living in the journey of stability, conversion and obedience.
- **Participating responsibly.** We are part of the economy of God's world by our participation in the human drama of creating, serving, and producing. There is faithfulness in the process of earning our own living and, for some, in contributing to the well being of a family.
- **Building community.** Holy joy can be experienced in relationship with other workers and being part of a workplace community. Every day offers opportunities for compassion, fun, and shared experience.
- **Finding value.** There is intrinsic meaning in the work we do. Our work is of value to the world. It matters to the well-being of people that this service or product is available. We may want to be generous and broad in what we are willing to include here. There is often a narrow puritanism that defines the life and work of others as being sub-Christian. Even products and services that seem very superficial and light may bring some of us great joy.
- **Bringing change.** Some Christians thoughtfully and quietly take action to influence their organizations toward a more humane and just way of operating. This may include humanizing the work place for employees and clients or customers. It might also mean finding ways to facilitate the organization in taking a socially responsible stance. This involves us in a "ministry to structures."[3]

The workplace apostolate may find its richest completion in an understanding of communion and holiness. Brian Jordan is a Franciscan, a Roman Catholic priest, whose work includes New York City construction workers. He spent weeks at the World Trade Center site after 9/11. His dad, like mine, was a member of the Teamsters Union. His father would speak of "solidarity." My father put it this way when challenged about corruption in the union, "Yea, they're crooks, but they're our crooks." His father said, "When we go to church, we pray together. When we do a job, we work together. When we stand up for something, we stand together." In one of Fr. Jordan's sermons he said, " 'As a surgeon has sacred hands while performing a medical operation, as a priest has sacred hands while celebrating the Eucharist, so are union

---

[3] "Ministry to Structures" is the name of a paper by Robert H. Bonthius that was delivered to the Department of Ministry of the National Council of Churches in 1968. Bonthius was then the Director of the Urban Ministry Internship Program for clergy at Case Western Reserve University. He was making a case for an "ethic of organizational responsibility" and learning "how to change these structures from within." His work was part of a an ecumenical movement in the churches that included several American industrial missions, the World Council of Churches study on the Role of Christians within Changing Institutions, and my 1972 Audenshaw Document, "Ministry of Laity as Agents of Institutional Change." Those efforts were in turn a building upon the earlier lay academies and worker-priest movements of the late 40's and early 50's which arose in Europe in reaction to the generally poor showing of the church in Nazi Germany.

construction workers with their sacred and skillful hands' doing godly work by building hospitals, schools, family homes. 'I am not stretching the imagery of sacredness, I am simply stating a fact.' " (drawn from NY Times 5/17/08)

Apostolate in Civic Life

A way of thinking about our apostolate in civic life is to place it on a spectrum. At one end are the basics, e.g., be a good neighbor, vote, attend the town meeting, serve on juries, pay our taxes, in times of crisis give our time and money to those in need. Further along on the spectrum might be joining a civic association, serving on the local school board, and contributing to the conversation about the issues of the common good. Even further along would be that place where civic life and vocation meet, e.g., becoming a political leader, a judge, a union or community organizer. The more basic forms of civic involvement are the minimum, and possibly the maximum, that most of the baptized will do.

Even that minimum form of involvement is seen as too much by many people in our society. A *Washington Post* article by Brooke A. Masters explored the difficulty in getting people to serve on juries. "There are probably a lot of very good people who are very reluctant to serve on juries, to take that kind of time out of their lives, and then there are some that want their 15 minutes of fame," said Linda A. Foley, a psychology professor at the University of North Florida who studies juries. "You're getting a jury that isn't representative of the population." (4/2/04)

The article suggested that the reasons for the reluctance had to do with concerns about privacy and time. The difference for the Christian may be as simple as beginning with a stance that assumes civic involvement as one expression of how Christ acts in and through his Church in God's love for the world. That stance is a starting point from which we engage what needs to be engaged and seek to balance life with all its demands and possibilities. The stance opens us to grace. Our participation in the affairs of the world will at times be experienced as a burden, even a cross, but might often be occasions of surprising experiences and relationships with people we would not otherwise know.

As Episcopalians we come out of a tradition that values civic engagement and responsibility. We see it in our history of the disproportionate percentage of Episcopalians serving in Congress and in our involvement in the Christian socialist movement. We see it in our parishes where so many give their time to feed the hungry and serve on school boards. Our attachment to the Incarnation and a sacramental way of understanding life provides theological and spiritual grounding for our involvement. "God loved the world," writes John. During the Eucharist in some parishes the priest and people make a solemn bow or genuflect at the Creed's words, "by the power of the Holy Spirit he became incarnate from the Virgin Mary, and was made man."

We have ways of engaging civic life that tend to differ from some other Christian traditions. I'll use the Southern Baptists as an example and I'll make several observations about how the following event might be understood to illuminate the Episcopal Church's approach.

In June of 2006 the Southern Baptist Convention rejected a resolution calling on its members to leave the public schools in favor of home schooling and private Christian schools. Instead they affirmed an approach that would "engage the culture of our public schools systems" by exerting "godly influence," to include running for school boards.

The stance of the Episcopal Church has been rather consistently one of assuming that Christians are to be involved in the decision making of the society. We have encouraged engagement and adult responsibility among our members. The Baptists have a long history of withdrawal from civic life. In more recent times they have moved to be more active, but even at that, their ambivalence about involvement keeps reappearing when they gather in convention, as it did in this case.

The Episcopal Church has continued to avoid an over-identification with one set of views or one political approach. In recent times the Baptists have become more engaged but primarily on the side of a very conservative political stance and have also aligned themselves with the Republican Party. Lay Episcopalians involved in civic life range widely in their views about politics and civic affairs. They are Republicans, Democrats and Greens. What they often seem to have in common is a more moderate and pragmatic approach to the political task. That stance was reflected at the 2006 General Convention when one of the primary speakers was John Danforth, an Episcopal priest and the former Republican Senator from Missouri. Danforth's message in recent years has been about the danger to both the nation and the church for a political party and a religious movement to be bound up with one another.

When Episcopalians gather in convention we are more likely than not to take social positions seen by others as moderate or liberal. These statements are the discernment of the bishops, clergy and laity who have gathered. They are one aspect of the church's voice. All of us are called to prayerfully consider what the church gathered in convention discerns about the moral vision. But those statements are also only that, something to consider.

When parish clergy provide instruction related to society it's usually more about how to prepare oneself for civic life rather than telling members what specific views they are to hold. So we are more likely to hear that we have a responsibility to be connected to civic life, to inform our ethical and moral thinking from within a disciplined spiritual life, and to open ourselves to the authorities of Scriptures, tradition and reason; and unlikely to hear that we are to vote for a particular political party or hold a certain view on abortion.

See Resource section for understandings of the Church's corporate responsibility to influence society in "The Church's Influence in Society"

In the political struggle between Hamas and Fatah, Muhammad Dahlan, a leader of Fatah, described a meeting between leaders of the two factions about the crisis they faced. The Palestine Authority president asked the leader of Hamas, "What's your program? How will you get us out of this crisis? What can you tell us?" Dahlan went on to say that Hamas always says, "God will help us." His response was "Fine. We all believe in God, but politics requires an answer."

Episcopalians tend to be concerned with how to be a devout Christian and also to accept and learn from the discoveries of science and anthropology; how to be a person of prayer and also be engaged in making the difficult political decisions that require respect for the views, dignity, and power of others; and how to be both an instrument of God's love and also have the pragmatism needed to live in and improve life in the world. In Liturgy and prayer we are a people enchanted by the love of God and the image of the Holy City. Our task is to see God's love and kingdom as it occurs among us, to point to it and give thanks for it, and in humility and with good sense and practical judgment serve it.

37

There's a great deal at stake in people's involvement in civic life. Helping members of the parish see and act on the value of participation is bound up with a variety of dynamics impacting our communities. A 2006 Associated Press – Pew poll examined the 45% of the population who are usually nonvoters. What they found was that nonvoters are disconnected from a wide range of connections with others. They are less likely to trust others, to have a strong network of family and friends or to know who their neighbors are. It's a reasonable guess that parishioners are more likely than most to vote and have stronger connections with others. So, this issue may well be one of evangelization. To enter into the community of the baptized, to live in the Trinity, and to do so as part of a parish community may have a relationship with how people participate in both their immediate communities and in the wider society.

Apostolate in the Church

Ministry in and through the institutional structures of the parish is a significant vocation for some people through much of their lives. The vestry needs members, children need a formation program, the liturgy calls for lay leadership in partnership with clergy, and many congregations have service ministries that need volunteers.

Most baptized people are not, however, called to an intensive investment of time and energy. For them it is something they take on for a period and then set down, a role in the stewardship of the institution to be played for a time. Most members have at least a minimal role to play as they pledge, occasionally give time to a project, and participate in parish meetings.

The church has the same temptation we see in all institutions. Those who are most invested in the organizational life of the parish may begin to see ministry primarily in terms of church-based activities. That tendency exposes itself in complaining about the "same few people that do everything." It appears on web sites when there is no mention of the primary ministries of the baptized. It is reinforced when dioceses offer programs in lay ministry that are almost totally about lay leadership roles in the church. We need to hear Dorothy L. Sayers on work, "The official Church wastes time and energy, and, moreover, commits sacrilege, in demanding secular workers should neglect their proper vocations in order to do Christian work—by which [the Church] means ecclesiastical work. The only Christian work is good work well done."

Balance in life? Authenticity and Joy

Most of us are familiar with the discussion in organizations and families about work-life balance. Many struggle with that dilemma. We want to see ourselves as responsible people. We would like others to think well of us. We don't want the conflict that comes when our workplace or family feels shortchanged.

The balance issue is also embedded within the Renewal – Apostolate Cycle. The model offers a perspective that suggests balance among several elements—first, between the processes of renewal and the apostolic activity of the faithful; then another balance among the daily life arenas of work, family, friends, civic involvement and church.

There's been a good bit of research and writing about work-life balance in an attempt to both understand the issues involved and to find ethical approaches to guide decision-making. Some of that work can help us here. An article on "Work Life Balance" in *The Journal of Applied Behavioral Science* (June 2007) shifted the discussion from assuming a one-size-fits-all approach to methods (such as flex-time) to the question of the ends to be achieved. For example, "…different groups requiring different solutions to achieve satisfying experiences in all life domains to a level consistent with the salience of that role for them," and "It is about assisting people to match their behavior to their values." An important consideration in developing a sustainable way to live the Renewal – Apostolate Cycle needs to be what the individual values and what methods best serve that person.

Is this working for you?

Rather than looking for some model that can be applied for everyone it might be best to look within and ask the basic question – "Is this working for me?" Our assessment might include the following:
- In each aspect of the apostolate are you able to show fidelity - loyalty, dedication, stability, and attentiveness?
- Do you find adequate satisfaction in each sphere? Is the difficulty about finding satisfaction related to balance or is it specific to that arena?
- Is it working for you in the sense of not just comfort but challenge and growth?
- Are the common negative consequences of a disordered life less in the picture – emotional and physical health issues, anxiety about being responsible in each area of life.
- Is one area crowding out the others? Is it claiming too much?

Accepting Responsibility for Your Life

At the heart of the issue is the need to accept responsibility for ourselves and our life. That's not about getting life "right." It's not about not being uncertain and confused. It is about self awareness, thoughtful reflection, and taking needed action.

Clearly, there is not some "correct" way to balance life. It's also the case that the people in the various sectors of our life will have their own answers as to what we should do with our time, energy and resources. They will want more time for themselves and may have a desire about how you engage the other parts of life. Your employer wants you to stay later and your daughter wants you at the school play. Your friend wants to see more of you and your spouse doesn't trust or like your friend. The parish has discerned that you should consider the permanent diaconate and you were thinking it was time for you to spend more time with your partner.

There's not any way you will ever make everyone happy whatever you decide (yes, you already know that). Others being upset about that will make you anxious (probably!). That seems to leave us with the task of accepting responsibility for what we decide and increasing our ability to manage our anxiety.

Do the others get a vote? Do others get to tell us how to live, how to balance life, how to be adult people? What we "owe" those we work with, our friends and spouse, our parish is to take seriously what they say they need and want from us. We are to listen with respect. We are to open ourselves to challenge and new ways of looking at things. We are to reflect prayerfully on the issues before us. But finally we each decide for ourselves. In this way we accept responsibility for our life in community. Any other course is an invitation to resentment, instability, and faithlessness.

There's an old book on my shelf, *When I Say No I Feel Guilty*. Most of us are easily driven by the demands and anxiety of others. We can become controlled and dominated by the desires of others. When we let them down we can experience feelings of guilt. Stephanie Dowrick in *Intimacy and Solitude* wrote, "In quite normal relationships one person can enslave another, not through cruelty, but ostensibly through love, making it difficult to spend time with others, denying them a life of their own which is not subsumed to the needs of the relationship as one person 'desires' the relationship to be." Dowrick's concern isn't something that is only present in interpersonal relationships. Employers, religious organizations, political movements, just as much as spouses and partners, can make demands and create pressures that claim too much.

We collude in our own enslavement if we measure things in terms of whether others are happy with us. Sometimes the claims being made on us are perfectly reasonable but we may still need to refuse them. None of us has enough time and energy to address all the claims on us, even if they have some legitimacy. And on occasion we will have honest differences about whether the claims being made are reasonable or legitimate. These circumstances may lead to separation from friends, family, voluntary commitments, workplace or church. Even though sad, and at times tragic, they happen and may be necessary.

On the other hand, there may be for some of us a temptation to push the envelope about self-responsibility and self-defining to a place where what we are doing is justifying a lack of connection with and responsibility toward some spheres of life. What to us seems like appropriate behavior to define ourselves is experienced by others as cutting-off and distancing behavior, even aggressive and hostile. Ways to test this behavior are: 1) Take an internal check—is this driven by anger? Is it an attempt to reduce your anxiety by reducing contact? Is it a form of emotional pressure on others? 2) See what others think about these things, and open yourself to honest feedback. 3) Consider whether you really are losing connection with the other. 4) Look for a pattern. Has one party been more the giver, the one to adjust to the other?

In our efforts to live a more responsible life, "Let your yes be yes and your no, no." (James 5:12b); live in community with others; ground yourself in the prayers of the church in Eucharist and Office; contemplate your life and seek to learn from your experience.

Mary and Martha: Balance or Rhythm?

An illustration of a common confusion about living the Renewal–Apostolate Cycle is in how many preachers approach the story of Mary and Martha. Jesus has come into a village and was welcomed into Martha's home. Martha's sister, Mary, "sat at the Lord's feet and listened to what he was saying. But Martha was distracted by her many tasks." In an ancient attempt to triangulate, Martha complained to Jesus about her sister leaving her with all the work. "Lord, do you not care …?" Jesus' response is clear: "Mary has chosen the better part, which will not be taken away from her." (Luke 10:38-42)

In spite of the text many people want to see this as an opportunity to affirm both Mary and Martha and by that action to affirm a variety of people in the congregation. Our instinct to support and accept people is one of the better things about most Episcopal parishes. But it can come at a cost. It can feed spiritual and emotional immaturity.

People can get driven, even obsessed, about some part of life. It may be situational or chronic. We focus on family to the exclusion of developing friendships or we do the reverse. We overwork and neglect the time needed by our family and friends or we do things the other way around.

In Martha's case she missed the opportunity in front of her. Here was Jesus in her house and she was missing the chance to be with him. Some preachers like to give what she is doing a form of cover by suggesting she is engaged in a ministry of hospitality. But Martha is missing what's happening. This is a time for regeneration and rebirth. It's a time for contemplation and being fed. This isn't about how Martha's role is as important as Mary's or about how we all need to "balance" life between the contemplative and active.

We can also become religious or spiritual fanatics so caught up in our own journey that we forget the rest of life. Most clergy have the experience of people wanting to hang out at the church as a way of avoiding something difficult at home or in their inner life. They may busy themselves painting a wall or coming to every opportunity for spiritual growth. This may even have a useful function if it's a temporary thing. We certainly need to take care about how we understand what is happening with a particular person. The same behavior that suggests a life "out of whack" for one may be a healthy form of rhythm for another.

This then has to do with discernment and finding a rhythm that works for us and seeing what the priority is at a particular moment. It's about what works and has priority in the sense of what works to help us grow and mature rather than what works in some self-oriented manner.

Parish Action

Parish leaders can help people address the issue by taking actions such as:
- Accept and affirm people making decisions about how they develop a rhythm or create a more balanced life. Provide support when a member decides to run for political office and needs to do less in the parish.

- Monitor and focus the energy and time demands the parish makes on people. For example, consider reducing the number of standing committees, learn group methods that allow for effective shorter meetings along with a few longer sessions, and consider reducing the number of vestry meetings. This last requires us to figure out the vestry alignment issue so we are asking for the time needed given the role of this particular vestry in this particular parish (See "Vestries: Choices and Alignment," Gallagher and Heyne, 2007. Documents at www.CongregationalDevelopment.com)

- Provide spiritual guidance and workshops for members to increase their competence in how they live the Renewal – Apostolate Cycle. Include in that effort work on self differentiation. Teach the church's normative ways of renewal—the rule of prayer.

How the Parish Contributes to Baptismal Renewal and What the Parish Does to Nurture People for the Apostolate

There are three areas we need to attend to — 1) the parish's culture and activities as supports for the formation of adults and children; 2) addressing patterns that tend to distort the Cycle; and 3) staying focused on the primary task.

Structures, Processes, Climate and Culture That Support Formation

- Nurture and coach people in their own renewal. Help people make use of the resources of the church for their spiritual life. Once people grasp and are grasped by the Eucharist, the liturgy and the whole pattern of Eucharistic living, then the Sunday Eucharist may become the most important contribution the parish makes to a person's apostolate.

- Shape the congregation's competence for Eucharistic worship. Teach people how to participate. Let them know how it can help to put down the Prayer Book and bulletin for most of the Liturgy and direct their attention to the liturgical action. Note which prayers it might help for them to memorize. Have them experiment with various ways of using their bodies in worship—standing and kneeling, using the sign of the cross, showing reverence in bowing or genuflecting. Help them gain a sense of the rhythm and flow of the worship.

- Offer ways for members to shape their own spiritual life. Provide opportunities for reflection on spiritual life and discipline; to develop a rule of life; and to participate in schools of prayer.

- Provide opportunities for members to explore aspects of their apostolate with family and friends, in the workplace and civic life. A workplace exploration might include having people reflect on and share their experience of common workplace graces such as: actions of compassion and justice, improved listening and other signs of respect in meetings, the joy many experience that comes from being in relationship with others at work, action in the organization to humanize the workplace by increasing the worker's voice, improving safety, getting the organization to be more socially responsible, and enhancing understanding between management and labor. These themes might be used in sermons, an adult forum, as a faith-sharing exercise, and in a quiet day.

- Weave into parish life frequent acknowledgement of the daily life apostolate. Provide examples in sermons. In the parish web site section on "ministry" begin with and emphasize the apostolate in the world before mentioning the apostolate within the parish. Design the Prayers of the People to make explicit reference to daily life ministries. The priest can make a point of informally commenting on and affirming the apostolate of members in their daily life. In all sorts of classes and gatherings facilitate connecting exercises in which members get to know something about the life and apostolate of one another. Use a brief exercise at coffee hour in which you pose a question such as, "Share something about your work life—what kind of work did you prepare for in school and what are you doing now?" or "What you have fantasized about doing?"

- Establish support groups around workplace, civic responsibility and family life issues. For example: a large parish or several parishes working together can bring together people in business, or medicine, law, social work, teaching, etc. Smaller congregations will need to have cross-vocational groups. Such groups might range from a focus on contemplation and intercession to problem-solving and strategizing.

- Offer quiet days and retreats with a theme of "Family Life" or "The Spirituality of Friendship," or "Faith & Work." Keep the focus on the spiritual life of the participants in relation to the theme.

- Pay attention to shifts in the social and cultural context. At times the church can so over-identify with the dominant culture that we resist cultural shifts, even where the changes may have little to do with the core of faith and practice. As I'm writing this section I'm aware of having seen reports on several shifts in American culture around family and friendships: married couples have become a minority of American households for the first time, increasing numbers of women are now living without a spouse, among married couples the number of households in which the woman is the primary earner has doubled over three decades, gay and lesbian couples are increasingly married or in some formal arrangement such as civil unions, and among young people the percentage having a best friend who is of another gender has significantly increased. If these trends continue they will have an impact on the workplace, civic life and the church. Parish leaders need to decide whether the church will be a resource helping people live full lives in the society as it is or if the church will be the community scold.

- Provide ways for people to explore their inner life in relationship to the areas of apostolic life. Our various connections with one another touch the deepest levels of who we are becoming and what we value. Powerful emotions can be generated in us when we give our hearts to some cause or person. We find ourselves conflicted about giving time, money and energy to the workplace instead of to family. We may find ourselves caught up in strong emotions and engaging in what seems like odd behavior over some controversial event in the parish. The joyous and often painful struggles that naturally emerge in parish life can speak to us about God's way with us and within us. Parishes can provide group experiences for personal and spiritual growth, spiritual guidance, and referrals to therapists.

- How the parish clergy deal with all the above can have a powerful impact on parishioners. Here are some of the typical issues—a priest takes a part-time job teaching at a college or pours himself in beginning the city's soup kitchen; is he running away from the parish and/or enlarging his soul? The priest develops several close friendships in the parish; can the priest, the friends and the parish manage the dynamics this sets loose? Are there answers to these issues that apply in all situations or does it depend on the capacities of the priest and others involved? The primary act of responsibility is less about getting everything "right" and more about the priest making use of resources for self-awareness and discernment. As both human being and symbol the priest can serve the parish by engaging his own inner life and avoiding a facade of perfection and control.

- Do the work to ensure a critical mass of members understands the Renewal-Apostolate Cycle.

- Develop the image of the parish as being a resource for people's daily life instead of a competitor for it. We want people to see the parish as a source of assistance for living with compassion and integrity, rather than just another competitor for their time, money, and energy. What some parishes have done includes cutting the number of vestry meetings; using temporary working groups rather than standing committees; not jamming everything onto Sunday, thereby making it an occasion of busyness and rush; affirming the centrality of the daily life apostolate of the baptized; and avoiding whining about how the society understands Sunday.

- Equip people with skills for a more balanced life. In hundreds of interviews of parishioners conducted by CDI participants we heard again and again about the issue of balance in life. They talked about spouses and partners, children, friends, work, volunteer activities; they spoke of stress due to illness, the care of aging parents, alienation from family members, and the pressures they place on themselves about how to be and live.

  In the interviews people shared many of the skills and methods they had developed to cope with all the expectations and demands. Some examples are being organized, maintaining and developing friendships, learning to say no, routines about rest and meals, gardening, exercise, people to talk with about the pressures, prayer, growing in a capacity for engaged-detachment, reading mysteries, taking time for enjoyment, going out to dinner with a spouse once a week, learning to let go and release things into God's hands, meditation, being regular in participation in the Sunday Eucharist.

  A desire commonly mentioned that is related to the balance issue, and is addressed by the coping practices, was for a sense of perspective. The parish might assist by providing occasions to share how people struggle to achieve an adequate balance. Just sharing their own struggle and hearing about that of others often helps. It may be important to limit the size and duration of such groups so they don't just add to the problem.

  Two other perspectives that caught my attention—one woman said, "I'm not very good at balancing things. I simply try to live each day, and pray." Another woman reflected on how the very struggle about balancing life was a source of pleasure. It spoke to her of the value of her life and how she was valued by others.

Structures, Processes and Climate to Support the Formation of Children

The parish's children have their own way of living the Renewal – Apostolate Cycle and of participating in the Eucharistic community. They are in a process of spiritual development along with the adults.

One way of thinking about the formation of children is to use the same core elements identified on the first page of this section. The life and growth of children and adults involves accepting our dependence on God, responsibility for shaping our spiritual life, and interdependence with others in the Body of Christ. That acceptance is nurtured by and expressed in our openness to spiritual guidance, having a spiritual discipline, and living in Christian community.

I like the way Gretchen Pritchard approaches the formation of children in *Offering the Gospel to Children*. Here's some of what I take away from her writing.

• Children need to be with adults in the Eucharist

Pritchard notes both the promise of participation and the damage done by not having children participating.

> "Children learn by watching and imitating adults, and by projecting themselves into imaginary worlds. Our liturgy, with its rich mixture of verbal and non-verbal, of colors and sounds and smells and gestures, is the primary source of nourishment for our adults, and should also nourish our children." … "Children who are kept from the liturgy are learning that the parish is not an inclusive community but an adult club: that its sacred space is for grown-ups only; that its normative rituals need to be mediated through adult patterns of understanding before they can be experienced, or else must be watered down into kiddie versions."

She goes on to propose a change in the common adult stance and behaviors toward children in the Eucharist. She calls for "educating parents and other parishioners to see children as fellow-worshippers, not as intruders who have to be hushed or distracted so that adults are free to pray."

Part of the preparation for Eucharistic participation that she suggests is to have in the places used for child care and education "a child-size chalice and paten, a small font and Paschal candle." By the climate, methods and things used with children, an experience happens that in many ways mirrors what we seek in our participation in the Eucharist. What Pritchard proposes aligns with the Godly Play and Catechesis of the Good Shepard programs that many parishes use. My own experience is that these parishes seem to do a better job of incorporating children into the Eucharist. See below for a bit more on this.

• Imagination needs to be stimulated and affirmed.

Prichard quotes Robert Farrar Capon:

> "Christian education is not the communication of correct views about what the various works and words of Jesus mean; rather it is the stocking of the imagination with the icons of those works and words themselves. It is most successfully accomplished, therefore, not by catechisms that purport to produce understanding, but by stories that hang the icons, understood or not, on the walls of the mind."

For Pritchard this includes engaging the child's fears. She notes how some parents have an impulse to shield the cross from their children. Her claim is that children not only should not be protected from the drama of the cross but that children don't really want (need?) that protection. She writes, "It is not the cross that terrifies children, but the false gospel that bypasses the cross and leaves us forever alone with our pain and guilt."

- Attention needs to be paid to the climate created, the physical space, and the process. Following is another quote from Prichard.

> "Instead, a series of baskets filled with wooden or clay figures depicting the stories … Imagine that the children enter this space and sit in a circle. After a greeting and some singing, the teacher brings out one of the boxes or baskets and using the clay figures … tells in quiet and spare language today's selection from the story of God's people, and invites the children to wonder about the story's impact and meaning …Then the children choose how they wish to respond." … "When the time is almost over, they are called back together for conversation, prayer and a blessing, and they enter the adult liturgy at the peace, joining their families for the gifts of Christ's Body and Blood."

Marti Rickel was the coordinator of the Catechesis of the Good Shepherd at Saint James Church in Austin. "The children experience a Holy place to be, encountering God and 'coming closer to God, all by myself.' This is done through careful preparation of the environment, the leaders (called "Catechists"), and the children. The children engage in praying, singing, and working while in this prepared environment. They are able to choose what they enjoy doing and find fulfilling, all while using their senses and cognitive abilities. The Catechesis of the Good Shepherd is more accurately called Christian formation, forming one's inner and spiritual life and one's relationship with God."

Notice how in what both Pritchard and Rickel are doing there is a two-fold process of working with children as children while also helping them stretch and be able to participate in the "adult liturgy." You can see imbedded in what is happening the three core elements needed in everyone's Renewal – Apostolate Cycle—dependence on God, responsibility for shaping our spiritual life, and interdependence with others in the Body of Christ.

Identifying Distorting Tendencies

There are several ways in which the parish can cut across (i.e., sabotage, distort, block) people's Renewal-Apostolate Cycle. There is not any way for a parish to avoid having some of these tendencies present in its life. They are part of the larger social and religious culture. We absorb them. Our awareness of those that are most strongly present in our own parish allows us to better understand parish dynamics and take constructive action. Distorting tendencies that I've observed include:

- The parish gives the impression that the world doesn't matter. There may be a protective or sentimental piety involved. It's as though we are stuck on the renewal side of the cycle.

- The parish has a fearful spirit. The fears generated by daily life have an emotional upper hand. The irrational reactivity of the world has a grip on people, e.g., feeling safe by getting SUVs that are big but roll-over, or intincting at communion to avoid illness when we know that to be the more dangerous practice. If a parish is absorbed by this fearfulness it is likely to nurture a form of unproductive dependency in people.

- The parish seems to imply that our task is to force the society to conform to "Christian" views. The language of the parish may have an over-and-against quality. Sermons and newsletter articles attack the "secular" culture with an angry undercurrent.

- The parish functions as a place to reinforce and support already established and safe religious views. There is little challenge to the culture or conventional religious views.

- The parish operates as a reinforcer of secularism. It gives the impression that this world is all there is, that there is really no need for renewal beyond oneself. The focus is on achievement in this life, here and now. It may take on an activist stance for many good works of service and justice. It may have a stance that is wrapped around a desire for financial success or social status.

- The parish becomes just another demand upon people for their energy, money and time. Parish life seems hectic and overly busy. There is pressure on people to take part in parish activities; e.g., to serve on the vestry, attend the potluck dinner. There may be a weak sense of the centrality of participation in the Sunday Eucharist. A productive alternate message might be, "It is okay to come to the 8:00 Eucharist, participate in the daily prayer of the church, give financially according to your means, participate in an occasional parish town meeting; and to never serve on a vestry, teach church school, come to social events, or be on a committee."

- The parish has a climate that helps people avoid their deeper and broader self.

- The parish doesn't challenge people's being captured by the demands and expectations of workplace, family and civic life. It may even encourage them, e.g., workaholic behavior, or an idolizing of the family, or a restless activism about social justice.

- The parish gives the impression that the apostolate in the parish is of more value than the apostolate in the world. On the parish web site there is a lot of attention to the activities and people that serve the parish's life and there is little or no mention of the apostolate in the daily life of the laity at work, in civic activities, and with family and friends.

Often these distortions are supported by images of the church that are drawn from other institutions, such as businesses, clubs, social action groups, historical societies. This is a natural enough process. People want to make sense of things. One way of making sense of the church is to establish an analogy with groups with which we are familiar.

This may be a natural enough process but it comes with problems. In *Understanding the Faith of the Church*, Richard Norris wrote that people compare "various associations which are consciously and voluntarily formed for the pursuit of common interests, ideals or goals. The idea is that a group of individuals band themselves together because they find they have convictions, needs or aims of a similar, if not identical, sort; and they are prepared to cooperate in the cultivation of their shared purposes." The danger is that parishioners begin to see the parish as a "society created by human enterprise and designed to serve particular human ends," that the church itself is created by the "agreement of a number of individual persons who presumably define the terms of their association and its goals."

All this runs counter to the church's self understanding as the *ecclesia*, a gathering of people who have been called by God to be and do something in the world. So the parish isn't a club who gather to pursue an interest, like a country club or a bowling league. It's not a political or social change movement, or a voluntary association of people who share a common view and cause. And even though we use the image ourselves, the church is not really a family bound together by kinship or adoption. While the church may have aspects of any of these structures, and may even learn from how they operate, we need to take care to maintain our self understanding as being the People of God, called into being by God, for God's purposes

The distortions take shape in many ways. Two current forms are when a parish's worth is judged in terms of service ministries or by how "orthodox" its views seem. Both expressions of this distortion share life with a number of those mentioned above. While most Episcopalians are probably more annoyed with the self-proclaimed "orthodox," it is the service focus that may be our greatest problem. I'm suggesting this for two reasons—first, it may currently be the prevailing view in the Episcopal Church; second, it has been developing in western societies for a long time. Evelyn Underhill wrote of it 1926: "We are drifting towards a religion which consciously or unconsciously keeps its eye on humanity rather than on Deity—which lays all stress on service, and hardly any of the stress on awe: and that is a type of religion which in practice does not wear well." (*Concerning the Inner Life*, p 15)

Addressing the Distortions

What can parish leaders do to counter the distortions? The first step is awareness. Become aware of the mix of tendencies present in the parish. This might be done in a discernment process that offers a climate allowing people to open their minds to see uncomfortable realities. Parishes that engage in such a process are likely to have a high degree of emotional and spiritual maturity. But even in those parishes this is usually difficult work. Most parishes will benefit from using a consultant to facilitate this process. In the discernment process people will name the distortions most alive in the parish and explore ways to address them.

It's generally easier to see the distortions if you have a common framework that points to health. Teach various ways for understanding the parish's life and ministry. This might include a mix of Scriptural and theological study along with the models in this book.

Seek the paradox within the situation. For example, the American tendency toward forms of individualism that cut us off from ourselves and others might be addressed by accepting it as a starting point. If many are inclined to an inward spirituality that seems cut off from civic responsibility, instead of fighting it we could seek ways to transform it. Parker Palmer suggested an approach in *Company of Strangers: Christians and the Renewal of American Public Life*. "Perhaps the most important ministry the church can have in the renewal of public life is a 'ministry of paradox': not to resist the inward turn of American spirituality on behalf of effective public action, but to deepen and direct that inwardness in the light of faith until God leads us back to a vision of the public and to faithful action on the public's behalf."

What if the parish isn't ready for this kind of work? The community can back up a few steps and make it ready. All change efforts work with that mix of where people are at the moment and where they could be in the near future. Leadership and stewardship are about moving us toward the deeper life and the enlarged heart. There's a need for work that is appreciative of the people and gifts already present in the parish; that provides a good bit of training in core Christian competencies; and is very patient.

Focus on the Parish's Primary Task

The Book of Common Prayer Catechism describes the mission of the church as "to restore all people to unity with God and each other in Christ." We have that mission because we understand it to be God's mission. That's what God is up to -- restoring unity, reconciliation, forgiveness. God is bringing all things into harmony in a manner that at the same time enhances individual identity. The self is not absorbed into a unity but becomes more fully oneself within community. And God's method for doing that is the Cross. We lose life to find life. The mission and its methods are for the whole church throughout the world, for every parish church, and for each of us as baptized members of that Body.

The Renewal – Apostolate Cycle is a way of understanding the parish's primary task. It's the primary way in which the parish addressing the mission.

There are two common difficulties parishes have in focusing on the primary task.
1. There is confusion about the primary task. Parish leaders may have never had the opportunity to look at the issue. It may have never occurred to the leaders that among all the things a parish

does there are some that are more central and important than others. Or it may be something that has been explored but only in a rather abstract manner.

2. There is an ingrained pattern of collective behavior that disproportionately focuses parish energy and resources on activities other than those related to the primary task.

Among the activities that draw the attention of parish leaders away from the primary task are:
- Conflict that is beyond the ability of parish leaders to easily manage.

- Major institutional efforts, e.g., construction of a new building, significant membership growth, a capital campaign.

- Ways of thinking and working that place an emphasis on things other than the primary task. The most common is when routine institutional efforts and ministries define the identity of the parish. That could be the kind of service ministries mentioned above or excessive time in meetings about property and financial issues. In these cases the apostolate gets defined in institutional terms, our collective service or maintaining our internal life and its harmony, rather that on the daily life apostolate of the baptized.

These activities may be necessary for the parish's institutional well-being or as a legitimate, if partial, expression of mission and the primary task. Leaders do need to attend to them. But there is only so much time, money and energy. While we are engaging these things the work of formation may suffer. It can help if during these periods we do two things:
- Create a firewall between the activity that is necessarily consuming our attention and at least some core formation processes. So, we maintain the parish's pattern of Eucharist and Office and continue with the adult foundations course.

- Engage the activity in a manner that weaves formation opportunities into what is happening, e.g., having a brief Office before or after meetings; making use of silence during meetings; having faith sharing that is related to the activity. This assumes that the parish is already accustomed to these resources. It is usually a mistake to attempt to introduce them during a time when parish life has been disrupted by a special need.

Being aware of the ways in which we are distracted from the primary task is important. Even more important is how we can intentionally stack the energy and resources of the parish around primary task activities. We can use money and time for better liturgy, spiritual guidance, and adult foundations programs that equip people for spiritual growth and ministry.

Other Models

The Renewal - Apostolate Cycle is a model that focuses on our baptismal identity and purpose. There are a number of other models that highlight the oscillation or cycle dimension of the Christian life. Each can be used to explore congregational development concerns. Other models include:

Salty Christians

A model developed by Hans-Ruedi Weber and presented in a small booklet, *Salty Christians*, Seabury Press, New York, 1964. Weber offers a pattern of being gathered together and scattered, a rhythm of withdrawal from and return to the world—

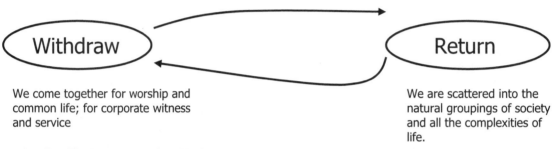

We come together for worship and common life; for corporate witness and service

We are scattered into the natural groupings of society and all the complexities of life.

The Grubb Theory of Oscillation

Developed by Bruce Reed of the Grubb Institute. Written up in *The Dynamics of Religion*, Darton, Longman & Todd, 1978. Reed suggests a movement between

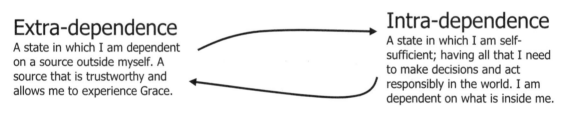

Extra-dependence
A state in which I am dependent on a source outside myself. A source that is trustworthy and allows me to experience Grace.

Intra-dependence
A state in which I am self-sufficient; having all that I need to make decisions and act responsibly in the world. I am dependent on what is inside me.

The Eternal Rhythm

Offered by Tilden Edwards in *Spiritual Friend*, Paulist Press, New York, 1980 --

Time to allow us to rest and to connect with "wisdom"

Compassionate action in the world

II. THE CHRISTIAN LIFE MODEL

The Christian Life Model: An Exercise

Do a quick assessment[4] of your parish.

1. **Overall satisfaction** with Parish Life and Ministry

I am very dissatisfied	1	2	3	4	5	6	I am very satisfied

2. *Worship* - How well we worship as a community. Also, how well the parish equips people for participation in the Eucharist and the use of the Daily Office and personal devotions

I am very dissatisfied	1	2	3	4	5	6	I am very satisfied

3. *Doctrine* - The parish's awareness of what has authority in the Christian Life. Competence as a congregation and individuals in relating those sources of authority to decision-making

I am very dissatisfied	1	2	3	4	5	6	I am very satisfied

4. *Action* - Corporate action of service, evangelization, stewardship; members' awareness of their apostolate with family and friends, in the workplace, civic life, and church. Parish's dealing with the tension between the parish's corporate ministries and the individual's apostolate in daily life.

I am very dissatisfied	1	2	3	4	5	6	I am very satisfied

5. *Oversight* - Competence and commitment of clergy and leaders for leadership and management, building community, and deepening the congregation's spiritual life; leaders serving, guiding, leading and managing the parish into an appropriate and full living of the Christian Life; bringing and preserving a proper order/shape in the parish's life; methods for reflecting, discerning and planning in parish life; lay-clergy relationships; parish sense of identity and direction.

I am very dissatisfied	1	2	3	4	5	6	I am very satisfied

6. **Look over your assessment.**
   - What are three things that could be done in the coming year to improve the life and ministry of your parish?

   - What would you need to do in the next year to move your "overall satisfaction" rating up one point?

---

[4] A somewhat expanded version of this assessment is in the Resources section

The Christian Life Model: A Diagram Overview

In a world where carpenters get resurrected, everything is possible.
Eleanor in *The Lion in Winter*

For many years Mother Mary Laney was vicar of Saint Gabriel's Church in the Olney neighborhood of Philadelphia. Olney is a community of African Americans, Asians, Arabs, Africans, Hispanics, and some whites, the remains of a once-large German American population. It is one if the most diverse communities in Philadelphia. It's also a community struggling with crime, affordable housing, and employment. It was a small parish dependent on the diocese for assistance, serving the Olney community with efforts of community organizing, employment and education, and holding together a diverse membership. Saint Gabriel's had a motto: "With God all things are possible". What held them together and allowed them to move forward in service? Liturgy and prayer were certainly at the heart of it. Another one of the tools Mary Laney used was this Christian Life Model. It offered a way of thinking about the elements and dynamics of life in a Christian community.

THE CHRISTIAN LIFE MODEL

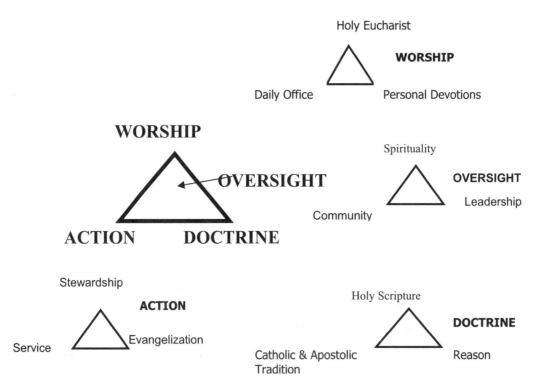

· Each element is a way in which Christ comes to us and in which we seek Christ. Each is an entry into, and participation in, the unity to which we are called. In them we are called into a deeper relationship with Jesus Christ - the heart of Christ, the mind of Christ, the work of Christ.

· The model can be used by parishes for self assessment, as a framework for planning, as a way to focus the parish on the essentials of the Christian life, and as a resource to individuals in shaping a Rule of Life. Each triangle is a system of mutual influence in which the elements strengthen and impact the other elements.

The Christian Life Model: An Exploration

The starting place for this model is what the Anglican bishops at Lambeth in 1978 spoke of as pattern of life: "This inextricable fusion of worship, of doctrine, and of action constitutes the distinctive contribution the churches of the Anglican Communion desire to make to the Universal Church of God in Jesus Christ." Martin Thornton points to it in *The Rock and the River* and in his description offers a process and systems perspective: "Moral action only flows from doctrinal truth by grace and faith, that is through prayer"

WORSHIP

Continue ... in the breaking of the bread and the prayers , BCP p. 304

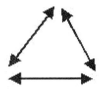

DOCTRINE

Continue in the apostles' teaching and fellowship, BCP p. 304

ACTION

To represent Christ and his Church to bear witness to him wherever they may be., BCP p. 855

Christian Life is life lived in Christ: "Christ in us and we in him." Christ comes to us and we seek Christ in worship, doctrine and action. Each is a pathway into a transformation of life, directed toward our union with the heart, mind and work of Christ; directed and our becoming a "new creation." [5]

Worship, doctrine and action are the means by which we participate in the life of Christ's Body, the Church, in her unity, holiness, catholicity and apostolicity. They are the means by which we participate in the Church's mission, "to restore all people to unity with God and each other in Christ." We are restored to unity, with God, others and ourselves as we are drawn into the prayer of Christ, the mind of Christ, and the work of Christ. In prayer, study, and work we become instruments of his holy mission. Through his baptized people he shares his life and draws all people to himself.

The parish as a corporate body can live these essentials of Christian life and ministry so that it becomes a "holy environment," a setting in which God's people may seek after him and find him.

---

[5] The hymn carries the right balance about the mission – the Unity and the maturity in Christ -- "changed from glory into glory, till in heaven we take our place, ... lost in wonder, love, and praise."

Worship

Continue in the breaking of the bread and the prayers
BCP p.304

HOLY EUCHARIST
The Gifts of God for the people of God, BCP p. 364

DAILY OFFICE
Day by day we bless you; We praise your name forever, BCP p. 98

PERSONAL DEVOTIONS
That in all the cares and occupations of our life we may not forget you, but may remember, BCP p.100

Our worship tradition as Episcopalians is based on a three-part structure. Michael Ramsey, the one-hundredth Archbishop of Canterbury, referred to it as the "Benedictine triangle." Martin Thornton called it the "Catholic Threefold Rule of Prayer." It is the Prayer Book's way of prayer. The three elements, Eucharist, Daily Office, and Personal Devotions, comprise the fundamentals of a disciplined Christian spirituality in the Anglican tradition.

The use of this pattern can help individuals and parishes move away from the attempt to base our prayer life on a self-made, unintegrated list of "rules" toward an integrated Rule grounded in *The Book of Common Prayer*. It is as a parish, as a local expression of the Body of Christ, that we may fully participate in and offer this threefold pattern. As individuals we will at times participate in this pattern, carrying others in prayer. At other times we will be carried.

The active relationship among *Eucharist/Daily Office/Personal Devotions* can be seen in how the Office is deepened and enriched by a person's personal devotions, how all three influence one another, and how the Office and personal devotions are focused and completed in the Eucharist. It's common for parish leaders to think about improving something by focusing on the thing itself. So, if we want to improve the parish's celebration of the Eucharist we might train those assisting at the altar to carry themselves with more grace and dignity, to hold their hands folded in front of the belly, and so on. Also, we might train the congregation for its participation. Both are worth doing and are likely to result in improvement. What we often miss is how dramatically our Eucharistic celebration is improved when a critical mass or even a core of those gathered has said the Office, in some form, that week and engaged in a way of personal devotions that nurtures and possibly stretches them.

What we bring to the Eucharist has a great impact on what happens in the Eucharist. This is a systems view of what takes palce in the Eucharist and of the process of liturgical renewal. Thornton notes the same reality, "Eucharist – Office – private prayer forms one whole balanced organic life," and "private prayer is absolutely dependent on the Office and the Eucharist."

Evelyn Underhill wrote of the role of Office and Eucharist:

> The peculiarity of the Anglican tradition is the equal emphasis which it gives to the Divine Office and the Eucharist; that is to say, to Biblical and to Sacramental worship. Where this balance is disturbed, its special character is lost. ...It is, I believe, by the balanced and instructed development of these two great instruments of Christian worship—carrying them forward without

deflection from their supernatural orientation, yet keeping them flexible to the changing spiritual needs and spiritual insights of the world—that the Anglican Communion will best fulfill its liturgical office within the Body of Christ. Here support and stimulus is given to the Godward life of the individual, while the solemn objectivity of true Catholic worship is preserved. (*Worship* by Evelyn Underhill, 1936, pp.335-336)

Underhill refers to the pattern we see in *The Book of Common Prayer*. About two-thirds of the book is taken up with the Eucharist, the Office, and materials to support those acts of worship (lectionaries, the Psalms). *The Book of Common Prayer* isn't a book of personal devotions, but its spirituality does assume that the Christian will find ways of personal devotion that are appropriate to their own personality and growth in love. The "equal emphasis" that she writes of isn't the distortion that many Anglicans once made of using the Office as an alternative to the Eucharist on Sundays. She's affirming a balance that is more to be seen in a parish that celebrates the Holy Eucharist each Sunday as its primary expression of worship and offers Morning, Noonday or Evening Prayer on all, or most, of the other days of the week.

The Holy Eucharist

The Eucharist sums up in itself Christian worship ..It seems to include everything. It combines Word and Sacrament; its appeal is to spirit and to sense ...; it is communion with God and communion with man .... Gathers up in itself the meaning of the church; its whole action implies and sets forth our mutual interdependence in the Body of Christ; it unites us with the Church of the past ...; an anticipation of the heavenly banquet. John MacQuarrie, *Paths in Spirituality*

There are five interrelated elements involved in strengthening the Eucharistic life of the parish.

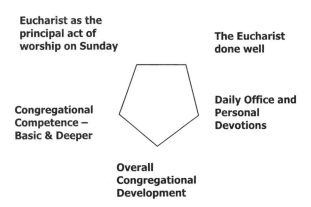

Eucharist as the Principal Act of Worship on Sunday

The parish can invite members to make the Sunday Eucharist a core part of their spiritual discipline, to commit themselves to join with the parish community in its celebration of the Holy Eucharist.

The Eucharist Done Well

Doing it well means spending time and energy to equip those with a special role in the celebration, e.g., cantor, lector, ministers of the altar, acolyte. Expect things to be well done. If a person doesn't have the gifts needed to do it well, help them let go of the role and seek something for which their gifts are suited. Attention to the issue of personal presence may possibly be the thing that will make the most difference in doing the Eucharist well and in the spiritual life of those assisting at the altar. We are seeking the presence of each in a manner that: lives in the paradox of seeking to do things perfectly while not getting agitated about mistakes; has a centered stance, confident and self–aware; doesn't intrude on the worship of the whole congregation by drawing attention to those serving; and doesn't seek to create particular emotions by the style of reading, preaching or presiding.

Congregational Competence

There is the basic competence that comes as we coach and educate the whole congregation to participate in the Liturgy by memorizing the prayers and responses, learning the physical gestures and movements, and becoming familiar with the flow of the Eucharist as done in the parish. We can bring them to the point where they do not need to have the Prayer Book or service leaflet in front of them for most of the Eucharist.

There is also a deeper congregational competence in what people bring to the Eucharist from their daily life. This is, in part, an understanding of what we do at the Offertory: the laying upon the altar our whole life (work, family and friends, civic life) and our whole self (mind and heart, virtues and gifts, faults and sins). It is also about our prayer life, our spiritual discipline. Deeper competence also includes various devotional acts members engage in to strengthen their participation (preparing for hearing the Word by reading the propers in advance, listening to the lector as she reads rather than looking at an insert).

Daily Office & Personal Devotions

The parish's Eucharist is deepened and enriched by the presence of a critical mass of members who join in the Daily Office and some form of personal devotions during the week.

Overall Congregational Development

The Eucharist shapes a healthier, more faithful parish, and is, in turn, shaped by that community. Invite and support people's cooperation with the parish's efforts to improve its life and ministry as one way to strengthen the Eucharistic community.

Work at developing competence and proficiency in liturgical leaders and in a critical mass of each congregation in the parish. The offering of the Eucharist and the Office in a competent manner is both a sign of a parish's spiritual health and also a means to nurture that health. Sloppy worship feeds spiritual immaturity and infects visitors and newer members. In addition to the problem of shoddy worship there are other ways in which we undermine the power of liturgy in many parishes:

1. Turning liturgy into a performance.

This typically occurs by focusing on what happens up-front and not equipping the congregation for competent participation. The other common expression of liturgy as performance is when the music dominates worship by having the choir located behind the altar, frequent solos or anthems, and cantors acting like song leaders.

2. Turning liturgy into an educational activity.
This happens when we disrupt the rhythm of liturgical life with instructed Eucharists or the use of historic liturgies. Both cut across the norm of "common prayer." They disrupt the congregation's ownership of the liturgy. Instead we can train people for liturgy within a foundations course, in special sessions after the Sunday Eucharist, and by occasional teaching sermons.

3. Turning the liturgy into a planned instrument of membership growth.

This is what happens when parish leaders misunderstand the relationship among evangelization, membership growth, and sanctification. We end up with "user friendly worship" or worship excessively anxious about everyone feeling comfortable. We end up undercutting the power of liturgy for personal transformation and our ability to attract members seeking a real liturgical life.

An alternate way of thinking about all this begins with not trading off one value for another. It is about managing polarities.

- Seek relaxed formality in liturgy rather than sloppiness or rigidity.
- Seek an integrated experience of grace and beauty on the part of congregation, the altar party, and musicians rather than a fragmented experience in which liturgy is divided into elements and turf.
- Seek a balance in parish life that respects the integrity of the liturgical experience and offers at other times training for those who want to become more comfortable with worship practices and flow.
- Seek another balance in parish life. Allow the liturgy to be a participation in the Mystery, a recreation of the Body of Christ, and an experience in which we offer ourselves upon the altar. Let the visitor's first experience of the Eucharist be that they are part of something that moves beyond their understanding and control; in a community that owns its liturgy as seen in the competent participation of the congregation; and that they are noticed and accepted.

The Sunday Eucharist can be an experience drawing people into the life of God. St. John Chrysostom wrote, "You cannot pray at home as at church, where there is a great multitude, where exclamations are cried out to God as from one great heart, and where there is something more: the union of minds, the accord of souls, the bond of charity, the prayers of the priests." (*De incomprehensibili*)

The Daily Office

The value of the Office is its objectivity. It is a means by which we pray with the whole church, uniting our prayer with that of millions of other Christians living and dead. This is true whether one is alone or in a group, for the Office is essentially a corporate act. It is objective too in that it does not depend on our feelings, but gives our prayer life a regularity and a disciplined framework. Kenneth Leech, *True Prayer*

An illustration of the power of the Office in forming a Christian is in Jonathan Daniels' story. Daniels was an Episcopal seminarian killed in Alabama during the civil rights movement. Not long before his death he wrote:

> I lost fear in the black belt[6] when I began to know in my bones and sinews that I had been truly baptized into the Lord's death and Resurrection, that in the only sense that really matters I am already dead, and my life is hid with Christ in God. I began to lose self-righteousness when I discovered the extent to which my behavior was motivated by worldly desires and by the self-seeking messianism of Yankee deliverance! The point is simply, of course, that one's motives are usually mixed, and one had better know it. As Judy and I said the daily offices day by day, we became more and more aware of the living reality of the invisible "communion of saints"—of the beloved community in Cambridge who were saying the offices too, of the ones gathered around a near-distant throne in heaven—who blend with theirs our faltering songs of prayer and praise. With them, with black men and white men, with all of life, in Him Whose Name is above all the names that the races and nations shout, whose Name is Itself the Song Which fulfils and "ends" all songs, we are indelibly, unspeakably ONE.

In *Paths in Spirituality*, John MacQuarrie made the same point about the Office as "a way by which we keep ourselves in constant awareness of the divine order; an order of love and justice which embraces and underlies all order."

Strengthen the Daily Office

There are four ways we can more fully engage the Office in the parish church.

1. Train and coach individuals to use it at home. Formally teach the mechanics of it, have people practice and reflect on its use.
2. Offer it most days at the church. This will connect the parish to the whole church's prayer and witness. It also offers support for the prayer life of individuals.
3. Help people make an affective connection with it. Look for resources that interpret and enliven the Office, such as the quotes or stories relayed here. Consider alternative forms to reach different types, such as this poem by Amy Hunter:

> these prayers are not woven by angels
> > but are built
> > every day every office anew
> by human voice and hunger
> the work of a people
> who have been doing this
> a long time
> *(The entire poem is in the Resources section.)*

---

[6] "Black belt" is a reference to the soil in that region of the south.

4. Teach the role of the Office in a balanced spiritual life: its function as a heartbeat for the Body of Christ, its detachment from our passing feelings and our engagement of duty. I may have first understood this idea when in my first week at seminary, Richard Norris, who taught historical theology, offered an orientation to the chapel. "The rule of the school is that you will be at the Eucharist and at Morning and Evening Prayer daily. That's the rule. Now I want to say something about your spiritual life. If you decide to ignore the rule and to only attend Evensong on Thursdays, then I hope you will attend *every* Thursday. You must not allow your passing moods and emotions to control your spiritual life."

> *The real significance of the Divine Office is that in its recitation the individual or group enters the ancient cycle of prayer, by which day by day and hour by hour the church in the name of all creation adores and implores the eternal God.* Evelyn Underhill

See Resources section "Daily Office"

Personal Devotions

> *Prayer must involve the unifying of the personality, the integration of mind and heart into one center.... Without self discovery there can be no further progress. 'In order to find God whom we can only find in and through the depths of our own soul, we must first find ourselves.' Without self-knowledge our love remains superficial.* (Kenneth Leech, *Soul Friend*)

There are a variety of ways of looking at Personal Devotions. Martin Thornton sees three forms:

1. Mental prayer, which is directed toward increasing our knowledge, love and communion with God.
2. Colloquy, which is saying our prayers in forms of petition, intercession, and adoration.
3. Recollection, which are momentary acts of prayer throughout the day; practicing the presence of God by habits of prayer such as a blessing before and after a meal or in a spontaneous response to an experience of the Divine Presence in a person or creation.

In *The Handbook for Prayer*, Lowell Grisham divides the types of personal devotions this way into *Kataphatic* (with words or images) and *Apophatic* (without words or images.)
He goes on to say that, "Styles of prayer tend to be distinguished by whether they concentrate on feelings or thoughts." The handbook then offers ways of meditating with Scripture (*Lectio Divina*, the Ignatian Method of Prayer), other forms of *Kataphatic* Prayer (A.C.T.S. Method of Prayer, Conversational Prayer), and *Apophatic* Prayer (Breath Prayer, Centering Prayer)

Regardless of how we categorize the various methods, Personal Devotions are about our unique relationship with God. While the Eucharist and Office are acts of corporate worship (even if we say Morning Prayer alone), personal devotions reflect how each person is drawn into the mystery in ways that fit his or her personality and spiritual development.

What the parish can do to assist people in experimenting with their personal devotions:

- Have printed resources available. Something brief like Father Grisham's *Handbook for Prayer* and a variety of material that deals with things in more depth.
- Offer a "school of prayer" every so often. This might be done as part of a larger Foundations Course. The sessions would be an opportunity for people to be introduced to various forms of personal devotions, to experiment with them, and to reflect on what they are experiencing in their prayer life.
- Use a personality instrument such as MBTI to help people explore the relationship between their personality and personal devotions. This might also include a look at how different personalities might enter into the Eucharist and the Office.

The threefold rule is a systems approach to prayer. It both assumes that the life of each person in the Body is interdependent with the life and health of the whole organism; and that each form of worship enriches and completes the others.

Doctrine

Continue in the apostles' teaching and fellowship
BCP p.304

SCRIPTURE
To hear them, read, mark, learn and inwardly digest (BCP p. 236)

CATHOLIC & APOSTOLIC TRADITION
Upon the foundation of the apostles and prophets, BCP p. 230

REASON
Blessed .. with memory, reason and skill, BCP p. 370

We are called to the transformation of our minds, to have in us the mind of Christ, to see our lives and our world through the eyes of Christ. Concrete ways for this transformation to occur are offered by Our Lord, within and through the Church, in the Scriptures, in the Catholic and Apostolic Tradition, and in the Holy Reason of the People of God. As Anglicans we give authority to those teachings that we can recognize in the Scriptures, that have come to be generally accepted in the Church through many centuries, and that can withstand the test of human reason in each age.

The Balance: A Threefold Stool, Cord, or Fabric?

In *The Challenge and Hope of Being an Anglican Today: A Reflection for the Bishops, Clergy and Faithful of the Anglican Communion,* Archbishop Rowan Williams wrote of the three elements of Scripture, Tradition, and Reason. In a possible tilt toward more conservative Anglicans he wrote of "a reformed commitment to the absolute priority of the Bible for deciding doctrine" and then, possibly in a nod to most Western Anglicans, noted that, "To accept that each of these (*e.g. Scripture, Tradition, Reason*) has a place in the church's life and that they need each other means that the enthusiasts for each aspect have to be prepared to live with certain tensions or even sacrifices…The only reason for being an Anglican is that this balance seems to you to be healthy for the Church Catholic, and that it helps people grow in discernment and holiness." Living and thinking in relationship to this paradoxical web is, as the Archbishop says, to live with "a habit of cultural sensitivity and intellectual flexibility that does not seek to close down unexpected questions too quickly" and therefore with "certain tensions." In an interview with the Church Times he offered a very Anglican and Benedictine way for the bishop's who where soon to gather for Lambeth, "Any kind of bishop has to do a kind of mediating job, a kind of: 'Have you heard what they are saying yet? Let's try and stay in the room for a little longer." (July 11, 2008)

That statement is the Anglican "thing"—an affirmation of the three sources of authority and an acknowledgement that it's difficult, but possible and productive, to live within the messiness and fuzziness. It's not just that we grow in faith by allowing our hearts and minds to be influenced by these sources; it's also that we grow by being in communion with people whose approach to the sources and conclusions differ from our own.

Scripture

The Scriptures of the Church have a special standing in relationship to the other two sources. There's an understanding in Anglicanism that we are not to require belief in anything that is not congruent with Scripture. This includes the idea that the Scriptures are to always be a significant part of our thinking about meaning and doctrine; but it's also that in our worship and prayer life we engage the Scriptures. The scriptural nature of the Eucharistic rite and ceremony, the rhythm of the Daily Office, and forms of devotion such as *lectio divina* are all expressions of this priority.

I experienced another way of expressing this priority when I was part of a city commune, all Episcopalians, that gathered weekly for the Eucharist. On one occasion, Bob, the urban minister for the UCC conference, joined us to preside and begin a shared homily. The lectionary for that day had us reading Paul on wives submitting to their husbands. As you might imagine there was a temptation to select another reading. Bob, however, insisted that we stay with what was appointed. "Stay with the hard passages. Engage them rather than avoiding them. It enriches life."

Tradition

Tradition has its roots in the emergence, in the early church, of the Sacraments, of a ministry of deacons, priests and bishops, and of the Creeds. It was continued in the writings of the Church Fathers and the first Councils. This work of the Holy Spirit continued through the ages as God's people have sought to understand God's movement in and among us.

The Church reveals another aspect of Tradition in the manner it has dealt with the polarity inherent in having to adapt while maintaining the Church's identity, integrity and internal integration. We came to understand our nature as one, holy, catholic, and apostolic as we faced the questions of circumcision and the gentiles, of what to do with those who sin after baptism, and of the validity of the sacraments celebrated by a priest of questionable views or virtue. The tradition is maintained and grows in this process. We adapt so we can survive and better engage the mission.

Reason

Timothy Sedgwick wrote, "Anglicans have consistently claimed that reason is the fulcrum by which the voices of scripture and tradition are lifted into perspective." (*Continuing the Dialogue*, Education for Mission and Ministry Unit of the Episcopal Church Center, 1988)

Reason draws upon the totality of the church's and humanity's experience and understanding. In its interaction with scripture and tradition it both interprets them and at the same time is enlarged by them. Reason in this setting is more than rationality and logic. It also calls upon our empathy and imagination in sorting out and deciding on meaning, and on what is moral and what is to be done in a particular situation. Reason is a form of practical wisdom grounded in reality. Our willingness to learn from our experience is an expression of reason.

Balance, Unity, Participatory and Community

Ways in which we connect with the sources of authority are in balance, unity, participatory engagement, and community.

Balance

Balance is maintained by seeing the three sources as intertwined rather than as separate and independent from one another. Each is indispensable. Anglicans seem to disagree about the weight each is to be given. Most Episcopalians appear to be eclectic in how the balance works; on occasion seeing all as being equally in play and at other times one element or the other having more importance.

Unity

The sources are aspects of one thing. Together they are a unity that points us toward Christian truth. None of the threads stands alone. They join together, sometimes in an easy affinity and at other times in troubled harmony. The three are woven into a fabric that differs in appearance depending on the community involved and the issues being worked. While the Scriptures are the ground for all essential doctrine, they need to be interpreted in the presence of Tradition and Reason.

Participatory Engagement

We misunderstand the workings of the Holy Spirit if we approach the sources as though they will in themselves produce a timely clarity or an answer to what we anxiously seek certainty about. Our spiritual growth comes by our engagement with the sources. Engagement both in the more passive sense of allowing ourselves to be immersed in it through liturgy, prayer and life in community and in the more active sense of doing the hard work of thinking on our own and with others. In both ways we submit ourselves to that authority.

In practice this approach doesn't come out with "the answer." Most parishes will include people with very different views. All these members have been shaped to some extent by the sources of authority. Even those who have approached some moral or doctrinal issue in a very prayerful and thoughtful manner often arrive at different conclusions. As a parish priest my role was not to get others to accept my position about abortion, the Resurrection, same-sex marriage, the virginity of Mary, or the latest war. I certainly have my own views and I do share them. But my concern was for the community's participation in the process of discernment.

Community

In the Episcopal Church's history there have always been attempts by one group or another to claim the truth of a particular way of approaching the sources of authority. For the most part

Episcopalians with differing emphases continued to live in community with one another, having friendly arguments and responding to differing emotional and intellectual needs. We prided ourselves on this diversity. On occasion, small groups have become so entrenched in their "truth" that they break off from the larger body. Now we may be experiencing the consequences of one party having seen an opportunity to have its way triumph over the others.

In my own life I have found it useful to do two things with all this. The first is to stay light, even humorous about it. The second is to come at the question from within a particular context. My primary interest as a priest is to equip members of the Body of Christ to engage, individually and collectively, the sources of authority. I want them to ground themselves in the web of Scripture, Tradition, and Reason. I want them to listen to the prayerful thinking of the larger church—of our bishops, General Convention, Lambeth and our theologians. I want them to hear the feelings and ideas and discernment of others in the parish. I want them to make up their own mind, to accept their role as responsible adults, and to continue to listen and engage. And I want them to stay connected to one another and the wider church as they seek understanding.

Former Presiding Bishop Frank Griswold said, "Truth is discovered in communion. If we want to know the mind of Christ, we have to do it together." That brings me back to how it is that we are to "have in us the mind of Christ, to see our lives and our world through the eyes of Christ." Regardless of all the polemics about how we are to understand the relationship among the three sources, there is not any real agreement about the matter and there is unlikely to be a consensus. It is by grace that we have one another: in discernment and disagreement.

I appreciate how the Conservative Jewish movement deals with defining acceptable teaching. The Rabbinical Assembly has the Committee on Jewish Law and Standards. It's made up of a committee of 25 rabbis with vote and 5 lay people without vote. If any six of the rabbis agree that a position is valid, then it's valid. When more than one position is validated, the rabbi of a congregation functions as a local authority who adopts for that congregation the position he or she considers most compelling. In late 2006 six agreed that scripture forbids homosexuality. A different six agreed on ordaining gays and same-sex marriage. What a generous way to handle times of transition. No one is pushed out of the community. Of course, no one gets to claim all the truth, except God.

Acceptance of Reality

We seem to be living in a time of literalism that comes from all corners. The right wants the Bible to do our science for us and the left wants utopian reform—all in the name of Scripture, or at least while quoting Scripture. From all sides comes pressure to "change the world" in someone's image and vision of scriptural truth. Literalism shows itself in making scientific and historic claims about the poetic and mythical language of scripture and liturgy. That language is used to express the eternal meaning and truth of the church's faith. The right and the left both seem invested in using language in its most literal and flat-footed sense.

I've been considering for myself the claim of reality-based living, which is an approach to life that is cautious about our tendency to eject our own prejudices into the church's theology and the government's laws. We are living in a time when facts and rational analysis are under attack in the name of religion. The faith I see rising from the interplay of Scripture, Tradition and Reason is one that respects rational analysis and understands facts as holy. It looks at the real-world results and consequences of what we teach and how we live.

The church is always in a struggle within itself and in the world about the balance of Scripture, Tradition and Reason. That effort is inevitable and useful. It is part of how we stay faithful. Living deeply in the words of scripture and understanding them in relationship to the church's ongoing attempt to apply them in each age is essential. But also essential is our need to hold fast to reason. Aquinas understood it as a "regard for and openness to reality," as an "acceptance of reality." Jeremy Taylor wrote, "He that speaketh against his own reason speaks against his own conscience, and therefore it is certain that no man serves God with a good conscience who serves him against his reason."

We may, of course, need to sort out different kinds of "realities." There is the day-to-day, concrete reality that can to some extent be verified and tested. This is the reality that allows scientific and anthropological research, that allows juries and courts to function and the routine exchanges of life to occur with some degree of harmony. And there is also what Paul Tillich called Ultimate Reality, allowing us access to what is eternal and life in the Glory.

The Episcopal Church can offer the world a form of reality-base living that engages and respects both realities. On the issue of science and faith, Presiding Bishop Katharine Jefferts Schori stated, "Religion and science are both ways of knowing, but they go at it from somewhat different perspectives. Science asks questions about how things happen and where they've come from. Religion and faith traditions ask questions of meaning, about why we're here and what we should do with what we have here, and how we should relate to the rest of creation." (Bill Moyer's Journal, 6/8/07)

Worship Shapes Belief

The way we worship shapes our identity and expresses what we believe. To know what Episcopalians believe, look at *The Book of Common Prayer*. To really know, participate in a parish's Sunday celebration of the Eucharist. To experience the depth and breadth of it, use the three-fold rule of prayer in shaping your own prayer life.

This suggests, then, a pathway for us. The best and richest way to allow the sources of authority to be internalized, to be on our heart and mind, is to engage Scripture as part of liturgy and prayer. This is more our way than Bible study or attempts to memorize passages (as useful as they may be for some).

The day-by-day, practical issue in doctrine is less one of deciding on some set of beliefs and more about allowing the filters we see through to include the church's scripture and tradition. This process of internalization, in our tradition, happens as we hear the Gospel read and preached, participate in the daily heartbeat of the Office readings, and open ourselves in *lectio* and other forms of scriptural-based reflection. That process is ongoing, so our internalizing is ongoing. Over time our understanding may be deepened and changed.

The Scriptures seem to scare some Episcopalians. It may be a fear that they will fall into a pit of intolerance, a pit with narrow walls and little light. It's a good fear to have. All too often, the Scriptures have been used by both conservatives and liberals to beat-up others and to protect themselves from change.

I have noticed that many of the Episcopalians who are apprehensive about how the Bible is used in debate seem comfortable with it when used in worship. Engagement of the Scriptures as part of the community's liturgy and prayer is not only our particular way but also a more effective means of allowing its influence to become inwardly absorbed.

In the Eucharist and Office the words of Scripture are in the liturgic text and are read during the liturgy. In the traditional physical acts of reverence that are part of our worship we take on a stance of wonder and awe toward the Word. In these ways the Scriptures become less "out-there", standing outside us, and more inward, gently working a way into our hearts and minds. In this context, they are less about being confronted as an individual, and more about a particular Child of God, from within the People of God, being fed for the journey.

In spiritual reading and *lectio* the emphasis is on reflection, and listening, and enjoying the presence of God.

In prayer, in the presence of the Christ, our minds are opened. In prayer, alone or with others, but from within the community of the baptized, the Spirit overshadows us and our transformation is set in motion.

Bring Our Empathy

In John Noonan's book on the development of Catholic moral teaching (*A Church that Can and Cannot Change*) he makes a case that the church's growth in understanding and ability to usefully respond to the human condition comes out of the engagement of our experience and our empathy. This is not to say that our experience is a fourth source of the church's authority but that it is a common human source of authority. We do give authority to our experience. It is what we bring to the table and many of us struggle to learn from it. In the field of experiential education we frequently say that you don't learn from your experience but by disciplined reflection on your experience. I'd modify that and suggest that such learning may not always be disciplined, but it is always related to the filters, the mental models and emotional patterns, that we bring into our learning process. An old hymn suggests that "new occasions teach new duties." That's an affirmation of the impact of experience. As we engage our experience with the filters of scripture, tradition and reason, we may see a new thing that may open up new choices for moral living.

Noonan reminds us of Paul's instruction "that your love abound more and more in knowledge and insight of every kind so that you test what is vital." (Phil 1:9 – 10) Noonan sees in this a web of love, knowledge and insight. Part of how we grow in moral vision and behavior is to allow ourselves to be empathetic to the experience of others as well as our own experience. In Anglican terms it means understanding "Reason" as including a process of thinking and feeling by which we engage the human experience. It is authentic engagement we seek, not some disembodied type of thinking that distances us from ourselves, others and God.

To Be Formed in Christ

There's a common confusion in our pastoral theology and practice that shows up as some try to use the Doctrine corner of the Christian Life Model. Some have been inclined to substitute "education" or "formation" for the word Doctrine. That misses the point. The measure is whether people are allowing the sources of the church's authority to influence them. The measure is not how many educational programs we have. Education, training and formation programs are ways of assisting people to access worship, doctrine and action. All three elements can make good use of such programs. Education is not the only way that this happens. For many people, it is by living a spiritual life grounded in the church's Rule that they have come to the mind of Christ. I'd suggest that people are more likely to intuitively "get" the Creed by singing it in the Eucharist than by reading a book on it. Aidan Kavanagh wrote, "The liturgy, like the feast, exists not to educate but to seduce people into participating in common activity of the highest order, where one is freed to learn things which cannot be taught."

Our concern is to be formed in Christ. The issue is: What will we allow to influence and shape us on a regular and frequent basis? Formation includes the development of habits of prayer and behavior that flow from who and whose we are in baptism. Formation also includes the way we think and decide. We are called to a life in which the Church's sources of authority are engaged often and in a recurring pattern. Our task is to discern and respond to the movement of the Holy Spirit in our lives. And to do that from within the Body, including those who see and feel differently from ourselves. Our experience is to be reflected upon in relationship to Scripture, Holy Tradition, the wisdom and knowledge of the larger human experience, and our own logic and good sense.

The outcome of formation is orthodoxy and participation in the divine life. Kenneth Leech wrote, "Orthodoxy is about being consumed by glory; the word means not 'right belief' (as dictionaries tell us) but right *doxa*, right glory. To be orthodox is to be set alight by the fire of God." (*True Prayer*) In her 2006 Christmas message Katharine Jefferts Schori said, "Irenaeus and Athanasius insisted that the gift of Incarnation was that 'God became human, that we might become divine.' You and I are bearers of the image of God, and you and I share in Incarnation, for Jesus has walked this way before us. God is born in us as well."

Humility

One danger that keeps reappearing in the church's life is confusing faith with our longing for certainty. Apostolic Christians are people of faith characterized by, among other things, a stance of humility. It is to stand before God and humanity with doubts and in wonder on the one hand and with courage and persistence on the other. John Stuart Mill caught the balance: "There is no such thing as absolute certainty, but there is assurance sufficient for the purposes of human life."

The Episcopalian's inclination to deal with doctrine through prayer and liturgy is a way of acknowledging that we live in the mystery of God. It is the humility to sing the Creed even when questioning its phrases; to say the Office even when uncertain that God cares; and to offer intercession while wondering if there is any result from such effort.

As individuals and a community the church needs to engage society and itself with whatever wisdom we have at the moment. We may find it useful to our spiritual growth to include in all such statements a caution about the limits of that wisdom. What we are to think and do about marriage and foreign policy is worthy of debate and discernment and can manifest something of God's love for the world. It may, however, be more important that we occasionally offer, with open hearts and minds, a special intention in the Eucharistic Offertory around the nation's foreign policy and our marriages and relationships. Life is given holy order by our prayer more than by our thinking things through.

The invitation to humility arrives from all corners of life. Elissa Ely, M.D., reported on her own experience in the early 90s with a patient's mother who resisted the use of the standard anti-psychotic medications because of what she understood to be the side effects. Acting in what

69

they believed to be the best interests of the patient, the doctors had the mother removed as legal guardian. The data were on the side of the doctors. And the patient became better with the medications. Later they learned that the patient developed diabetes. Studies eventually confirmed an association between such medications and diabetes. Dr. Ely ended the article with this: "Kierkegaard wrote that we understand backwards but we live forward. ... The facts we had then were incomplete, even if we didn't know it at the time. We were right but we were wrong, innocent but at fault, acting in good faith with bad results." ("Medicine, Constantly Redefined and Redefining Lives", *New York Times* 7/24/07)

The whole church, and especially the Roman Catholics, has faced a very painful experience in part because they acted on their mistaken assumptions about redemption and the possibility of cures and healing for priest sexual predators. And from what we know now that was a costly mistake. Leaders are always taking action based on what they know at the time. Nations go to war or fail to resist aggression, parishes invest institutional funds, politicians seek to balance a variety of interests, all based on the forces, emotions, and information known at the time. Parish leaders take action seeking harmony and then Freidman and Steinke suggest that approach may undermine parish maturity. We have borrowed membership growth strategies from more evangelical traditions and later learn about organizational culture and appreciative inquiry as essential elements in creating any change effort. We begin as a Jewish sect and learn that God wants a Catholic church.

"But that's the perpetual tragedy of life: the owl of Minerva flies at dusk. Wisdom comes from suffering and error, and when the passions die down and when observation begins." (David Brooks, *New York Times* 3/8/07) Brooks was picking up on Hegel's use of the image in philosophy; it would also seem to serve those concerned with theology and ethics. We learn after the fervor of the moment. As our mind clears, we receive new information and have new thoughts, and our capacity to use a broader range of filters returns.

In the immediate situation leaders must act on the information and wisdom they have at the time. In what appears to be a reflection on his involvement in the plot to kill Hitler, Dietrich Bonhoeffer wrote, "I believe that God can and will bring good out of evil. ... I believe God will give us all the power we need to resist in all time of distress. ... I believe that even our errors and mistakes are turned to good account. ... I believe that God is no timeless fate but that he waits for and answers sincere prayer and responsible action." And on the meaning of free responsibility he wrote, "It depends upon a God who demands bold action as the free response of faith and who promises forgiveness and consolation to the man who becomes a sinner in the process." (*Letters and Papers from Prison*)

Action

To represent Christ and his Church; to bear witness to him wherever they may be.
BCP p.855

SERVICE
Seek and serve Christ in all persons, BCP p. 305

EVANGELIZATION
Proclaim by word and example the Good News of God in Christ, BCP p. 305

STEWARDSHIP
You formed us in your own image giving the whole world into our care, BCP p. 373

Christian action is participation by the People of God in the work of God. This is a process of being drawn into a deeper relationship with God, into service to others, and into responsible participation in the care and ordering of the creation. To be a Christian is to be a servant, evangelist and steward. This is most properly understood as a way of being rather than as a list of things to do. Those shaped over the years by participation in the life and ministry of Christ's Body, nurtured by Word and Sacrament, grasped again and again by Mercy and Glory, become his light and salt and leaven. Martin Thornton touches on this in *Spiritual Direction*: "Aquinas got it right: prayer is 'loving God in act so that the divine life can communicate itself to us and through us to the world.' Christian action is not action of which Jesus approves but action that he performs through his incorporated, and therefore prayerful, disciples."

The context within which we are servants, evangelists and stewards is our daily life and work. Because of who we are in Christ, we are—in our work, community and family—instruments of his compassion, his inviting, and his order.

The particular way in which we are servants, evangelists and stewards will depend on the needs and opportunities present in our work, family and neighborhood. It will also take on a particular shape due to our order (laity, bishop, priest, deacon), our particular vocation(s) in the Church and world, and our gifts. The parish is to facilitate an awareness of and support for the lay apostolate of service, evangelization and stewardship while also engaged in appropriate corporate expressions of each.

The central expression of Christian action is what flows in the Renewal–Apostolate Cycle of each person. Most of a parish's ministry is accomplished in the daily lives of its members. The secondary expression is what we do collectively as a parish community. In the material below I give more attention to the corporate expression of Christian action and allow the chapter of the Renewal–Apostolate Cycle to speak to the more primary form of action.

Evangelization

The principal evangelical tools of the church are (1) mature individuals grounded in the spiritual life of the church; and (2) parish churches exhibiting a joyful stability in their common life and liturgy. These are the things that touch the more adult and faithful elements of people's personalities. It's an organic form of evangelization. The "real life" of the faithful can attract people to faith. The spiritual health of individuals and the parish community can set loose a "buzz" from within the parish that carries over into the routine conversations of members with others.

The baptized man or woman who lives the apostolic spirituality of the church has an impact on others. For some it is an attraction, for others it puts them off. There's an influence that comes not by argument but by being. The faith is not a debate but a life. The faith is caught much like a cold. There's a contagious spreading from one to another. Of course, at some point each needs to find an adult, intelligent way to understand and own faith but the starting place is often seeing the fruits in another person.

There is also a thoughtful and intentional element to this. The apostolic Christian will not only draw people to Christ by their being but will also find in themselves a sensitivity about when there is and isn't an openness in the people with whom they work and live. The conversation will come when the time is right. Because we know Christ, we can introduce Christ to another at the right moment.

The parish's corporate work of evangelization is about attending to the whole process of a person's formation, from doing what you can to draw people to the parish's life and worship, to nurturing them as Apostolic Christians. The parish needs to know how it is approaching all the various needs around inviting, greeting, orienting, incorporating, and sending. That doesn't mean having a massive planning document; it means knowing what you are trying to accomplish and how you intend to go about it.

In that aspect of evangelization that is about membership growth there are a few things most parishes need to focus on:

Develop a Healthy Parish

Set aside the life of grumbling and loneliness and seek the life of community and solitude. Let go of anxiety about making members happy and serving their needs and turn instead toward making members holy and being a community of compassion and justice.

Some parishes have a climate that is grumpy or angry or whiny. If you project that climate, you will bring in people drawn to that. So, your parish may grow numerically but it's not really set up for success in the formation of people. I had a parish client that spent a lot of its energy being unhappy with the diocese and with the Episcopal Church as a whole. I ended up telling them that they had to agree to knock it off if I was to be of any use to them as a consultant. I told them that such behavior just made the parish unattractive and would impact its growth and health. So far, they seem to be making progress.

In other situations I have noticed that a rector's preaching has a frustrated and judgmental tone. In one case, it was a conservative priest complaining about American culture, keeping Christ in Christmas, and so on; in another case, it was a liberal priest complaining about how the parish didn't do enough for the homeless and poor. I doubt either approach did much for the listeners.

If the Episcopal Church wants to survive and grow the starting place is for parish churches to live in the best of the tradition. We need to focus on what is already healthy and sound in the parish; expand that and build upon it. The parish also needs to draw on the best of the Episcopal

Church's tradition. Find and live what has health and hope. Attend to those things and the parts that are unworthy and distorted will weaken and fall away. This isn't about aggressive and audacious planning or action. It is about the courage, patience and wisdom needed to see what is health, to trust that it is the Spirit's work, and to live it.

Here are a few things you can do to create a healthier parish.

1. Ground the parish's life in prayer
2. Stay focused on the primary task of a parish; serve people in the renewal of their baptismal life.
3. Build the capacity of the parish by training leaders in congregational development and decision-making as part of a team.
4. Give attention to strategic issues like building relationships and knowing three things that need to be done in the next two years to increase health. These matters are usually not urgent, even if they are important. Accordingly, there is a tendency to put off strategic issues.
5. Nurture a climate that is mature and enjoyable. Work at trust development. Teach leaders how to deal with triangulation and cope with their own and others' tendencies to play "cynic, victim or bystander." Laugh, dance, eat and drink together. Openly share the times of tears and pain.

Do Sunday Well

The primary Eucharist and the coffee hour need to be well done. In many places we need to improve the Sunday morning experience. That requires attention to the liturgy, preaching and the social connections being made. In liturgy attend to beauty and flow in music and the liturgical movement of those around the altar. Build the liturgical competence of the congregation so they can participate without prompting. That allows people looking for a church to experience the best of us. Figure out a way to get people to the coffee hour for great coffee and tea and an opportunity to meet a few people who show an interest in them. In both worship and coffee hour we need a form of hospitality that doesn't destroy the liturgy or connection among members with excessive concerns about "comfort" and "user friendliness." You are seeking to create an experience in which visitors who are ready for spiritual growth find themselves a home. One visitor to such a parish said, "the experience caught me up in something beyond myself; it blew me away."

Avoid falling off the ends of polarities that are inherent in the Sunday experience. You must *manage* the polarities and pay attention to elements from both ends.

Worship that has the structure, climate and rhythm of Apostolic faith. It needs to require some competence. It needs to have the potential to catch people up in something beyond themselves; to feed wonder and awe. Avoid worship that is oriented to the most tentative among visitors. Attempts at "user friendly" or "seeker" worship almost always undermine the parish's primary task.	....	Attention to the experience of visitors. The need is for them to feel welcomed (e.g., at the door, in the bulletin, in an announcement, etc.). Acknowledge that the experience will be different for some of them; invite them to rest in the liturgy, to allow the congregation to carry them along for a few weeks.

A coffee hour that is primarily about the community's need for connection. A mostly informal time allowing people to wander the room and talk with a variety of people. Consider having most of the parish's spoken announcements here rather than in the Eucharist. It helps the flow of the worship, connects members and visitors to the common life, and puts announcements in the more informal gathering of the parish community.

....
....

Attention to visitors, and newer attendees, by making sure that they are not abandoned. Having lots of nametags available for members and visitors to put on (never just on the new person!). Some training of people in hospitality and listening. Encourage parishioners to go directly to coffee hour and not get in a line to greet the rector. Allow the line to the rector to be primarily visitors or people not going to coffee hour; the rector can directly invite the person to come to coffee hour. That will also get the rector to coffee hour a lot sooner.

Invite People

In most places you will need to market the parish if you are to grow. Four steps to take are:

1. Have a great web site. A person should be able to look at it and make a decision that the parish may be a "fit" for them or that it is definitely not a "fit". Orient the site toward potential visitors. Consider having one link that takes existing members to a page that deals with internal concerns and administration. Think of the rest of it in terms of what a visitor will see and how a visitor may respond.
2. Have a way to drive people to your web site. Advertise! Consider an ad on Google and in the phone book that will stand out. Have paid ads in the local paper, especially at Christmas, Easter and in the early fall. Become newsworthy! Have news releases from time to time on activities that are likely to be seen as interesting by reporters. For example, while your regular Sunday Mass isn't going to get coverage, beginning a jazz vespers or jazz mass series may catch the attention of the arts and leisure pages. Clergy might learn how to become sources for reporters looking for a comment about events in the news (need to come off as intelligent and clear, not angry or whiny). Mention your web address in everything.
3. Work through your new members. New members are more likely to bring other new members. Your long-term members are really not going to have new people to bring from among their friends. So, don't try to make them feel guilty about it!
4. Look to groupings of people who are most likely to be attracted to what we can offer. Parishes need to do that in terms of the context they are in. My hunch is that in the larger society we will look at groups such as: 1) People in their 20s (and all age groups) who have an "ancient – modern" orientation; 2) Lapsed Roman Catholics looking for good liturgy and openness; and 3) Evangelicals on the Canterbury trail seeking "God-centered worship" and tradition, along with more inclusiveness.

All this needs to emerge from the existing life and competencies of the parish and not be some experiment disconnected from the parish's identity.

Nurture a Spirituality of Hospitality

Increasing parish membership has a twist in it. If your primary way of thinking about it is in terms of "membership growth," you may find yourself struggling with your own demons about measuring success in terms of numbers or seeing new people as solutions to an institutional need such as money or volunteer time. But if you turn it around so the issue is about your spirituality, you may find yourself struggling with things such as your openness to the stranger, your clarity about why this Episcopal expression of Christian faith is worth sharing with others, and the power arrangements in the parish that make it difficult for newer members to be included in a timely manner.

We know that many Episcopalians are offended by the ways some Christians approach those without a church. That sense of offense may result in a resistance to "evangelism." That leaves parish leaders a choice between fussing about words and their meaning or getting on with attracting new members. Thinking about evangelization as a process of the spiritual life in which humanity is being drawn into the heart of God helps some people. Thinking of evangelization in terms of hospitality helps others.

Stewardship

The poet Gary Snyder has this way of defining stewardship: "Stewardship means for most of us, find your place on the planet, dig in, and take responsibility from there—the tiresome but tangible work of school boards, county supervisors, local foresters, local politics, even while holding in mind the largest scale of potential change. Get a sense of workable territory, learn about it, and start acting point by point." Snyder was addressing environmentalists in the early 1970s, but to my Benedictine spirit it sounds familiar. His "find your place", "dig in", and "take responsibility" are a lot like Esther deWaal's understanding of the vow of stability. "It raises the whole issue of commitment and fidelity." … "Stability means that I must not run away from where my battles are being fought, that I have to stand still where the real issues have to be faced." (*Seeking God: The Way of Saint Benedict*). One of a parish's tasks is to equip people so they can find their place, listen to, and accept responsibility for their lives.

What about the stewardship of the parish as an institution? The parish is a system. Health in one aspect of the parish's life may generate health in other areas. Our tendency to see things in programmatic terms ends up overwhelming the parish. We think we need programs in evangelism, service and stewardship. What we actually need is an understanding of the organic workings of the Body. So, while some parishes can benefit from having a stewardship program most need to be more concerned about building up the general health and faithfulness of the parish. People are inclined to support such a parish. They don't need a program to generate that support. But even if we take this approach, we still need to do a few simple things. We need to ask people to make their pledge each year. We need to have ways to invite planned giving. We need to have a regular assessment of parish life and ministry.

This relationship between stewardship and growth shows itself as new members are incorporated into the parish. Those who arrive at the parish with Apostolic Faith may start with a more sacrificial pledge. But most people who begin to attend are not of Apostolic Faith. We know that there's usually a lag in receiving pledges from newer members. Accepting the organic nature of the parish may help us be patient. Address the issue by helping people grow in faith and develop a stable connection with the parish.

As the people grow emotionally and spiritually they accept more responsibility. As they develop relationships they care about they become more reliable toward that community. A shift takes place and this becomes a community and institution they want to support.

Therefore we need to give ourselves to the basics:

- Work at formation processes
- Do Sunday well—liturgy and social connections
- Plan the budget so you are realistic about lag time
- Take an approach that brings people into contact with Christian maturity from their first encounter with the parish.

The larger concern for the faithful is our stewardship of society, especially of its institutions and wealth. The thinking of two popes suggests the pathway.

"Here once more we exhort our sons to take an active part in public life, and to work together for the benefit of the whole human race, as well as for their own political communities. It is vitally necessary for them to endeavor, in the light of Christian faith and with love as their guide, to ensure that every institution whether economic, social, cultural or political, be such as not to obstruct but rather to facilitate man's self betterment, both in the natural and in the supernatural order. And yet, if they are to imbue civilization with right ideals and Christian principles, it is not enough for our sons to be illumined by the heavenly light of faith and to be fired with enthusiasm for a cause; they must involve themselves in the work of these institutions, and strive to influence them effectively from within."   Pope John XXIII

"Faced with the abuses of economic power, faced with the cruelty of capitalism that downgrades man to a commodity, we have begun to see more clearly the dangers of wealth, and understand in a new way what Jesus meant when he warned against wealth." Pope Benedict XVI in *Jesus of Nazareth*

Deep prayer; accepting responsibility to influence what we can influence; and sound theology and social analysis are all components of stewardship.

Service

The idea of service ministries has become a kind of "should" upon the back of many parishes, producing more guilt and confusion than it does service. It's in that area of service that many carry a sense of burden. When I've asked parishes to complete assessment forms based on the Christian Life Model it is in the area of service that people seem most conflicted. Evangelism is often rated low but just about all the leaders agree that it is not being done well enough. But service is usually spread out from low ratings to high ratings. Frequently what is missing is a deeper, more grounded conversation about the question. Parishes feel pressure about it but haven't really engaged it. Or if they have, it has been at the level of the "liberals" keeping up the pressure and others deciding to let "them" have part of the budget or to do something individually in the name of the parish.

Here are a few suggestions a parish could use in sorting out its thinking.

- Every parish does not need to have a corporate form of service ministry to be faithful. The most organic method is in the Renewal–Apostolate Cycle of individual members.
- If the parish has a corporate form, establish an approach that is sustainable over time.

- Since most of the service ministry of the parish is accomplished in and through the daily lives of the baptized, we need to say that to others and ourselves. It needs to show up on our websites. The section on "ministries" needs to start with the daily life of members, with the parish's collective efforts taking second place. In many parishes this daily life apostolate may be the sustainable form of service that the parish expresses.
- The primary task of a parish is to nurture the development of the Eucharistic community: a people sharing in God's life and transformed by God's love. Our first responsibility is to shape the climate, structures and processes of the parish so that in our life together we are brought more fully into relationship with Christ. It may help to understand that a parish church is more a Benedictine than Franciscan system.
- People will be able to discern appropriate service ministries to the extent we have shaped a parish that renews its people.
- When referring to the corporate service ministries of the parish, call them "service ministries" not "outreach". The word "outreach" carries the unfortunate implication that there is a division between "outreach" and what some call "in-reach." The first is good while the second is selfish and regrettably necessary. This is simply a distortion of the renewal-apostolate dynamics of the Body of Christ.

To develop a common parish service ministry that is sustainable it needs to come out of a process that has:

1. **Explored all the information.**   Learn about the needs of people that we are in relationship with and some that we are not in relationship with. Use group methods in which we listen to one another about our hopes and dreams, our fears and anxieties. Create a vision of what is possible and an assessment of costs and benefits to those we serve and to ourselves. Explore the sustainability issue by asking about whether this can be carried for a number of years and whether it will be likely to survive the pressure to let it go because of the costs or because some have a new idea for a project.
2. **Considered the real options**. What might we do that meets real needs and that we have the resources to engage? Communities that decide on the basis of free choice versus emotional coercion or habit are more likely to stay invested.
3. **Ownership of those who must carry it out and those who must provide the resources.** That kind of commitment rests upon the first two elements of useful, open information and free choice in exploring the options. This is about discernment and political realism.

While the parish's primary acts of service are in the lives of its baptized members, there are reasons for a parish to have some form of corporate service ministry. Doing even a very small ministry can sensitize us to a bigger need and enlarge our hearts. It's also possible that a particular parish may have a charism for a specific form of Christian action. The feeding ministry of the Church of the Holy Apostles in Manhattan may be such an example. We confuse the parish's exploration about service if we allow places like Holy Apostles to become a standard by which we measure ourselves. That kind of large scale, major impact service ministry is a rare occurrence for a parish church. Each parish needs to discover what might fit its situation.

In trying to sort out the issue it may help to consider whether the parish has some particular charism. Charism has a couple of meanings. In the broad sense it is about the gifts of Christian life received in baptism—"an inquiring and discerning heart, the courage to will and to persevere, a spirit to know and to love you, and the gift of joy and wonder in all your works."

All parishes have this work of formation as the primary task. In a more narrow sense charism is about a specific gift received by individuals or communities. In this sense a parish may have a gift, or charism, for a certain form of service ministry.

We want to look for an energy that is of the Holy Spirit and that moves the parish again and again in relationship to some particular area of action. This isn't simply a strategy we devise to address for the moment an area of Christian Life.

The Organic Nature of Christian Action

Christian action is something that flows organically from the inner life of the parish. In the celebration of the Eucharist, and in the exchanges of the eucharistic community, we are taken, blessed, broken and shared. To the extent we have taken into ourselves something of the mind and heart of Christ we will show that in daily life.

Justice

It may be useful to think of our advocacy for justice as flowing from the organic connections formed in stewardship, service and evangelization. Each element will bring you to the claims of justice. Our stewardship of creation and institutions, our evangelization of those we are in relationship with, the evangelical call for all powers to genuflect before Christ in the Blessed Sacrament and his justice, and the mandate to serve the least of these—each lays a claim of holy teaching. Each is lived in jobs and families. Each is touched by parish churches. At the offertory of the Eucharist we place it all upon the altar to be transformed. The process is from doctrine though prayer to action. Faithful action flows from life in the community of the Blessed Trinity and the saints.

If a justice ministry comes out of this organic process I think we will see both joy and sustainability. We also want it to be truly useful and at least in some limited manner, effective. Here are a few examples of sustainable and useful justice-related activities in parishes.

- **A Compassion & Justice Award.** The parish gives a yearly award to a person or group in the region that has done outstanding work for compassion and/or justice in the past year. This allows the parish to point to, and affirm, the efforts already going on in the community. The award might include three elements: 1) A print done by a local artist that expresses the theme and has a small plaque on the frame noting the award and date. One urban parish made use of Alan Crite's work. The Boston African-American artist was known for creating drawings of a Risen Christ among the people of the city. Often he would include a small image of the parish. 2) A financial award of a couple of thousand dollars, enough to be meaningful and within the means of most parishes. The check is given to the person or group to be used in any way they think best. 3) Arranging for a newspaper article about the award. The news release and "pitch" to the reporter would focus on the work of the award recipient rather than the parish.

- **Community Organizing**. The best community organizing efforts are about helping communities develop the capacity to advance their own interests. This usually involves working with a professional organizer who knows how to train local leaders. A parish can work ecumenically with other churches in establishing such an effort. This might involve an Alinsky – IAF (Industrial Areas Foundation)-type effort that is about creating an organization of organizations that takes on a variety of issues over the years. When I lived in Philadelphia there were two efforts like this. One was metropolitan-wide, focusing on the needs of "senior citizens," and another was more focused on the needs of city neighborhoods. Or, it could be something that develops to deal with a specific issue the community faces at the moment. For example, a Seattle Presbyterian Church has played a catalytic and supportive role in an effort to get a community voice activated and involved in plans for the development of the neighborhood.

- **Community of Interest**. The parish could make space for one or more communities of interest in which a small group works on some matter related to justice. This could be a group that writes letters in cooperation with Amnesty International, environmental efforts, or an anti-racism group. The group uses parish facilities and is included in those whose work we hold in prayer. Beyond that the group exists based on the energy within itself. The parish doesn't pay any of its costs or recruit on its behalf.

- **Economic Development**. Invest some of the parish's funds in economic development efforts that benefit the poor and those more marginalized in society. Investigate opportunities in community loan funds, affordable housing efforts and programs that begin business in poorer areas. Provide a way in which parishioners can participate.

- **Opportunities**. Every couple of years gather information on opportunities for compassion and justice. Have a coffee hour with displays and handouts. The exhibit might include information on ways to integrate just habits in our family life and about groups outside the parish that people could join.

- **The Church's Position on Social Issues**. Provide occasions and materials that help members be aware of the formal positions of the Episcopal Church as stated by General Convention, the House of Bishops, or your diocese. Probably more important than taking note of the church's official thinking about issues is reading and listening to the thinking of Christian thinkers with a range of views. We can be surprised and challenged in that process.

- **Let Those with the Vocation Act**. A useful rule of thumb is to encourage those who feel called to act for justice to act. If a small group of people in the parish want to take responsibility for one day a month at the local soup kitchen, encourage them to do that. If several people want to engage in support activities for workers on strike, support their witness. It's also important that members who do not experience a calling to such activities not feel coerced into participating.

- **Seize the Moment**. Look for the opportunities to have an impact on public policy. Frequently that will require timely and bold action. Parish leaders will only meet the occasion if they are aware of the events and issues of their community, have the imagination and flexibility to act when the time is right, and are sensitive to what has to happen within the parish to build whatever political support is necessary. One parish in a small east coast city influenced the city over a swimming pool. The swimming pool in the neighborhood was not going to be opened that year because vandalism had created $3,000 to $4,000 worth of damage. City officials didn't want to spend the money and were publicly blaming the whole neighborhood. "If they want nice things they're going to have to protect them." In a news conference the local parish challenged the city by collecting

$3,000 from several Episcopal parishes and offering the funds to the city to help make the repairs. The next day saw a furious mayor calling the priest and yelling about being put on the spot. After a bit of negotiating, and mention of the local newspaper, the mayor decided that opening the pool was a grand idea. The city started an effort to work with residents to keep the park and pool well-maintained year round. Two local community organizations joined forces to get the park into shape. The city official who had earlier blamed the community now said, "This is what I was saying was needed. We need people in the neighborhood to get involved." All this was followed by a news conference and photo opportunity at the pool that included the mayor, leaders of the community organizations, the parish clergy, and lots of children. The whole process took one week from the news article about closing the pool to the news article announcing a cooperative effort to open the pool.

The starting place is to trust the organic working of the Body of Christ.

As Light Must Shine

The organic relationship of holiness and Christian action was expressed by James Huntington, OHC. "Holiness is the brightness of divine love, and love is never idle; it must accomplish great things. Love must act as light must shine and fire must burn."

Our parishes are not social work agencies. Our task is different. We are a local expression of the Holy Church, a holy people. In the Eucharist, education and the routine interactions of life in community, that holiness is expressed and formed. At the Society of Saint John the Evangelist the acclamation after the breaking of the bread and before communion is often this:

> Priest: Behold what you are.
> People: May we become what we receive.

The cycle of renewal in baptismal identity and purpose, and our apostolate in workplace, civic life and family, is the primary organic cycle. In the dismissal the deacon sends people back to their work, families and civic life. Of course, they would go there anyway. It's an organic rhythm of the Eucharistic people.

We gather and we scatter. To the extent we have been restored in our baptismal life, have renewed "an inquiring and discerning heart, the courage to will and to persevere, a spirit to know and to love you, and the gift of joy and wonder in all your works" – to the extent all that is restored, we carry it into our daily lives.

This organic life of the Body can have more play in our institutional life as we contemplate what is already present in our life as a parish. Seek within the commitments and decisions of regular parish life opportunities for compassion and justice. This may allow us to see the lonely, grieving, and overburdened among us. It may help us give attention to the day-by-day decisions that relate to compassion and justice. We can use union contractors and union businesses, provide meeting space for groups working for compassion and justice, and be more environmentally responsible.

We need to stop obsessing about having a parish program that makes us feel better. There are a few parishes that have had the gifts and opportunity to do something large that attracts public praise and attention. However, many parishes have the capacity to do something that has a significant impact on the life of a few people.

To measure ourselves by these large programs is a sign of pride rather than humility. Send money to those doing the truly remarkable work and provide the limited help you can to a local feeding program. Rather than looking to create a program out of a planning process we might slow down, sit in silence, and focus our attention on what is present in the parish's life now. Our attempts to create that great service ministry may in some cases actually cause us to miss what God has placed within our life.

Oversight of Parish Life and Development

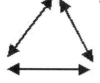

SPIRITUALITY
That in thy light we may see light, p. 832 BCP

COMMUNITY
A new people in Jesus Christ our Lord, to show forth your glory in all the world, BCP p.378

LEADERSHIP
To nourish Christ's people from the riches of his grace, BCP 531

Oversight is what knits things together in harmony and beauty. Oversight is expressed in the three threads of spirituality, community, and leadership. They offer richness and depth in worship, doctrine and action. Oversight provides strength and connection for the fabric of Christian life.

A Learning Organization

Oversight is also a process of reflection and action, a discernment process. It is the process of:

1. Reflection on the state of the parish, especially on the parish's productivity in its primary task of renewing people in their baptismal identity and purpose and sending them into their daily life; and
2. Action that creates the conditions from which the primary task is accomplished.

Oversight involves the creation of an organization with the capacity to learn from its experience, a learning organization. This is very different from the type of oversight that acts as though the task is simply to create a vision or strategic plan. It's relatively easy to get parish leaders to share their hopes and desires for the parish's future. It's much more difficult to get them in a disciplined process of looking at their common experience, assessing it and discerning God's presence in it, and stating what they are learning about the parish, themselves, their context, and the presence of God. It is out of such learning that a Christian community faithfully sets direction for its life and ministry.

The Three Threads

Spirituality

The task is to shape a healthy corporate spirituality. This includes:

- Enabling a pattern and climate that focuses the parish on Christ; that encourages people to discover the claim Christ has on them; and that helps people to trust and rest in God.
- Inviting the parish to contemplation, surrender and transcendence.
- Using models for understanding the parish's spirituality and skills for guiding the parish to a healthier spiritual life.
- Building competent common participation in the Eucharist and Office and providing ways of exploring forms of personal devotions that respect the unique character of each soul.

- Nurturing an adult parish climate in which people accept responsibility for their own spiritual life as part of the Body of Christ.
- Providing various levels of spiritual guidance that accept people where they are while inviting them into a fuller life. It is especially important to offer this for people of apostolic faith and practice. That group is often neglected in a parish in favor of serving the larger numbers of sacramental Christians. But it is the nurturing of the more mature in the parish that will help create the needed climate and set loose the energy that grounds the parish in its truest life.

See Resources section for several ways of nurturing parish spirituality

Community

The task is to shape a transforming community, a parish in which lives are made new.

- Enabling awareness that the parish is a local expression of the one, holy, catholic and apostolic Church; that it is the Body of Christ; that it has a mission given by God.
- Focusing the parish and each group in the parish on the mission of the Church.
- Teaching that through baptism we are incorporated into that Body and mission and in the Eucharist are transformed into instruments of the Holy Unity.
- Enabling a parish culture in which people may be transformed more and more into the likeness of Christ.
- Create and maintain a parish social life
- Being a caring community in which people bear one another's burdens and celebrate one another's joys.
- Clearly presenting the Church's expectations and standards.

In some parishes there is confusion over the place of social activities in building community. The conversation may become a debate between the overly rigorous and the "keep them happy" poles. The one tends toward a position in which all activities in the parish are expected to have a somewhat abstract purity of intention and effect. Everything gets measured by a narrow understanding of the formation task. The other pole seems to assume that because a number of people enjoy social activities it is obviously something to do and the more the better.

Personally, I like wasting time with people, hanging out, being with others just because it is pleasurable. I enjoy dinners with friends; drinks at a bar with a good jukebox; and conversations that drift about from politics to family to work interests to today's news. I also think it is a sign of parish health when people spontaneously gather with one another for these activities. These activities are also a setting in which the exchanges of the Holy City occur: where people encounter others' needs and desires, where they run up against each other, experience hurt and forgiveness, and are called into courage and patience.

Most of us understand how we meet Christ in the Mass. We understand that in the Eucharist we are restored to unity with Christ and each other. Many seem not to see that this work of Holy Unity is also accomplished in the seemingly non-religious activities of parish life. It isn't just the exchanges of the Eucharist that bring us to holiness and wholeness but also the exchanges at the breakfast after Mass, in the post-Foundations Class gathering at McHugh's Irish bar, and in all the spontaneous meetings of members in the local coffee shop. The Christ is among us in all the small exchanges of those occasions—in the meeting of eyes, in laughter and tears, in the touches, and in the words of support and challenge, and yes, even in the gossip. It's all part of creating the glue among us that is the binding together of the Body of Christ.

Some of the factors I try to take into account in deciding about the nature of those activities include:

- Begin with an assumption that all experience of being in community has some transforming potential. Parish social activities usually have the effect of building a sense of community and creating glue among people. We are part of something larger than ourselves. The natural give and take of a parish's social life is a sacramental experience of acceptance and challenge. The ways of the Eucharist show themselves as members are taken, blessed, broken and given to the world.
- Consider what needs changing in that social life. Has the parish allowed social life to overshadow other important activities related to the primary task? A clue to that is seen in parishes when there is little energy around spiritual life and growth. Is there a superficial climate? In such an environment leaders may want to connect social activities with programs that deepen spiritual life. It's not that social events need to be reduced but that spirituality needs to be increased.
- Explore how to use social activities as an entry point for some new members and in the early stages of incorporation.

Leadership

The task is to move the parish's people and energies toward increased health and faithfulness. This also involves effective management and administration and includes:

- The ability to do the parish's routine work effectively, to engage strategic issues by sorting out priorities among all the challenges and opportunities, and to maintain a network of professional and personal relationships that provide both a sense of perspective and connections to additional resources.
- The capacity to decide on a direction to move in and mobilize the human and financial resources needed to get someplace.
- The emotional and mental flexibility to move easily between working with one person around her spiritual life, shifting to another working on the strategic issue of bringing the parish's finances into alignment, while responding to a third person's question about whether it's acceptable to move an icon from one room to another.
- Use of the knowledge and methods of organization development.
- Regular assessments of parish life and ministry. "Let the data speak," is a phrase used by some organization development practitioners. It means that in the process of assessing our life and work we need to trust the community to interpret the information that has been gathered. Few things catch people's attention as much as coming up against what they have said about themselves as a community or vestry or committee.
- Development of an informed, self-disciplined, faithful lay leadership.
- Clear decision-making and discernment processes.
- Effective financial, property, and office management.
- Clear and appropriate use of authority.
- Conformity, without rigidity, to the standards of the Church in regard to business methods.

There's a kind of political wisdom, a social intelligence, needed for effective leadership.

The Archbishop of York, Dr. John Sentamu said:

> Gracious magnanimity is the quality of the person who knows that regulations are not the last word and knows when not to apply the letter of the law…A church meeting may sit with the book of practice and procedure on the table in front of it and take every one of its decisions in strict accordance with the law of the Church; but there are times when the Christian treatment of some situation demands that the book of practice and procedure should not be regarded as the last word.

There were just a few times when as a consultant I'd enter a meeting room and see a book of canon law sitting in front of the rector. It was always a sign that we were in for a long evening. An essential leadership quality needed by parish leaders is a mix of what Archbishop Sentamu calls "gracious magnanimity" and what most of us mean by political smarts.

A resource I have found useful is the work of Karl Albrecht on social intelligence. He looks at five areas of competence: 1) Situational radar—the capacity to read situations and act effectively based on that; 2) Presence—a sense of confidence; 3) Authenticity—behaving so you and others see yourself as honest; 4) Clarity—being able to express ideas and feelings in a way that persuades others; and 5) Empathy—the ability to create a sense of connection with others.

Creating Holy Order: Weaving the Threads into a Fabric

Our oversight has the purpose of advancing the "holy order" of Christ. We are to enable a parish life in which people may rest in God, offer their lives to God, give themselves to the mission they share in the Body of Christ, and be transformed more and more into his likeness. We are to enable a parish life that is a Eucharistic life. In *The Mystery of Sacrifice*, Evelyn Underhill described the shape of it. "For the fully Christian life is a Eucharistic life: that is, a natural life conformed to the pattern of Jesus, given in its wholeness to God, laid on His altar as a sacrifice of love, and consecrated, transformed by His inpouring life, to be used to give life and food to other souls."

Important understandings and resources for weaving the three threads into an integrated, responsive and stable Christian life include:

- The parish priest
- A foundations course
- Spiritual balance and organizational focus
- The mission and nature of the church

The Parish Priest

If the parish is to develop into a healthier and more faithful community, what do we need to look for in the parish priest?

1. Leadership ability. This is the ability to get others to move; to listen and respond to one another, to the needs and opportunities, to God; political common sense; to occupy that role in a parish's life in such a way that the parish is moved toward greater health and faithfulness.

2. Emotional maturity. Including an awareness of your own emotions; accepting responsibility for how you act on your emotions; an understanding of the impact of your behavior on others; self-confidence; self-control; the ability to stay with something while being flexible; the capacity to negotiate with others; the ability to be part of the group as well as to stand apart from the group.

3. Spiritual maturity. Being a person of Apostolic Faith, including maintaining a spiritual discipline

4. Competence in many of the skills related to effective priestly ministry. Presiding at liturgy, preaching, spiritual and pastoral guidance, Christian formation, etc. In each there are skills related to designing as well as implementing.

5. Priestliness. The person has something of the enchanter about them, can be "with God with the people on your heart," sees the "inward and spiritual grace" within the life of individuals and the community and accepts being human and being a sacramental person. One of my friends has offered a caution based on her experience with one priest who seems to fit the "enchanter" description. We need to see the difference between the healthy enchanter that Terry Holmes wrote about in *The Priest in Community* and the narcissistic leader who's more about looking good and being right.[7]

When a parish is in a search process for a new rector or vicar they might focus on these characteristics and pay attention to the experience of candidates. The best indicator of a capacity for leadership, emotional intelligence, spiritual maturity and priestliness is evidence of their exercise in previous situations.

A Foundations Course

Most parishes can make good use of an adult foundations program, which is a substantial educational offering that grounds people in the thinking and practices of the Christian faith as lived in the Episcopal Church. It can serve multiple purposes, including being used in place of all "inquirers" classes or adult baptismal or confirmation instruction.

A foundations course is a resource for moving people into a more Apostolic expression of faith and practice. There needs to be enough substance to it that it has the potential of taking participants to a new place in their spiritual life. Some parishes have nine or ten sessions. Others have modules that extend over three years (see the Resources section for more on Foundations Courses).

The course is a tool in creating a "critical mass" of members who have some competence for living the life. So, it's important that it be experiential and include skill training.

Spiritual Balance and Organizational Focus

While you want to use the Christian Life Model in moving toward balance and wholeness, you don't want to pursue an artificial balance. It's not about each element being allotted equal attention and resources. It's more about providing for strength in each element in a way that emerges from and serves the parish's context and organizational culture. St. John's in the Village in Manhattan puts a significant amount of money into liturgical matters such as environment, music, and resources. They, and many other Episcopal Churches, stack resources

---

[7] There are two books I find useful in seeing the distinction. In *The Priest in Community*, Seabury Press, 1978, Holmes writes of the priest as "one who raises and expands the consciousness of those he serves" and as being "the 'hook' on which we 'hang' certain symbols or archetypical images." In an appendix he offers a chart of character traits that suggest readiness for priesthood and others that suggest the opposite. So, Holmes' enchanter priest also has humility, humor, earthiness, flexibility, compassion, is nonconformist but interdependent, responsible and forgiving. The opposite is self-righteous, heresy hunting, certain, oriented to activity for its own sake (particularly in the face of death), status oriented, secretive. The other book is Peter Steinke's *Congregational Leadership in Anxious Times*, Alban, 2006. In a postscript called "People of the Charm" he writes about narcissistic clergy. He notes that it's a relational activity. Some "congregations attract narcissistic clergy because they need someone outside themselves to motivate them." He sees a connection between the charmer and the charmed – the functioning is one "of mutual reinforcement and self–deception." Signs of the dynamic include no checks and balances, groupthink, avoiding outside influences (might be consultants or a lay leader with too many questions) demonizing those who might uncover the truth. Some of the characteristics of the clergy involved include: expert at disguise, appears to be in command of situations, cleaver charming, persuasive, star quality, fun to be with, articulate, unable to use self examination, and exploitatively ambitious. The task is to sort out Holmes enchanter from Steinke's charmer.

87

toward having a wonderful liturgy which has value in itself as worship, forms the hearts and minds of people, and attracts new members.

Looking at the budget as a way to look for balance doesn't reveal the underlying balance. It's in looking at the totality of parish life, at the outcomes in worship, doctrine, action and oversight that you see the balanced life. In the case of Saint John's in the Village the parish has stressed worship as a kind of driving engine for its formation and evangelization. There are parishes that have seen the same general results by devoting what may appear to be a disproportionate amount of resources to education for all ages or to Christian social action. What the model can do is remind us of the interdependence of all these elements and so allow us to shape the underlying balance.

Many parishes have used the Christian Life Model as the outline in developing a strategic sense of direction (in a plan, vision, or other method of clarifying direction). One parish used it in thinking about the relationship between the life of its members and the parish's process of assessment and direction setting. "The Christian Life Model encourages us to evaluate the life of our parish in terms of a balance between worship, action, and doctrine. Our strategic plan calls for ministry that provides for a variety of opportunities for our parishioners so that they may develop a balanced Christian Life."

Three things to keep in mind:

1. Establish a process of reflection, planning and acting in the fabric of parish life. Become a parish that can learn from its experience.
2. Root decision-making in prayer, Scripture and the Holy Tradition of the Church.
3. Use the Renewal–Apostolate Cycle, Christian Life Model and other models to help the parish focus on the essentials of the Christian life.

The Mission and Nature of the Church

As mentioned earlier some parishes have a special charism. A charism is the work of the Holy Spirit in a community that gives it a special identity and purpose. People are attracted to the community because of the charism. It's not given to all parishes. But clearly some have a charism for liturgy, others for education or service. I've mentioned the feeding program of Church of the Holy Apostles. The liturgy at Saint Paul's in Seattle moves many to feel as though they have never worshipped as deeply or as fully. The parish attracts students of liturgy from the city's academic institutions and seminaries. There is clearly a special force at work in parishes with a certain charism. Trinity, Seattle has a large service ministry and a heart of compassion. Trinity's liturgy is fine and includes some wonderful music but it's not as graceful as St. Paul's. Trinity also has a more tangible sense of human dignity then seen at St. Paul's. So, parish rest rooms are open for the homeless to use most of the day. On occasion that creates a mess and other problems. I came to see the significance of Trinity's gift when I was conducting a workshop at the parish over a two-week period. I'd be in that rest room when a mess was being made but more often when men were doing simple things like brushing their teeth or washing their hair.

Other parishes can be inspired by and learn from these parishes. We get into trouble when we begin to measure ourselves against them. A charism is a gift, not an accomplishment. As a gift it needs stewardship and development. It will be adapted to different times and to the socio-cultural context. In time it may be lost and a different form of emphasis and life will be available.

Not all parishes will have a special charism, but all share in the holy mission and nature of the Holy Catholic Church. All can grow and develop.

> The development of a parish is a process of entering more deeply into the life of Christ and the nature and mission of the Church. A parish is being renewed as it enters into and reflects the mind, heart and work of Christ. A parish is being renewed as it enters into and reflects the unity, holiness, catholicity and apostolicity of the Church. A parish is being renewed as it pursues the mission of holy unity. Parish development is our striving, as a community of Christian people, toward God. It is not primarily something we do, or create, or make happen. It is the way in which a parish, a local manifestation of the Holy Catholic Church, shares in the Divine Life. It is living the Christian life, not simply as individuals, but as a people. The movement of a parish into a comprehensive and deep expression of the Christian Life is the result of years of striving, submitting and molding. It is the responsibility of clergy and lay leaders to monitor the life and ministry of, the parish and to take initiative in increasing the faithfulness and effectiveness of that life and ministry." (From *Power from on High*)

The Christian Life Model was the topic of *Power from on High: A Model for Parish Life and Development*, published by Ascension Press, 1983. Still available from Ascension Press.

See Resources section for two assessments related to the Christian Life Model: Assessment of Parish Life and Ministry, and the Parish Oversight Assessment .

Other Models

The Christian Life Model is in one sense a list of the essential elements of a full and healthy life in an Episcopal/Anglican parish. It can be compared with other lists that might be called a "factors" or "key elements" approach (see below). At their best they are thoughtful and grounded in the experience of Christian communities. At their worst they are simply a laundry list of things to do.

When these other models are the result of research that highlight elements of healthy churches, such as the U.S. Congregational Life Survey List, they can fruitfully be used in combination with the Christian Life Model. Each will inform the other.

In general, the Christian Life Model differs from the others in at least two ways. First, it is a systems model and approach. It allows us to look at the dynamics of a parish, the relationship and interaction among elements, at issues of balance, and at the culture. It implies an approach to intervention in which action to improve things might begin any place within the system.

Second, the model is grounded in our tradition. It assumes that the development of a healthy parish culture rises out of the strengths of the existing culture. It has an appreciative stance toward our heritage and seeks new and innovative ways that rise from the best of our common life. Several of its components are long standing systems used among Anglicans, such as the Benedictine Triangle and the sources of authority.

Next Step in Mission

In 1982 at the 67th General Convention, the then-Presiding Bishop John Allan introduced *The Next Step in Mission* and the SWEEP model. This model was a way of suggesting essential areas the parish might focus on its life and ministry. The categories were widely used for awhile.

- **S**ervice
- **W**orship
- **E**ducation
- **E**vangelism
- **P**astoral Care

New Directions in Ministry

This model comes from Philip Turner's *New Directions in Ministry*, Forward Movement, 1981. It suggests that the abiding pattern of the church's ministry includes five constants. It is this pattern that can be used as a lens through which we may view the life of the church and test it for adequacy.

- Worship
- Evangelism
- Service
- Formation
- Intercession

Natural Church Development

NCD fits in the same class as those above because its focus is on church health rather than numerical growth. It takes the approach that such health is the key to membership growth (as do other models in this class). It's an evangelical, non-Anglican model.

Eight qualities that define healthy churches:

1. Empowering leadership
2. Gift-oriented ministry
3. Passionate spirituality—prayer, enthusiasm, and boldness
4. Functional structures
5. Inspiring worship service
6. Holistic small groups— that meet the real needs of people
7. Need-oriented evangelism
8. Loving relationships

The U.S. Congregational Life Survey List

This is based on a survey of more than 300,000 worshipers in over 2,000 congregations. Cynthia Woolever and Deborah Bruce identified ten strengths found in above-ordinary congregations:

1. Growing spiritually
2. Meaningful worship
3. Participating in the congregation
4. Having a sense of belonging
5. Caring for children and youth
6. Focusing on the community
7. Sharing faith
8. Welcoming new people
9. Empowering leadership
10. Looking to the future

A Single Element or Factor Approach

These approaches are usually more implied than directly stated. Rick Warren's focus on clarity of purpose in *Purpose Driven Church* might be an example. What we hear is that if the parish will just do this one thing, everything else will fall into place. When challenged the presenter usually acknowledges more complexity but the single right action lingers in the air.

III. THE BENEDICTINE PROMISE

The Benedictine Promise: An Exercise

1. Thinks of an event or experience in the parish that seems significant to you. It may have been something that produced a lot of anxiety or emotional energy among people. What happen and who was involved?

2. **Stability** – In what ways did you want to flee from the experience? What did you do? What was in the experience that was graceful? How was God's presence seen and acknowledged in the relationships or circumstances?

3. **Obedience** -- What listening took place? What was it that that you didn't want to hear? What was your response? How did you experience God's presence in the listening and responding?

4. **Conversion of Life** – What was in the experience that was a call to a new way? How did you experience God's presence in that new possibility?

5. Other thoughts? For example -- Is there a way in which the others compensated for a rub in one of the elements? Was there some dynamic or interaction among the elements?

The Benedictine Promise: A Diagram Overview

The three elements of the Benedictine Promise, and the whole of Benedictine spirituality, can help us see some of the hidden dynamics of parish life.

STABILITY As a parish we find God here and now in the relationships and pattern of our life together.

CONVERSION OF LIFE
As a parish we find God on our journey together and in the new places we will go as a parish; in losing life to find life; in our openness to transformation.

OBEDIENCE As a parish we find God as we listen deeply to the world; to Scriptures; to the church, now and through the ages; to each other; to the creation; and to the deepest longings and prayer of our heart.

Benedictine spirituality is part of our Anglican DNA. It's the way of the Prayer Book and is embedded in much of the way we function as parish communities. We can make use of it in the work of congregational development: 1) as a way to see and enter into the depth of our own culture as Episcopalians and 2) because it is the spirituality of particular communities that have developed a capacity, over time, to maintain their integrity while renewing themselves in adaptation to the environment.

Looking at the dynamics of parish life

You might think in terms of the whole parish or of a specific event or experience.

What is the predisposition you see in the parish's behavior toward stability, change, or listening processes? Which direction do we generally tilt towards? Which is our anxiety often focused upon?

In the parish's expression of stability, conversion of life, and obedience what seems healthy to you, what unhealthy? Is the stability simply being static? Is the conversion simply being driven by an impulse to change? Is the obedience endless listening and process, too little listening, or a facade of listening?

Developing a parish culture that is marked by:

Stability – Especially seen in Liturgy, prayer and relationships.

Obedience – Seen in our openness to listen, and respond to, one another, our bishop and the larger church.

Conversion of Life – Out of our life of stability or obedience we see and act on new challenges and opportunities for mission and building up the Body of Christ.

The Benedictine Promise: An Exploration

A life that is vowed to simplicity, appropriate boldness, good humor, gratitude, unstinting work and play, and lots of walking brings us close to the actual existing world and its wholeness.
Gary Snyder

The Benedictine tradition includes a promise of stability, obedience, and conversion of life. That "promise" is not only a commitment made in community, it is a lens into the inner life and dynamics of a community. We have seen the health of a parish that is grounded in a rich and complex prayer life; in which there is deep listening, both interpersonal and in communal discernment; and where there is an openness of minds and hearts to the future that God offers. We have also seen parishes that seem to express a shadow side - where stability is turned to frozenness and obsession with parish traditions; where obedience has either become legalism or has no hold at all; where conversion of life is the cover for self-absorption in which change is driven by sentimentality or political ideology. We know of parishes where there is an obsession with change and others with maintaining traditions.

Members of an Episcopal Christian community, the Order of the Ascension, take a three-year promise "to seek the presence of Jesus Christ in the people, things and circumstances of my life through stability, obedience and conversion of life." This is one group's way of making the traditional Benedictine promise, which establishes an orientation toward their own spirituality and in their leadership of creating a healthy parish culture. The Benedictine tradition joins these three aspects of spirituality into one promise and a mystery. The promise is a way to assess the congregation's dynamics and structures. It is also a guide in shaping the culture and climate of the congregation.

Parish Culture

The work that's been done on organizational culture can be a very useful tool in relation to Benedictine spirituality. In looking at this I'm relying on the work of Edgar Schein[8] and other theorists and practitioners in the field. Organizational culture is a web of shared ways of being and working, stated values and deep underlying assumptions about the nature of things. Within the organization this defines "reality" for people. And as part of that reality, culture offers a sense of identity and meaning; and the ground upon which the organization can have some sense of integration among its various elements. Benedict's *Rule* and the tradition of Benedictine communities provide all the essential aspects of an organizational culture.

In what follows I'll offer a variety of specific ideas about how to shape a parish culture grounded in Benedictine spirituality. Let me begin with the broad strokes. What shapes the organizational culture of a parish church? There are the more obvious things—the liturgical space, its beauty and functionality; the way the liturgy is done and the degree and form of congregational participation; the feel of and what is available in the rest of the parish property; how meeting rooms are arranged and what resources they provide; the stories that get told and retold; formal statements of belief and values; and the way the decision-making is structured. The greatest impact on shaping the parish's culture is in what leaders do. How they deal with crisis and other critical situations, how they stack the resources of the parish in one direction or

---

[8] See Schein's *The Corporate Culture: Survival Guide,* Jossey-Bass, 1999 and *Organizational Culture and Leadership*, Jossey-Bass, 1992.

another; and what they pay attention to, measure and reward. The leader's efforts at training, education and coaching are also central parts of forming the parish culture.

In the church we seem to over-rely on the more obvious things hoping that ritual and stories will have more impact then they can. When relying on these things we avoid the harder leadership work that's needed. The week-by-week process of making decisions, influencing people, and maintaining direction and norms is difficult and demanding. The priest and lay leaders can simply get weary and wary.

From time to time we hear voices in the church suggesting that either the Episcopal Church will make radical changes in its culture or it will die. Overblown rhetoric rarely produces much lasting change and in this case it's based on a limited grasp of what it takes to change organizational culture.

Organizational culture can begin to undergo significant change when the system experiences a major crisis. That crisis needs to be experienced within the parish in a way that brings the crisis home, which is real and compelling in the experience of parish leaders. That's part of why there is little local response to all the statistics and negative forecasting by some national and diocesan leaders about the need to dramatically change our culture in order to address the membership decline. There are three primary reasons for this. 1) It doesn't feel real. Even if there is a decline in parish membership it's often gradual. 2) Changes in culture mean changes in identity, organizational integrity and integration. It's a sign of health for people to be cautious about such change. Most Episcopalians seem to value the existing culture. 3) Members don't have the competencies needed to function in the culture being proposed. They don't know how to live in that place and aren't sure they want to.

To use Edgar Schein's categories, in all organizations including the church, the learning anxiety is usually higher than the survival anxiety. Schein looks at the two anxieties this way. "… there's an inherent paradox surrounding learning: Anxiety inhibits learning, but anxiety is also necessary if learning is going to happen at all. …There are two kinds of anxiety associated with learning: "learning anxiety" and "survival anxiety." Learning anxiety comes from being afraid to try something new for fear that it will be too difficult, that we will look stupid in the attempt, or that we will have to part from old habits that have worked for us in the past. Learning something new can cast us as the deviant in the groups we belong to. It can threaten our self-esteem and, in extreme cases, even our identity.

"You can't talk people out of their learning anxieties; they're the basis for resistance to change. And given the intensity of those fears, none of us would ever try something new unless we experienced the second form of anxiety, survival anxiety—the horrible realization that in order to make it, you're going to have to change." Schein goes on using a rather dramatic image to show just how hard this is for people, "Like prisoners of war, potential learners experience so much hopelessness through survival anxiety that eventually they become open to the possibility of learning. But even this dejection is not necessarily enough. Individuals can remain in a state of despair permanently."

Having an impact on parish culture is usually a slow process requiring:

- Persistence, patience, and courage
- Dealing with the learning anxiety especially related to competencies and social connections (and avoiding trying to increase survival anxiety by scaring people).
- Rooting the changes in 1) the best of the parish's ways and values and 2) the best of the Episcopal Church's ethos and traditions of liturgy, spirituality, and community.

If we are interested in creating healthier congregations with an increased ability to effectively form people in Christ and to attract new people to that life then we might look to Benedictine spirituality as a resource in that work.

The Benedictine Promise and the Dynamics of the Spiritual Life

I want to begin with looking at the elements of the Promise and the dynamics among those elements in a living community of people.[9]

STABILITY To find God in the current relationships and circumstance of our life

CONVERSION OF LIFE
To find God in a new life; in the changing relationships and circumstances

OBEDIENCE To find God in contemplative listening to others, self, creation, and God; to hear and respond

Each element of the Promise is rooted in recollection and has certain internal dynamics. In stability, obedience and conversion of life there comes an awareness of God's presence. Speaking of it in general usage rather than in relationship to the spiritual life Edna O'Brien, an Irish writer, said "Recollection ... is not something that I can summon up, it simply comes and I am the servant of it." It is the Spirit praying within us.

The Promise draws us into recollection of aspects of God's presence. Each also carries within it dynamics that can draw us into maturity in Christ.

	Recollection	**Inner Dynamics**
Stability	God in this community, these people, this situation	Entering into a deeper acceptance of self and others; turning away from illusions drawing us into boredom, resentment, a desire to escape. Learning about the grumbling of our hearts, about how and why we flee self, others and God.
Obedience	God in this "word" to me	Living in the reality of death and resurrection, of losing life to find life. Learning to live in relationship, to listen deeply, to respond.
Conversion of Life	God in the new community, in the new life	Being on the journey that calls us into continuous change, a life-long process of being transformed into the likeness of Christ. Learning to find joy in the new life instead of weeping for the life that has passed or never was.

---

[9] I think the best resource for looking at this is Esther de Waal's *Seeking God: The Way of St. Benedict*, The Liturgical Press, 1984, 2001.

In the parish's life as a community these elements of the Promise will touch and press upon one another. The static parish might find a new stability out of having listened and responded to its own fears and longings; that is to say out of being obedient and open to a new life. The excessively anxious-to-please parish might experience a conversion of life if leaders establish the stability of the Prayer Book Pattern (Eucharist, Office, Personal Devotions). Living for a time in the Rule may allow the space for the Spirit to move and be noticed.

Parish development leadership involves seeing the dynamics as they exist in the parish and acting to shape parish life so the needed balance exists in its structures and processes.

Benedictine Spirituality and Parish Development

There are at least three reasons for congregational development practitioners in the Episcopal Church to gain some understanding of Benedictine Spirituality.

1. It is a significant part of our Anglican root system. It's part of our organizational DNA. If we increase our understanding of Benedictine Spirituality it may help us increase our understanding of Anglican liturgy, prayer, and the nature of community life. We may come to better understand and appreciate ourselves as Episcopalians and as parishes in that tradition.
2. It is the spirituality of particular communities that have developed a capacity, over time, to maintain their integrity while renewing themselves in adaptation to the environment. Maintaining organizational integrity and being a self-renewing organization is a central concern in organization development.
3. Benedictine communities have a defined, integrated organizational culture. We need images of such communities.

We want to develop congregations that are effective communities of Christian formation. In terms of the Benedictine Promise, the task is to shape the structures, process and climate of the parish so there is an active dynamic of stability, conversion and obedience.

Hints for Parish Development

The way into this web of Christian stability, obedience and conversion is not through our feelings or our thinking, though they will play their part. A comment attributed to Jesse Jackson goes, "It is easier to walk your way into a new way of thinking than to think your way into a new way of walking." So, let's look at how we might walk our way into real life as a parish.

Stability

Well, I don't believe we go to heaven, I believe we become heaven. Martin Sheen, when interviewed on The Actor's Studio

I'll begin with the process of incorporating people into a parish's life. There needs to be adequate attention to the incorporation phases of inviting, greeting, orienting and incorporating. If we do that well it will contribute to stability. Because part of creating a healthy stability in parish life involves enabling a stability of relationships we want to: facilitating the speedy incorporation of new people by orientation to the liturgical and social ways of the parish and having ways that allow them to develop relationships. There's a useful synergy between the phases of incorporation and giving special attention to nurturing stability in relationships in the parish. We usually see all this as something the parish does. There is however a third element -- the attitude and behavior of the person coming into the parish.

The person who wants to become part of the parish can take initiative in that process by joining in a stance and behaviors needed by all members. Invite everyone in the parish, clergy and lay, new and long term members, to:

- Accept this particular community, this parish; seek out and appreciate the best of it. Give yourself to it. Your alternatives are to either enter into parish life as it is or to engage in the illusion that you will make it become what you want or living a half presence in which you feed your resentment.
- Ground yourself—take responsibility for making yourself "at home" with this parish community. Deal with the paradox that this calls on you to find that rhythm of solitude and intimacy, apartness and togetherness; for stillness and centering along with engagement and action.
- Persevere—stay with it. Pray for patience and courage in the task of making this a home by negotiating your participation in it.
- Accept as a norm — "We will live in the ways of the wider church." When the church changes, we will change. When there is a new prayer book we just send in the order form. It's a decision to do things as the Episcopal Church does them, at its best, in this time. This will also mean helping people see the difference between the essential and the non-essential. This norm is also related to the other two elements of the Promise.

Four other things I'd highlight that can help establish and maintain a healthy stability.

1. Create structures and processes that encourage mutual responsibility for common life by being more inclusive and participatory.

2. Increase skills in the parish for trust development and conflict management. That needs to include establishing expectations and competency for maintaining and quickly restoring relationships.

3. Build a parish culture that is "centered" and has a pattern of prayer grounded in the Prayer Book, especially work with those ready to go deeper in faith and practice. For people to move into a deeper spiritual life there needs to be a basic stability in worship. The community needs to trust that stability. The stability allows the mind and heart the freedom to go deeper, to not be caught up following the details of the Liturgy.

4. The priest's own spirituality and leadership have an impact on all this -- personal stability, a capacity to be centered and present; acting like you are here and with the parish, as though it is for the long-term, not always seeking new and "better" calls.

Obedience

Listening creates relationship ... Listening moves us closer, it helps us become more whole, more healthy, more holy. Not listening creates fragmentation, and fragmentation is the root of all suffering. I love the biblical passage: "Whenever two or more are gathered, I am there." It describes for me the holiness of moments of real listening. The health, wholeness, holiness of a new relationship forming. I have a T-shirt from one conference that reads: "You can't hate someone whose story you know." You don't have to like the story, or even the person telling you their story. But listening creates a relationship. We move closer to one another. Margaret J. Wheatley

- Become a listening parish. Teach skills for contemplation, communal discernment and interpersonal listening. Establish a pattern of opportunities to listen deeply to God, creation, others and self. Learn methods and tools that facilitate collective listening.
- Coach people in how to be open to influence in their spiritual life while also accepting responsibility for their spiritual life in a manner that fits their situation and life commitments.
- Provide opportunities in which people can reflect on and shape their spiritual discipline.
- Listening to God and each other opens onto the other elements. It is in listening that a parish can move beyond the distortion of the Promise as a struggle between change and stability.
- The Gospel mystery in which we lose life to find life is activated in the process of listening.

Conversion of Life

Nothing is more surprising than the rise of the new within ourselves. We do not foresee or observe its growth. We do not try to produce it by the strength of our will, by the power of our emotion, or by the clarity of our intellect. On the contrary, we feel that by trying to produce it we prevent its coming. By trying, we would produce the old in the power of the old, but not the new in the power of the new. The new being is born in us, just when we least believe in it. It appears in remote corners of our souls which we have neglected for a long time. It opens up deep levels of our personality which had been shut out by old decisions and old exclusions. It shows a way where there was no way before. ...Suddenly we notice it within us! The new which we sought and longed for comes to us in the moment in which we lose hope of ever finding it. That is the first thing we must say about the new: it appears when and where it chooses. We cannot force it, and we cannot calculate it. Paul Tillich, *Shaking of the Foundations*

Our life of stability and obedience will bring forth new challenges and opportunities related to the church's fully living its nature and mission and the baptized person's living his or her identity and purpose. It can happen in the normal exchanges of parish social life. People arrive at stability in their relationship with the parish as they develop friendships, establish a sound spiritual discipline, and begin to see themselves as part of the community's history. At some point we come up against ourselves. Our way of looking at or doing things is challenged or the parish has a crisis or makes what appear to be radical changes. For a time we can be in a kind of emotional and mental gridlock. Nothing is moving. We seem unable to make decisions. We may feel numb. These are moments of hard grace; invitations into new life. We may avoid the invitation by abruptly leaving the parish, by withdrawing into ourselves and limiting our involvement, or by entering into fantasies about the way things should be or use to be. We might also face into the invitation and find new life. That new life may be a renewed life within the parish or it may be one that we will need to find in another parish or tradition.

- Establish processes that develop a sense of vision and direction. This is openness to our future. We can share with Sara and Abraham the trust and surprise that God is also over the next hill, that God is in the new place. Or as Ann Richards, the late governor of Texas, put it, "If you always do what you've always done, you'll always get what you've always got,"
- Enable practical action. The norm is to respond to God now, do mercy now, forgive now, show compassion and justice now. It is openness to God in the present, in the here and now. This is I think related to Benedict's understanding about meditating on death. In the late fall of 1961 Susan Sontag made a journal entry that read, "The fear of becoming old is born of the recognition that one is not living now the life that one wishes. It is equivalent to a sense of abusing the present."
- Build up those of apostolic faith to accept responsibility for their life and journey; to make a commitment to their own maturity in faith and practice, in emotional life, and in the competence to perform the "work we have been given to do."
- Develop the parish's own uniqueness, its own wonderful oddness. Flannery O'Conner wrote "You shall know the truth and the truth shall make you odd."
- Help the parish tell its story as one of change. John Henry Newman said, "To live is to change, and to be perfect is to have changed often." We can intentionally begin to speak and write parish histories as accounts of how well the parish has adapted to changes within and around it; stories of courage, vision and persistence.

Shaping Parish Culture in Benedictine Spirituality

Shaping a congregational culture is done by: 1) leaders teaching, training and coaching members in competencies and practices that express and undergird the culture, 2) creating structures, processes and a climate, that incarnate the values and assumptions of the culture you are seeking, and 3) where leaders, especially the rector, focus their attention.

Creating a culture that lives in the Episcopal Church's Benedictine roots is helped by teaching ways of thinking about parish life and dynamics grounded in that spirituality. I'm going to focus on three things:

1. Teach several models with Benedictine roots
2. Leadership attention
3. Define and shape a parish culture with Benedictine characteristics (including listening, grumbling, deciding to be in community, and healthy stability)

Teach Several Models with Benedictine Roots

Train and coach people in how to use the models to see and nurture the dynamics of their corporate and individual spiritual life.

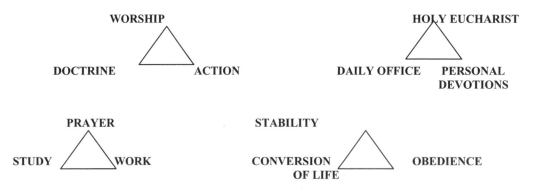

People in their corporate and individual spiritual life will use the models in two primary ways.

The first may be as an "overlay" used to assess and make decisions about what to nurture in their spiritual life. An individual might conclude, "I want to give more attention, at this stage in my life, to learning and experimenting with forms of personal devotions." A vestry and rector reflecting on the parish's corporate spirituality might decide, "We have focused most of our worship life around Sundays and the Eucharist. We need to train people for personal devotions, provide settings for exploring spiritual discipline and developing a rule of life, and provide instruction in the use of the Daily Office that allows people to see how to adapt it to their personal style and schedule."

The second is by seeing the models in a more holistic and relational fashion. So in looking at *worship-doctrine-action,* note the dynamic that Martin Thornton suggests, "Moral action only flows from doctrinal truth by grace and faith, that is through prayer." We might explore it in terms of our tendency to think that if we just get our thinking correct, moral action will result. Yet our experience suggests a more complex dynamic in which what we may understand as true life, as ultimate reality, is not automatically transformed into authentic living and acting; as though we merely had to "get our head straight" to live a whole life. The connection between our thinking and acting seems to be facilitated by our life with others in the Trinity. The community of prayer, compassion and justice is a source of integration and authenticity for doctrine and action.

Regarding *obedience-stability-conversion of life*, Esther de Waal writes about the paradox of Christian life as including our living in the tension between stability and change, action and contemplation. She also proposes that it is in the context of stability and obedience that forces arise in the common and personal life that call communities and individuals to move forward in the Christian journey. Conversion springs from lives of stability and obedience. Of course, it's also true that stability and obedience will be deepened as conversion takes hold.

The relationship among *Eucharist-Daily Office-Personal Devotions* is seen in the Sunday Eucharist when a number of people have said the Office during the week, meditated on the readings, or at the Offertory are pouring into the cup a life that has been reflected upon that week. In that parish community the daily offering of prayer and thoughtfulness are focused and completed in the Eucharist.

Leadership Attention

An essential component of the work is for the rector and other key leaders to learn how to be in-role. Leaders, especially all parish priests and deacons, and wardens and the treasurer, need to accept that the position they hold isn't about their personal preferences but about service. So effective parish leaders give themselves to the patterns of prayer, listening, and not colluding with grumbling. They do that not because it is always comfortable or because it always fits their own views, but because it helps the parish community live a better and more Christ centered life.

I want to revisit Edgar Schein's research about organizational culture. He suggests that while many things contribute to shaping a culture some are more important. For example, the focus of leadership attention is more important in shaping culture than the parish's stories and rituals. People notice what the rector acknowledges and affirms. Here's what Schein's work suggests about the elements that have the most significant impact on shaping organizational culture – what leaders pay attention to, measure and work to influence regularly; the observed criteria by which leaders allocate rewards, recruit others into positions, and allocate scarce resources; and how the leaders react to critical incidents and crisis.

Here are some of the other activities that help to shape culture—rites and rituals, stories and myths, the physical space, statements of belief and values. All these things need attention. A problem we have in many parishes is that leaders operate as though just doing these secondary things will be enough. But people notice what leaders affirm and reward. If there is a positive relationship between leaders and a critical mass of the congregation this process of attention, rewarding and allocating resources will shape the culture.

Pressures on a priest to affirm everyone and everything are often designed to weaken the culture of a parish. Leaders who fall into this trap may become overwhelmed and end up resentful. Leaders need clarity about what will have an effect and adequate boundaries to avoid being consumed by the neediest or most insistent members.

A key to shaping the culture is for leaders to work at training and coaching people in how to competently accomplish what a healthy parish culture requires. Resistance to change can have many causes but one of the most significant is that people are afraid they will look and feel foolish, that they will not know how to effectively function in the new way of doing things.

We can see the process when clergy introduce silence and stillness in liturgy. Some people are uncomfortable with silence and not use to being still. It feels unfamiliar and they are uncertain of what to do. They need instruction not only on why silence and stillness (physical silence) is part of our spiritual life but also in behaviors to do and avoid.

- Do be physically at rest.
- Do decide for yourself on an approach of either using silence as "resting in God" or as a time of reflection (on a reading or an action in the liturgy).
- Do see silence and stillness as behaviors as active as noise and restlessness.
- Avoid rustling paper and looking up pages in the Hymnal.
- Avoid looking at others.

Getting accustomed to a new practice takes time and encouragement. And it is the parish priest who needs to be patient and persistent, and so provide the time needed. And it is the parish priest who needs to occasionally comment on what is settling in for people and where there are still difficulties. One of the actions leaders can take is to build the critical mass needed to sustain a change in practice by offering special coaching to and explicitly asking for cooperation from sub groups in the parish like the choir, lectors, all serving at the altar, those who attend mid-week liturgies and the vestry.

The Model in Action: A Case Study

The Promise also offers leaders a way to see what they are doing in relationship to developing the spirituality of the congregation rather than as a question of whether to go along with the desires of a group within the parish. Here's an example from an Anglo-Catholic parish that had in recent years reduced its use of incense at the Sunday Eucharist. It was now used about 2/3 of the time. There was rationale about different uses at different seasons but it was largely driven by some who didn't like or had an allergic reaction to incense.

In an apparently unrelated process the parish profile used in the new rector search expressed division and ambivalence about the parish's Anglo-Catholic heritage. From the perspective of organizational culture the link is obvious. You are changing the culture when you begin to alter "the ways of being and doing" that express and reinforce the culture. Reducing and being tentative about the use of incense was for this community part of weakening parish identity.

When the new rector arrived she decided to claim the progressive Anglo-Catholic legacy of the parish and proceeded to revise and restore practices that were part of that tradition, including using incense at the primary celebration every Sunday. Developing a stronger organizational culture with a clear identity and more integrated practices helped the parish in its membership growth and spiritual life; incense was just one aspect of that.

In terms of the Promise, what did the priest need to consider?

The most obvious issue was stability. Before this rector arrived the parish was static with an underlying spiritual health but an uncertain cultural identity. The uncertainty and vagueness about the Anglo-Catholic identity of the parish had left the congregation without the excitement and energy that can attract members and ground the common life. It was an excessive anxiety about the feelings of current members. It either failed to consider the impact on membership or assumed that watering down the cultural strength would be beneficial. It also didn't understand the actual behaviors members were likely to engage in relationship to their feelings - were they really going to leave if the Anglo Catholic heritage was affirmed? A big factor in creating the new vigor has been the claiming of the parish's identity. Making that claim real means using practices that are of that tradition, in this case, incense every Sunday.

There has been some complaining about the incense. For some it's about a feeling that they are excluding members who have allergies. A few have even begun to complain on environmental grounds. This "building a case" is likely to continue among some people. They will find more and more reasons about why they are right. The underlying issue about this being a parish that had settled for an identity that was weak and had limited attraction may get lost in the clamor about "inclusion." Leadership is needed that stays clear about issues of culture and direction, that understands what real parish health looks like in both emotional and spiritual terms, and that can maintain a reflective and thoughtful position.

Leaders can easily lose track of the larger questions at stake when people we care about get upset. In this case it was essential that leaders hold onto having an organizational culture with power and depth that can attract people to it and transform lives; having a stability that is sustainable; and remembering the impact on the parish when that was lacking.

A somewhat hidden part of this is that the culture question isn't simply about a particular form of liturgical and spiritual expression. There is also the question of if the parish can live in a more complex and healthier process of leadership and influence.

Here's another parish example about leadership and shaping culture. In the past there would be occasional attempts to improve how Evening Prayer was done in the parish. It was said or sung most nights at different times and in different ways depending on the officiant's preferences. When someone would suggest making it more accessible for the whole congregation they were always stopped by someone else's concern that one of the officiants would be upset. So, to have Evening Prayer at the same time every day, at a time people might be able to attend, was to take away from John's ability to "have a night" because he didn't get off work until a later time. To ask people to follow a standard format making it easier for others to grasp the flow and participate was attacked as undercutting the richness of the Office. The static stability was trumping real stability. Leaders found it difficult to set a direction that would reshape the culture around the Daily Office because they were trapped in trying to please the people present in the room more then they were motivated by the potential for more people who could become involved if the change were made.

Another dimension of the situation is the approach some rectors have taken regarding obedience through listening. These priests have instituted processes and structures that help the community in its listening. There are community meetings, survey-feedback processes, and action-learning methods used. The rector makes an effort to connect with people when they are disturbed around an important issue. And around questions that are not appropriate for the larger congregation to weigh-in on, such as liturgical practice, the rector consults with a smaller group that has agreed to a disciplined method of exploring such issues.

In such parishes there's more listening happening then ever and the impact has mostly been to increase acceptance of change. But in some, under the surface, there's a growing unhappiness among a few and a mild concern for a larger group. You hear the old familiar refrain, "The rector doesn't listen to us!" As leaders in any parish know, in many cases this might more properly be expressed as, "The rector isn't doing what I want him to do!" That's certainly part of what's happening.

My read in one case is that it also may be driven by a personality difference between the rector and many core members. They are more introverted, the rector is more extroverted; they are caught up in their feelings about the happiness of existing members, the rector is more focused on the decisions needed if the parish is to grow and be more truly inclusive. The rector may be exactly the person needed to bring balance to the parish's decision making but will also in that process tend to generate resistance. A successful lasting outcome may hang on the rector's ability to demonstrate empathy for others and to retain humility concerning her judgments and decisions, while also maintaining a direction that serves the parish's long-term purposes. An issue in this and other places is that on occasion the rectors don't really engage the information they receive from people. For example in one parish the rector would conduct a survey and then allow the material to sit in the office not collated and unexamined for weeks. There are other cases where rectors use listening processes as a means to pacify people. Putting on a facade of listening can be maintained for a long time if the rector is skillful and careful.

So, a rector may care deeply that a few people are made uncomfortable by the incense while continuing the practice because it serves important corporate purposes. For some people when they have empathy for others they automatically move to find a way to end the discomfort of the other person. In some cases what is happening is that the leader may have empathy but not be effective in expressing it to others while maintaining a direction. Or the empathy may be introverted and therefore not seen. Or the leader may be incapable of holding to a course of action while openly sharing empathetic feelings and thoughts.

Sometimes leaders can address the tension by finding creative solutions. In the case of the incense an option in some parishes is a third liturgy with music and ceremony but without incense. Such alternatives can be very useful but they also may represent ways of avoiding the work that develops a healthier culture around leadership and participation. At times leaders do need to find these third-way options allowing the parish to accomplish goals while maintaining harmony. But if a parish is to have a mature health we also need occasions when hard choices must be made, when some will be left unhappy.

Define and Shape a Parish Culture with Benedictine Characteristics

What we are trying to do is help the community understand itself in terms of certain characteristics. So that when parish leaders say, "This is how we do things at St. E's", what we hope to hear is a self-definition that is rooted in the characteristics of Christian community rather than the habits of a religious club.

I'm going to discuss four such characteristics: listening, not grumbling, deciding to be in community, and healthy stability.

Listening

Benedict writes of listening carefully with "the ear of your heart" and wants what is received in the listening to be "put into practice" or accepted "willingly and carried out vigorously." It is about translating what we have heard into action. This process of listening and responding is obedience.

An assumption in organization development (OD) is that information that is engaged will create pressures and expectations in systems, that information has a catalytic effect in organizational change. OD consultants have all heard the advice to "let the data speak."

If we are to hear God, the society we live in, one another, and ourselves the parish needs structures, processes and a climate for listening. If the data is to "speak" the parish needs to be a listening community that nurtures listening people.

We need concrete ways to do that listening and responding. There are several ways parishes might "listen to the world."

Each year use a different method to engage in a disciplined contextual analysis. One year do a broad analysis that identifies the forces and trends that impact the parish. What is happening in the wider society (global, national), in the region, in the wider church? As part of this process invite your city/town planner to come to the part of the process related to regional trends. Another year look at a way of segmenting the population by values orientation or generational groupings. How does this show itself in the congregation? What groupings will be most drawn to this particular parish?

Many parishes have study groups that explore issues present or emerging in the society or church. That's a way to help the parish stay sensitive to trends. Or we might ask members with experience in various sectors of society to share their view of the trends. Listen to people from health care, government, education, and business. Expect them to do some research so that what they share is based in its own listening process.

Another form of study group would be to have leaders read a book that relates to some issue the parish needs to address. It might be around spiritual life, the parish as an emotional system or membership growth. The process would need to include some reflection about the parish's related patterns and an attempt to apply the ideas in the book to the parish. As a consultant I was asked to lead such a session in two parishes using Peter Steinke's *Congregational Leadership in Anxious Times*. The one parish had an acknowledged pattern of reactivity when people disagreed with a direction. The other had an unacknowledged pattern of overloading life with too many good things to do and ending up burdened and frustrated because they had a hard time saying "no."

There are forms of prayer and worship that play a role. Train and coach the congregation to include in their prayer life the concerns of the workplace and civic life along with those of the family and self. For example, help people learn how to imaginatively engage the offertory of the Eucharist with the whole of their life. Or, teach and have people practice a form of contemplation and intercession that attends to the broader society. Relate this to the Prayers of the People in the Eucharist. Work with the congregation on offering thanks for the signs of God's movement in society. Beware of the tendency for prayers related to the world to be focused on what people see as the "negative" part of their life.

Another way of using prayer to listen to the context is to conduct a contemplative walk around the town or neighborhoods the parish serves. Walk in silence. Invite participants to simply listen, see, and feel. Return to a meeting place to share what you have experienced. Explore any surprises, places of pain or joy. Celebrate the Eucharist or say an Office.

There are also structures, processes and a climate involved in learning to listen to the parish community. When leaders talk about "communication issues" in the parish they usually mean - "How can we communicate from the top, or center, to the rest of the parish?" While we do want to do that well it's the wrong starting place. The first issue is how the parish community can better listen to itself. Leaders have a responsibility to help the community communicate with itself and to take what is explored into account as they make decisions in vestries and committees. The leadership will want to establish listening processes within the vestry and other groups. Not all issues belong in front of the whole parish community. Here are a few ideas.

Leadership Conference or Retreat

Each year have a leadership conference. The idea is for leaders to take the time to get their "heads above water" and to see the parish in broader and deeper ways. This can be at a retreat center or at the parish. It might just be the rector and vestry or could be open to anyone who was willing to participate and help with follow-up work in the three months after. It helps to use an external consultant at least every two or three years. I've recently been working with one diocese and several parishes to do this with three parish vestries. All three vestries attend the same weekend. Working with all three at the same time allows them to afford the services of a more experienced consultant. It's a three-year contact which both allows us to build on what was done the previous year and gives me the opportunity to understand and get perspective on each. I take the vestries through an agreed process of some work together and a lot of time in for each vestry to work on its own.

A leadership conference needs to include time in prayer and activities that build connections among those present. It's a time to explore parish dynamics, strengths, and opportunities in relationship to the primary task and core processes. Use tools such as the core frameworks -- Renewal-Apostolate Cycle, Christian Life Model, Benedictine Promise, and Shape of the Parish. Consider using one or two models each year. These processes can include ways of looking at dynamics such as trust and inclusion. There can also be a long-range assessment of the parish's institutional life including finances and property. All this can be the base for identifying strategic issues and goals. My own bias is to avoid creating elaborate plans. Focus on developing a sense of direction and a deeper appreciation for the community's life.

In one parish I was the consultant for their leadership conference for fifteen years. That helped me and them gain a sense of the broad dynamics present in the parish. That parish required the vestry to attend and invited any members to participate as long as they would attend all the sessions and help with the follow up work. By being that open about participation they did three things. First, it expanded the amount of listening and response. More people contributed to and owned the direction. Second, it helped build a sense of community by creating stronger relationships among people. Third, it allowed them to identify people with the gifts for leadership. The rector and wardens could see who had the gifts and would tap them later to be on the vestry or take on projects.

Channeling Process

Parishes require more ways to identify and focus on needed conversations and issues than just yearly leadership gatherings. Some have established a "channeling process" that allows the parish to gather people's concerns, new ideas, and insights about emerging issues and put them in a channel, a pathway, toward decisions and action. One way of doing that is at every third vestry meeting, and at most meetings of the parish community, set aside time to have small groups record on newsprint "concerns" and "wish we would do" lists. Share the lists and have the whole group prioritize items. If the group is small and/or has good group discipline and skills, this could be done as a whole group. The process can be done about the totally of parish life or a segment. The key is for the community and its leaders to carefully listen and respond. We don't want to miss opportunities or to allow issues to fester or become centers of anxiety.

Testing Process

Another practice that can be used regularly is a "testing process." This is used in setting boundaries on how emerging issues will be engaged.

The process in too many parishes is one of listening and responding to the most anxious, cynical and passive people in the community. The clergy, wardens, the vestry, or even a whole parish community can get so caught up in trying to please or pacify a few people that disproportionate time, energy and resources get tied up in issues that are not really in the parish's best interest. This misdirection also usually leaves a resentful undercurrent in the community while not really addressing the anxiety of those who raised the initial concern.

Even when leaders know who is raising an issue, without a broader listening process they usually do not know whether it is an interest of just those people or of a wider segment of the community.

A "testing" process helps a community cope with situations in which a few persistent voices press a concern or idea that would have an effect on the community's life. What they are saying may represent a widely shared view or it may simply be their view. Those expressing the issue may not really know how many they represent. Imagine the informal one-on-one coffee hour discussion. Someone is making the rounds, letting others know about an important problem in the parish. People are listening and even nodding. Is it agreement or politeness?

The use of a "testing process" requires leaders to use sound judgment in deciding when the process is likely to produce valid and useful information as well as help the community manage its anxiety. Overuse may result in an increase in the community's anxiety, less listening, and ineffective action. However the danger in most parishes is not overuse but the absence of any way for the community to define itself in relationship to emerging issues. A rule of thumb might be to use a "testing process" about four times/year with the whole community and possibly ten times with the vestry.

The "testing process" can be done for a few minutes at the community's coffee hour, at vestry meetings, in working teams and at community meetings. It will usually be most effective if done when the group is gathered rather than in a paper survey. Face to face processes are usually more effective in promoting careful listening and effective response.

A possible process is to identify the issue, and put it on a spectrum of some sort. Have people indicate where they are on the spectrum, and summarize the result, along with what the next step will be, if any.

For example, in a parish where several people had been complaining about the extent of the parish's involvement in the arts.

A spectrum was created regarding the parish's involvement with the city's art community:

Too Much Involvement	About Right	Too Little Involvement

The 80 parishioners at the meeting came forward to register their opinion. The result was:

Too Much Involvement	About Right	Too Little Involvement
////	//////////////// //////////////// //////////////// /////////	/////

There was no judgment that those who had raised the issue were "wrong," only that most people in the community had a different opinion. Those who had raised the issue saw that their position was not widely shared.

It was not just the pet project of the rector and a few members. This involvement had wide ownership. The process allowed the community to know its own mind. The anxiety in the community about "people being upset" was put into perspective. No next steps were needed.

Community Meetings

Some parishes have started having community meetings three times a year. These are opportunities to have all those willing to gather focus on one significant issue. I've seen parishes do it around things such as hospitality, membership growth, and finances. The meetings are usually about 1 ½ hours long. They may include "channeling" (gathering prioritized lists of issues to address and moving them into a channel for action) and "testing" processes or some other way to gather information related to the topic.

Training in Skills and Methods

A listening climate can be encouraged by training people in how to use processes of faith sharing, circle discussions, and discernment that require respectful and careful listening. It helps to provide training in one-to-one communication skills, methods for teams to gather information and make decisions, and basic facilitation and group participation skills. Nurture the community's competence for being together in silence and stillness is part of establishing a listening community.

Encourage the practice of people speaking only for themselves. Teach people how to use "I" messages. Discourage "manipulative confidentiality" norms that allow people "to poison the community well" without being accountable for what they say. Leaders need to develop the practice that when someone comes carrying an invisible group's message they ask, "Who is saying this. Will you join me in meeting with them?"

Gathering Information Rather than Making Assumptions

Parish's can get stuck in a pattern of operating off of assumptions about what people want or why they are doing what they are doing. Four members resign from the vestry with a few months of one another. Is it coincidence or is a reaction to the rector or a difficult person on the vestry? The parish averages ten visitors per month and retains only a few each year. Is it that the liturgy and preaching is poor, that members overwhelm or ignore visitors, or is it something else?

We can get closer to finding out what is really happening if we can find an appropriate way to gather information. For example, the parish could seek information from people who visited the parish but did not return. Interview them to find out what went into their decision. Explore what you hear in terms of:

- Was it a matter of "fit"? The culture of the parish just didn't match what was being looked for. The parish was being its "best self," but it wasn't what this person wanted.
- The parish wasn't being its "best self." We were not showing our values and vision. For example, there was a lack of hospitality by either a lack of attention or overwhelming attention.
- The parish doesn't have a "best self."

Obedience to One Another

Obedience to one another is another thread that can make up a Benedictine fabric to strengthen parish life. This is part of developing a "listening parish."

The Latin word "oboedientia" comes from a root concerning hearing. Obedience is about hearing and responding to what we hear. In the people, circumstances and things of community life we are able to listen for God, for God's will, God's rhythm, God's spirit.

Obedience is about caring for those with who we are in community. Joan Chittister's translation of the Rule states, "Obedience is a blessing to be shown by all, not only to the prioress and abbot but also to one another ...."(Chapter 71) and later, "try to be first to show respect to the other (Romans 12:10) supporting with the greatest patience one another's weaknesses of body or behavior, and competing in obedience to one another"(Chapter 72).

"Obedience to one another" is a process of listening and responding to what we hear. That calling, if heard by a literalist spirit and an unskilled community, can become a pattern of communal dysfunction. Training people in skills for contemplation, discernment, intercession are part of the competency base needed. A related understanding is of how organizations develop and express unhealthy cultures in patterns of dependency and counter dependency, over involvement and under involvement, enmeshment and distancing and can improve by moving into patterns of interdependence, self-differentiation, and engaged-detachment.

Face-to-face, Two-way Communication

One method that might be especially useful for leaders to hold in mind is the power of communication as a face-to-face, two-way process.

Earlier I mentioned how in many parishes when there is talk about "communication" what is meant is communication from the leaders to the members, e.g., newsletters and sections of the web site. When leaders receive complaints about "communication" in the parish the discussion frequently moves to how the leadership can increase the methods and amount of information being shared with parishioners. We need a broader view of what is happening if we are to improve communication in the parish. To what extent does the leadership needs to change how it offers information and what is offered? To what extent do the members need to be directly challenged to pay attention to the information already available? Even more important may be exploring how the communication takes place. Try expanding the occasions of face-to-face, group, two-way communication, e.g., "testing processes" at coffee hour, regular parish town meetings that include a "channeling process" and a process for the community to focus its attention on some matter of common interest.

To increase the amount of face-to-face, two-way communication:

- Use survey-feedback processes rather than a survey-closed discussion processes. Four rules of thumb: 1) If you survey people, report the results back to them—don't gather information that only a leadership group then explores; 2) Report back in a face-to-face manner, such as in an open meeting; 3) Don't ask for data you are not really open to hearing and acting on; and 4) Increase the relationship between data gathering, analysis, setting direction, and taking action by doing it all at the same time. The immediacy creates more ownership and investment that can translate into understanding and action.
- Develop your ability to decide when it is appropriate to just receptively listen and when there is a need for conversation.
- Use the methods, e.g., "testing processes," "channeling processes," parish town meetings, external consultants from time to time.

The more immediate the data collection and feedback, the more likely you are to increase the community's energy for follow through. For example, if you hold one meeting in which you survey, report back, and also begin initial thoughts about planning, you are both more likely to engage those who have expressed an interest and to able to use that energy to get something accomplished. Delays between data gathering and feedback are not necessarily deadly but they will create an energy drain as people have to be brought back up to speed.

Also avoid the compulsion to survey everyone, thereby focusing on artificial inclusion rather than action and energy. The people who show up for the open meetings are the ones more likely to be involved and participate in subsequent actions. Focusing on making sure everyone was surveyed usually results in leaders feeling a need to accommodate all those opinions. It's healthier and more likely to lead to effective action if those filling out survey forms are the same people gathered in a face-to-face setting that allows exploration and the possibility of being influenced by others. Survey-feedback processes do require small group follow up activities. Working groups begun at an open meeting can stay with the project for a few months and leaders will need to monitor movement and make adjustments.

Grumbling or Murmuring

A second theme that has a strong connection to the listening climate is how leaders and members deal with the grumbling in our hearts.

Benedict's passion for listening and mutual self-giving in community is made clearer and tougher by his objection to "grumbling" or "murmuring." Parish leaders know all about this way of complaining. New ideas and problem solving will not create, in themselves, a healthy community that stays healthy. The parish must attend to its spirit. Grumbling is often the manifestation of communal cynicism and passivity, of a victim stance. In individuals it can become an addictive behavior that eats away at the person's integrity.

Our listening and responding builds community when freely given to one another and to the whole community. In the Rule our obedience is only "acceptable to God and agreeable to people" if it "is not cringing or sluggish or halfhearted, but free from any grumbling ...." The Rule also speaks of responding gladly because if people respond only "grudgingly and grumble, not only aloud but in their hearts, then even though the order is carried out, their actions will not be accepted with favor by God, who sees that they are grumbling in their hearts." (Chapter Five of the *Rule of Saint Benedict*)

Addressing the issue of grumbling might include at least seven elements.

1. Develop those listening and problem-solving processes mentioned above. There needs to be a healthy process for people to cope with the feelings, frustrations and ideas they have; a process that is an alternative to the grumbling. This is a way of doing what Benedict did in taking counsel with others in the community around truly significant matters.

2. Establish a "no grumbling" norm. We need to ask people to honor each other and the well being of the community. If the community has ways to listen and to work together in improving its common life, members need to be asked to use that process. There needs to be an explicit invitation to exercise self-discipline over what and how we speak in addressing issues and especially when things don't go our way.

3. Actively nurture emotional and spiritual maturity. There are a couple of very conservative women I have frequently talked with during the years of fighting in the Episcopal Church. They are in a minority in the church and in their own parishes. One is a priest, the other a lay woman. Here's what I have heard from them about what allows them to remain in a church that they disagree with over several very important issues. In reference to our friendship, "I would not want to be part of a church that would not include you." (We have different opinions.) "I don't want to do anything to harm the unity of the church." And, "I have changed my mind before, so I don't want to be so arrogant as to assume that

I might not change my mind about these things." They each exhibit humility and self-awareness. The parish's work of formation needs to include shaping this kind of maturity. We need to be clear about what we are doing in formation. It is about the virtues and Christian character. It is not about getting people to agree with our view on current issues in the church or society.

4. Train and support leaders in their ministry with chronic grumblers as well as those who are especially insistent around a particular issue. Train leaders in how to: listen to upset or anxious members, explain the parish's position, and invite people to participate without trying to take responsibility for convincing people. Have leaders learn to be firm in inviting members to offer their concerns and ideas in the community's normal processes for channeling and testing rather than having the leader accept responsibility for the member's issue. Make sure that leaders know that polling members behind the back of the rector is a big "no-no." The destructiveness of such behavior lingers in a parish community and poisons relationships.

5. Accept that grumbling will take place. Even in parishes that have done all the above there will be times of grumbling, times when the pressures within the community will erupt. Responding with a legalistic "we have a no grumbling norm," or a moralistic, "This is very harmful behavior," is likely to only make the situation worse. Even the most mature communities will have difficult emotional and spiritual periods. We are all "grumblers" sometimes.

6. Confront the chronic grumblers. Every parish seems to have a few people who live under a cloud of unhappiness with the clergy and/or the parish. At some clergy gatherings there is occasional joking about trading grumblers or asking the diocese to establish a special parish to transfer all these people into. In one parish the leadership identified two people fitting the category. Each had an idealized parish they carried in their head. For the one it was an innovative parish that attracted "funky" people, for the other it was several Anglo Catholic "flagship" parishes. Each had their complaint about "inclusion." The one wanted an approach to communion allowing the non-baptized to receive, the other felt "conservatives" were not welcome enough. Each had particular issues they would name when engaged. If an issue was addressed the complaining would shift to a new topic. The parish leaders noticed two constants. The first was that there was a history to the behavior. Years could pass, leaders could change, but the grumbling stance was maintained. The second was that each was unable to cope with the authority of the wider community. Neither could graciously live in something real that was larger than themselves and their own imagination.

7. Watch out for scapegoating. It's often a sign of something being "off" in the parish's listening process when there is a pattern of scapegoating by the leaders. In some parishes a "no grumbling norm is used as a cover for not listening and engaging fully. Face-to-face discussion is avoided and members are either forced out of the parish or marginalized.

A healthy parish confronts the constant grumblers. It's a process of challenge and invitation. A challenge to change the stance they have taken, to put on kindness and patience. In John Gardner's terms it's to become loving-critics, rather than unloving-critics, toward the parish and its leaders. The invitation is to a fuller and more real life, to experience the embrace of the Blessed Trinity from within the parish's life. This work is in the best sense "pastoral." It is pastoral care for the individual, and pastoral oversight of the parish's life. It's also pastoral self-care for the clergy and lay leaders. Few things wear on a priest more than parish habits that enable and reward the constant grumblers; that some clergy grumble in return only adds to the problem. The need is for skills in listening, trust development, and conflict management.

We also need to take note that Benedict has a bias. He's a leader of a community and he writes from that perspective. Parish rectors get it—how nice to eliminate the constant noise of people complaining and suggesting all their new ideas. For a no-grumbling norm to have integrity Benedict's call to consult with others needs to be effectively implemented. There are at least three things needed.

1. **Availability.** This is accomplished by a pattern or routine of listening processes. People need to experience survey-feedback, testing processes and community meetings as things that happen regularly. When I know the time to say my piece will come I can hold my peace. When the issue has urgency and importance, or there is possible harm to a person or community, that calls for a more timely response.

2. **Appropriate to the issue and circumstances**. Some issues are best dealt with by the routine listening processes. Ideas about how to improve parish life or add some new element may be managed by asking people to bring them to the next community meeting when we will collect all such thinking. A person enraged about something the rector did to them requires a more personal and immediate response. At times we need a face-to-face conversation. Other cases call for a third party to mediate or facilitate.

3. **Genuineness.** Listening and its benefits are not just accomplished by using the right methods and skills. The listening needs authenticity. It must be real. People can tell when the leadership has no "in-box." Some rectors function in a strongly narcissistic manner. In *Congregational Leadership in Anxious Times,* Peter Steinke points to a pathological narcissism. He defines that by quoting Alexander Lowen, "excessive investment in self at the expenses of others." Then he notes seventeen characteristics, a few of which are reproduced below.

   - "The person is capable of seeing only her own perspective, is intolerant of disagreement, doesn't discuss ideas but imposes them, is single-minded, believes in her own superior wisdom, and doesn't need help from others."
   - "The person is ruthless toward those who do not reflect back his projected image of specialness. He is vindictive, vengeful, devaluing, and abrasive. He publicly humiliates others and wants others to be wholehearted supporters."
   - "The person is prone to lying and an expert at disguise."
   - "The person presents herself impressively. She is clever, charming, seductive, persuasive, self-assured."
   - "The person is more interested in being admired than loved."

If the vestry avoids availability, appropriateness, and genuineness in what it does then the priest can be the balancer. More often it will be the wardens who need to help the priest get perspective and engage what needs to be engaged. This doesn't need to be a confrontation with the priest but an empathetic intervention when the stress of the work and life get overwhelming.

In general wardens function best when they see themselves as the rector's collaborators and supporters. They can help the priest be his best self. At other times they need to ask hard questions, challenge and occasionally insist on alternatives with a strong rector. That can require wisdom, courage and a high degree of social intelligence. We've seen wardens who want to micro-manage the priest and those who side step any confrontation with her. When the priest cuts off listening and communication it may be up to the wardens to intervene and help the priest move toward a more open and listening stance.

When lay or clergy leaders cut off two-way communication for any reason they risk more conflict in the parish. Not being receptive in spirit, lack of empathy, or refusing to meet with someone, may set off troubles that could have been avoided.

Speed Lees has a model of conflict levels that assumes that if we fail to skillfully address conflict at one level it is likely to press onto a higher level. For example, we can take what he defines as a level two disagreement, in which the energy is about solving the problem, or a level three "contest" in which the parties want their way but don't want to hurt others, and push it to a level four of five. Level four is "fight/flight" in which people are willing to hurt others, and level five is an "intractable situation" in which significant damage can be done to the someone's reputation, position, and well being. If leaders fail to listen when a person or a group connected to the parish requests it, they become responsible for what happens when those people seem to go crazy.

It's easy to blame the "crazies" because their behavior seems so over-the-top or "emotional." But what choices have we left them with? They need to submit to a situation that seems mistaken or even unjust or they need to press their case at the risk of damaging himself or herself or the parish. Leaders need to work at keeping level two and three conflicts at those more manageable stages by empathetic listening, a collaborative sprit, and an attempt at mutual problem solving.

This is about the well being of the whole parish community and about each individual's growth. The community needs to not have its attention and energies constantly taken away from its common life and work by having to deal with the complainers. The single most important thing a parish does to manage this is to have reliable listening processes and genuineness in the listening. It is these processes and that stance that sorts the healthy challenges from the chronic grumbling.

The individuals most given to complaining need to be in an environment in which they might come to terms with themselves and life in community. For that to happen leaders need to help the parish learn to tolerate discomfort at those times when there is tension and conflict. It is at those times that a community can develop its ability to persevere and live in stability of life. And it is the stability of the leaders and the parish community that offers its most troubled members a chance to find a new life.

Decide to be in Community

The parish will be a healthier place if members can own that they have decided to be in community and that they have decided to be in *this particular* parish community. Benedict's position about grumbling is in chapter five where he reminds members that they have chosen to live in community. The Rule seems to assume that some things come along with a person's decision to join, things like no grumbling, balance, worship, silence, and humility. In deciding to join a community we also decide to live within the particular ways of that community. How do we help people accept responsibility for the decision they have made?

Be explicit with potential members of the parish that to join is to decide to be part of a living community, to open oneself to the process of being influenced and shaped by others, and to participate in the mystery by which you will influence and shape others. It is to enter into the rhythms of the community's life that will, in time, work their way into your mind and heart. We lose life to gain life, die to rise, become empty so we might be filled. The central mystery of Christian life is lived in the context of community, community with others and with God.

The Rule's assumption is that the community is the setting within which conversion takes place. That conversion is shaped by the give and take of life together; in the example of others; by giving oneself to habits of listening, balance and humility; and by the occasional confrontations and upheavals that life with others always brings. That conversion is a gradual process; that holiness comes bit by bit, and it is best when not noticed. Parishes need to tell new members about how it works. New members often need a picture of what is possible in a parish and guidance in how to engage those possibilities.

The Rule's approach toward new members may seem strange, even wrong, to parish leaders who have been encouraged to go all out in bringing people to Christ and the Church. Benedict writes, "Do not grant newcomers to the life an easy entry..." (Chapter 58) The process of admission includes: knocking at the door for four or five days to test patience and desire, a few days in the guest house, then time with those in training. The Rule is read to the person after two, six and ten months. The person reflects on the Rule (you need to think about what you are getting yourself into). Only after all this comes the commitment of the person and the community.

What the Rule is getting at is the need to, "Test the spirits to see if they are from God" (1 John 4:1 and the Rule, Chapter 58). The community has an interest in maintaining its capacity to be a place of formation. That means it can't constantly be struggling with new members over the central culture of the community. There needs to be an adequate degree of stability.

The potential new member needs to be a wise steward of her or his time and energy. Is this a place (a climate, a culture, a people) in which the person's spirituality will grow and mature? Or should another community be considered that would be more of a fit with the person's needs?

For example, the Order of the Ascension is a Benedictine community of Christians in the Episcopal tradition that I've been part of for over 25 years. Its members take a three-year Promise "to seek the presence of Jesus Christ in the people, things and circumstances of my life through stability, obedience and conversion of life." The Order has a shared commitment to parish revitalization and the struggle for justice. Its members gather yearly for five days of retreat, education and social time. All its members have received a significant amount of training in congregational development.

In its Rule, the Order lays out a process of entry that includes: a five month discernment period of reflection on the Rule, developing an understanding of the relationship between the Promise and the person's daily life, and a series of questions for both the applicant and the community, including the following:

- Is there obvious common ground between the person's and the Order's orientation to parish life and the spiritual life?
- Does the person have an adequately disciplined spiritual life, and sufficient self-esteem and support from colleagues, family and friends, so as to be able to benefit from what the Order does offer in vocational support without holding to unreasonable expectations of the support such a life will provide?

- Is membership in the Order likely to have beneficial effects on the person's work, family, friendships?
- What does the person bring to the Order?
- To what extent is the person making an act of free commitment, choosing to devote energy in this way and pattern? To what extent is the commitment "clouded" and "divided"?

A parish church is not a monastic community. It may be a dispersed community in the same way as the Order of the Ascension, but it doesn't have the same purposes and therefore doesn't require that level of training and commitment for membership. However, parish leaders do need to explore the same underlying and interdependent issues, such as:

- The parish is an instrument of God's mission of Holy Unity and people becoming fully alive. The parish's purposes emerge out of God's purposes. The life that glorifies God and forms women and men in the divine image is shaped in the rhythm of what I've called the Renewal-Apostolate Cycle.
- Given the purpose and task of a parish community, what is needed from new members so they are in relationship to the community in a manner that advances the community's purpose, as well as the person's growth?
- What does the community need to communicate to potential members so they can make an informed decision about membership? What does the community need to ask of the potential member? What training and education needs to be provided to incorporate the person into the way this community lives its life and forms people in the Christian life?

Dealing openly with these issues may help a parish create an entry and incorporation process that has integrity, is effective and efficient.

The need is to develop an invitation process that communicates the nature of the parish community to people before they come to visit, and that helps people make an informed choice about whether it even makes sense for them to visit. Good marketing is done in a manner that allows people to make informed and free decisions about the use of a product, a service or membership in an organization. Good marketing helps people focus their energy and make more lasting commitments.

There is also a need to have a process of greeting, orienting and incorporating people in a way that is consistent with what they will experience as a member and begins to equip them for full participation in this particular community.

So, if the parish is striving for a culture in which people are both accepted and challenged, people need to see this early in their relationship with the community. It should not be all acceptance with the challenge appearing after you're "hooked." If the parish is serious about its task of Christian formation, then visitors and people considering membership need to experience opportunities for faith sharing, exploration of questions and doubts, and for training in Eucharistic worship and living. They need these experiences early on in the relationship rather than the all-too-frequent experience of being recruited into parish groups and jobs, and given a sense that the focus is on the institutional life of the parish rather than on its purpose. If the parish is really a place of deep prayer, then the environment of the space, the community's competence for worship, and offerings to train and coach people in prayer life need to strike new people early in their time with the parish.

The reason most people leave places of work is a lack of "fit" with the organizational culture. The person may be seeking a work environment that is participatory and empowering while the company's management style is more controlling. The same thing happens in parishes. Cultural issues (e.g., the style of spirituality and worship, the range of leadership styles commonly used, the degree of acceptance vs. challenge as part of the climate, openness to differences, the way in which the dynamics of closeness and separation are managed, and expectations about participation and giving) are matters over which people commit themselves or withdraw.

The entry and incorporation process needs to assist potential members and the parish community in making educated choices about a particular person's membership. The issue is not one of creating artificial or high standards. A parish church is by its nature a relatively open system. For the most part people make a decision to join and we accept them. We want people to make a right discernment, a wise choice about the parish they join. Parishes are not interchangeable.

Healthy Stability

Most organizational life cycle models suggest a development that moves from creation through formation to a place of maturity or stability. The model I frequently use differentiates between healthy stability and static stability. Healthy stability is maintained by addressing the tasks of parish formation in a spirit of, and with the behaviors of, obedience and conversion of life. The parish's stability doesn't come about by pursuing stability in itself but by being a listening community and engaging the issues and people that invite us consider when we need to let go of loved ways and secure places.

In times of healthy maturity, some people will yearn for those times of institutional formation with the adventure of dreams and significant work to accomplish. Some will so miss the excitement of institution and community creation that they will avoid the work needed during the healthy stability phase. Others simply get anxious during this phase because they don't know how to live in it and may lack the associated competencies. They may be tempted to focus on institutional and administrative goals. The work of membership growth, building projects, special attention to financial management, and great service ministries all need to be addressed at some points in a parish's life. At other times these projects substitute busyness and a desire for institutional success for the ongoing and primary work of Christian formation.

The primary task is the formation of the People of God at all stages of their life. It is *always* a needed ministry but it is all too often done as though it were simply one program among other programs. There is a kind of half-life that is generated in churches that stay caught up in some institutional scheme. There are clergy and parishes that find themselves always seeking a new challenge in a new project, a project defined by a sense of numerical or physical accomplishment. Instead, choose to make the liturgy an experience of delight and enchantment; choose to create an adult foundations program that equips people with a capacity for spiritual discipline and ways of thinking that rise from what is eternal. Choose to have many opportunities in which those who are Christ's own come to know themselves and each other as people of curiosity and discernment, of courage and perseverance, of joy and wonder, and lovers of God.

Static stability is characterized by an inability to effectively address being on a plateau in membership or spiritual life; seeing planning methods as a way to control the future; fussing over small things; not responding to new opportunities; losing a sense of vision and purpose; and an identity that is increasingly focused on the past and can seem bland.

If that condition isn't turned around the parish will usually slide into decline characterized by denying that we are really in trouble; avoiding the needed conversations and resources to have the conversation; increased levels of stress; a nostalgic climate; low or fragmented energy; and a "fear-blame" cycle in which people begin to search for someone to blame (the priest, the diocese, the people who left for another parish, the change in the neighborhood's demographics). Leaders may step away from accepting responsibility. Or new leaders may emerge with a narcissistic orientation in which they are all too ready to take control and "save" the parish.

The ministry of parish development frequently involves helping churches move out of static and declining lives and engage the tasks of formation in a manner that fits the here and now life of the parish. But it also is about how to serve the many parishes in a state of health stability. How do we help them stay healthy and faithful?

The work of formation whether from a place of decline or of health includes shaping a new vision or sense of direction and managing the polarity of maintaining parish identity and integrity while making adaptations that serve survival and mission. Parish formation embraces the task of grounding the parish in its organic reality as a microcosm of the Holy Catholic Church, attracting new members, developing new leaders, and nurturing a deeper inner life among individuals and the whole parish community. This work is always with us.

A stable and healthy parish can find itself no longer hoping for a new and better life. It can stop being attentive to the movement of the Spirit. The fact of its health and faithfulness can undermine its continued health and faithfulness. We can lose touch with Newman's, "To live is to change, and to be perfect is to have changed often." How does the healthy, mature parish do just that? How do we change often and be stable?

In most cases the starting place is among the current members. Leaders and consultants can provide an environment and processes that help members identify and give voice to their deeper hopes and longings. This work takes some care. It's easy for traditional exercises to generate either an image of the new that is really just the current way repackaged or a radical and utopian dream that brings more judgment than hope. As useful as mutual ministry reviews and leadership retreats can be they are rarely tools that bring a parish closer to its depth and uniqueness. The longings and energy of the People of God need a gentle space in which they can emerge. We might try more of these kinds of things:

- Interviewing processes with individuals and then shared in small groups. Use ways that invite people to come at the parish's life indirectly and through their own experience. So, don't begin with "What are your hopes for the parish?" but with "What is God doing with you that is making you more human?" or "What as happen in your life this year that caused you to want to run away from people or things that you need to face into?" or "What has died in your life that you need to bury?"
- Increase the times and places of silence and stillness in parish life.
- Allow more space for mystery and awe in liturgy. Increase the gracefulness and beauty both in what happens around the altar and among the congregation. Pay attention to movement, music, and silence.

- Help families make space for wonder and awe, especially with children. For example, it is critical that young children participate in late-night or pre-dawn liturgies at Christmas and Easter. The experience of this being something very special, something that is part of the adult world that they get to participate in, can provide needed experiences and memories of mystery. Children may, even more than many adults, "get" the power of rhythms in darkness—light, movement—stillness, silence—sounds.
- Create a parish history that is a narrative of how this local expression of God's people has experienced the presence of Christ in stability, obedience and conversion of life. Tell the true story with kindness but honesty. Step away from the history being about the buildings and rectors. Tell the story of how we have faced occasions of defeat and decline and persevered into new life, of how we have been estranged and in conflict and brought to new trust and life in community. If the parish has some real saints in its history, tell their stories, speak of how these fragile beings were used as instruments of God's love.
- Pay attention to times of receptivity and fear. There are moments in parish life that are like the period between darkness and dawn, sleep and awakening, in which something new might be seen. This can be especially true in times of transition, including before and after the departure and arrival of priests, the death or departure of parish saints, a noticeable trend in the membership of the parish (up, down, stuck on a plateau, demographics), significant conflict, the destruction of parish property, and major financial threat.
- When holding leadership retreats and ministry reviews, seek out a third-party facilitator with significant skills in congregational development and consultation work—someone with an awareness of the hidden parish dynamics and a vision of what is possible in the Body of Christ.

If we have the eyes to see, a new energy will break into parish life during times of health and stability. The first expression may come from the chronic complainers or those driven to fix everything around them. They may not have the emotional intelligence or political smarts to make much happen on their own that is truly fruitful. But if you listen closely to what may be mostly an expression of anxiety you may also hear a yearning that comes from a deeper place within the parish system.

Pay attention to the moments of confusion and trouble, to the accidents and missteps, to the parish fools, strangers and enchanters, especially those who have been with the parish for some years. Notice times of loss, death and grief. Listen to those who see life as an adventure.

Take in the way in which the polarities present themselves in times of maturity. Believe that the people of the parish carry within themselves those polarities. They long for the journey and for home, seek intimacy and solitude, and want change and stability. If you believe this you will see it and you will stir up those forces within the community. By allowing, affirming and pointing to the polarities leaders can create within the parish a climate that provides the freedom for individuals to be where they need to be and to move when ready to move.

Within what may appear to be the carefully controlled life of maturity can surface the new security of a transformed home, of new love, new friends, and new work.

Other Models

Poverty – Chastity - Obedience

The Congregation of the Sisters, Servants of the Immaculate Heart of Mary in Scranton, Pennsylvania, offered the following as a way of understanding the traditional vows. I can imagine a parish developing itself around these vows.

"The vows are meant to be a public witness to Gospel values. They are not meant to be restrictions on our lives, but rather attitudes toward life and signs of hope. While our understanding of the vows grows and develops, we generally see the vows in this way:

Poverty—a call to live for the sake of the poor, to act for justice, to advocate against oppressive policies, to embrace a simple lifestyle.

Chastity—a call to love well and non-exclusively, to care deeply for and about others, to love totally for the sake of others.

Obedience—a call to listen to the voice of the Spirit in all of life, to search for truth.

Change and Stability

Many organization development practitioners approach their work as one of managing the dynamic between change and stability in an organization. Organizational culture change efforts are cast as increasing the possibility of the organization's success by managing the needs for adaptability on the one hand and system integration and integrity on the other.

In *Organization Development and Change*, Cummings and Worley write about "contingencies related to the change situation…and the target of change" as including:
1. Readinesses for change – For example, is there adequate dissatisfaction with the status quo and are the needed resources available?
2. Capacity to change – For example, is there the ability to motivate and lead change?
3. Cultural context – This is the need to take into account the cultural values and assumptions of people in the organization.
4. Capacities of the change agent – They write about the many failures of change efforts "when change agents apply interventions beyond their competence." For leaders, managers and consultants this is partly a matter of self-awareness and partly one of ethics.
5. Organizational issues and levels – This involves assessing and selecting the parts of an organization in which to intervene.

Dealing with these contingencies is in Benedictine terms a matter of obedience; there is listening to self and others, and there is a kind of submitting to the claims of professional and ethical standards.

IV. The Shape of the Parish

The Shape of the Parish: An Exercise

Following is an exercise for assessing your parish. My experience is that it provides the base you will need to understand and use the model. Please follow the steps below:

1. Using the circles below, in circle #2 put your parish's average adult Sunday attendance. Be sure to include all acts of corporate worship from Saturday evening through Sunday evening. For the most part these are the people you see frequently and regularly. They may range from weekly to every few weeks in their participation in the Eucharist.
2. In circle #3, first put the parish's adult attendance at Christmas or Easter.
   - Then subtract the number you have placed in circle #2. Put the result in circle #3
   - This makes up those people who relate to the church primarily through the major holidays; also possibly through family occasions such as baptisms, weddings and burials.
3. For circle #4, you will not place a number here. Instead, make a few specific notes of ways in which people relate to the parish but don't ever attend the regular corporate worship of the church. It may be people who are connected through family who are members or because they are part of a group that makes use of the property or are in some way served by the parish. You may be able to name some of these people.
4. In circle #1, write the number of those that you see as having a deep, mature faith & practice.
5. Then subtract that number from what you have in circle #2. Place that number in circle # 2 in place of the earlier number.

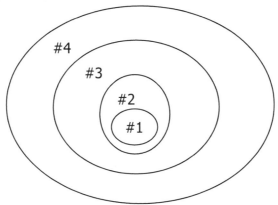

The numbers now in the various circles represent "the shape of the parish". Continue reading the document to explore the dynamics, issues and strategies that can emerge. I'll begin with the basic diagram.

The Shape of the Parish: A Diagram Overview

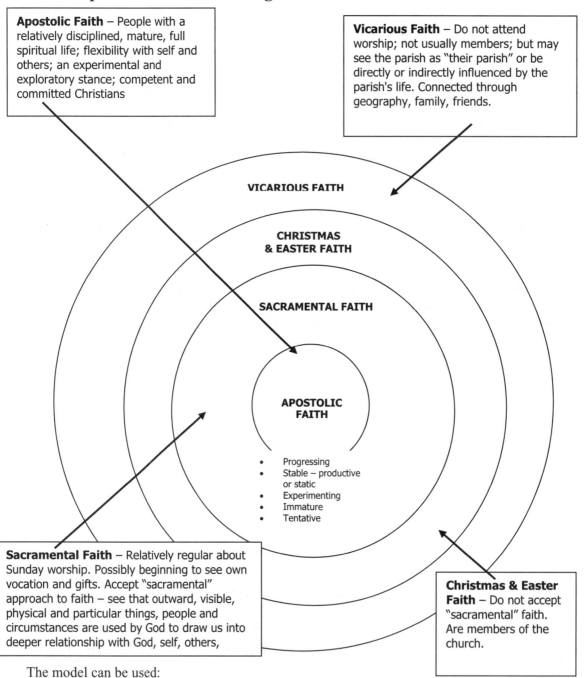

Apostolic Faith – People with a relatively disciplined, mature, full spiritual life; flexibility with self and others; an experimental and exploratory stance; competent and committed Christians

Vicarious Faith – Do not attend worship; not usually members; but may see the parish as "their parish" or be directly or indirectly influenced by the parish's life. Connected through geography, family, friends.

VICARIOUS FAITH

CHRISTMAS & EASTER FAITH

SACRAMENTAL FAITH

APOSTOLIC FAITH

- Progressing
- Stable – productive or static
- Experimenting
- Immature
- Tentative

Sacramental Faith – Relatively regular about Sunday worship. Possibly beginning to see own vocation and gifts. Accept "sacramental" approach to faith – see that outward, visible, physical and particular things, people and circumstances are used by God to draw us into deeper relationship with God, self, others,

Christmas & Easter Faith – Do not accept "sacramental" faith. Are members of the church.

The model can be used:
- To assess the health of a parish, and
- To develop a strategy that deepens the parish's spiritual life, while staying open to the various places people are in their faith journey.

"Shape of the Parish" Diagram -- Robert A. Gallagher/Mary Anne Mann, 1983; Revised RAG 1999, 2003

The Shape of the Parish: An Exploration

We must believe that it is the darkest before the dawn of a beautiful new world. We will see it when we believe it. Saul Alinsky

The Church (it was early decided) was not an organization of sinless men but of sinful, not a union of adepts but of less than neophytes, not illuminati but of those that sat in darkness. Nevertheless, it carried within it an energy not its own, and it knew what it believed about that energy. Charles Williams, *He Came Down from Heaven*

A Critical Mass Model

The "Shape of the Parish" is a critical mass theory. Critical mass theories are used by many Organization Development practitioners. The model suggests building the level of commitment, competence and emotional maturity at the center of the organization so that it grounds the system in a mission orientation and an organizational culture that supports the mission. The grounding then is enfleshed; made real in the lives of men and women. It's in the habits of people rather then statements of leaders.

Critical mass models draw the attention of leaders away from obsessing about "fixing" the problems and dysfunction at the edges and toward building the center. We can all too easily find our attention drawn toward the "difficult people" or those who constantly demand personal attention. A critical mass model suggests that we give much more of our time and energy to developing the center.

In the Shape of the Parish the "critical mass" has the effect of pulling people into a deeper relationship with God and the church. By their behavior and character those closer to the center contribute to establishing a climate, "an energy not their own," that attracts some others toward the center. In addition, leaders need to facilitate and strengthen the "critical mass" by firmly and gently tilting the structures, processes and climate of the parish toward maturity and health. The whole atmosphere of the parish says that there is more; more than we have yet experienced and known.

All critical mass models open up the question of what a system's practices need to be at the center and to what extent members of the system need to be fully in the center. Or in this case, does everyone need to be of Apostolic Faith for the nature and mission of the church to be fully engaged? Three thoughts: 1) I believe that the Holy Catholic Church is a body with fuzzy boundaries and gray lines. It includes people at all stages of the journey. And, that condition is God's intention for the church. 2) The church's mission is advanced by the reality of the church's life. The process of sanctification, of being brought more and more into the Holy Unity and the completeness of self, happens not in spite of the messiness, but in some sense because of it. 3) It's not possible for a parish to have all its members be of Apostolic Faith without having everyone pretending things that are not true.

A Caution

This particular model needs to be used with care. More than all the others it has the potential of setting off in some people either judgment towards others or defensiveness about themselves. Leaders need to consider limiting its use to people of a mature enough faith that it will be used as a tool in spiritual and congregational development.

Elements of the Shape of the Parish

The model is based on observable characteristics, specific patterns of behavior and attitudes, connected to various forms of faith and practice. Parish leaders familiar with the church's tradition of spirituality, and present in a particular parish for several years, are usually able to make reasonable guesses about where members are in relation to this model. Caution needs to be taken in the process of making such assessments. Leaders need a stance of spiritual guidance and pastoral oversight rather than judgment and control. It is also important not to become literal in the use of the characteristics. Think of them as pointing in a direction: a person may fit a form of faith and practice without all the characteristics being present, and there are characteristics not mentioned that will be related to a particular stage.

Apostolic Faith

People of Apostolic Faith are those who reliably live a grounded, mature faith and practice. In relationship to the Renewal – Apostolate Cycle they will generally move in the cycle in a graceful, effective and efficient manner. They "own" their practice of faith. It is no longer what someone else has asked or expected of them, but it "belongs" to them. There is an adult acceptance of responsibility for their spiritual life. This is a responsibility that isn't taken in isolation but from within the community, as a baptized person incorporated into the mystical Body of Christ. Another sign of such faith might be a sense that "there is more"—more to God, more to others, more to themselves, than they yet know or understand.

Those of Apostolic Faith are also likely to accept that they are sinners. Stuart Hazeldine, a writer involved in a movie of *Paradise Lost*, explored what Milton did in his writing and Scorsese did in his movie *Goodfellas*. He said, "You can't understand the nature of the fall until you've tasted some of the exhilaration of sin and crime. Scorsese makes you feel the rush of being in the Mafia—what it's like to be special, get the best table at a restaurant, kill someone and get away with it." (*New York Times*, 3/9/07) The Apostolic Christian "gets" what Hazeldine is saying. To accept that we are redeemed sinners is an act of humility and realism.

There are then three broad elements present. The first is behavioral. People of Apostolic Faith regularly and frequently engage in the church's practices of the spiritual life. The second is a stance or attitude that includes openness and humility. They would understand Auden's words, "You will love your crooked neighbor/With your crooked heart." Third, is that the characteristics of the new life are more stable: "an inquiring and discerning heart, the courage to will and to persevere, a spirit to know and to love you, and the gift of joy and wonder in all your works."

The existence of a critical mass of these people in a parish can orient the parish toward Christ and away from its preoccupation with the more trivial aspects of religion and parish life. By living the faith they draw others deeper into God. They become a means of grace for the parish by their contagious influence.

Additional characteristics of Apostolic Faith are the following:

- **Living by Rule**. The Apostolic have a spiritual discipline. For most Episcopalians that will mean that they have adapted the Prayer Book pattern of prayer to the circumstances of their own life. Eucharist, Daily Office and Personal Devotions all have a place in the person's spiritual discipline.
- **Responsibility within community**. The person has learned to adequately manage the polarity of being a self and of being in relationship. This entails acceptance of individual responsibility along with an acceptance of being in community with others. In other words, I am responsible for shaping the Rule that I live, while allowing the Rule of the Church to influence me in creating that pattern.
- **Responsibility for the community**. People of Apostolic Faith accept the duty of being a prayerful center of the parish. This is an organic dependability rather than something achieved by appointment or election. It is accepting that you pray even if others don't. That in some sense you pray on behalf of all who don't pray; and you pray more consistently and deeply for all who pray superficially and sentimentally. And all this is done without complaint but graciously and thankfully. Please note this job is not an

institutional matter. It is a responsibility that is about the natural functioning of the Body of Christ, the activity by which the church is a channel of grace for the world.

- **A more humble, open stance**. There is an increased acceptance of the diverse ways in which people live the faith journey; an acceptance of its complex, ambiguous, and paradoxical ways; openness to a broader range of expression about faith. In some sense we know less than we used to know; we are caught up in the mystery of God's loving embrace. Frequently, those in earlier phases in the pilgrimage are more certain about the right way to understand God, humanity, and the church.

- **An integration of mystery and apostolic living.** In Evelyn Underhill's *Concerning the Inner Life*, she writes about that integration: "... one's first duty is adoration, and one's second duty is awe and only one's third duty is service. And that for those three things and nothing else, addressed to God and no one else, you and I and all other countless human creatures evolved upon the surface of this planet were created. We observe then that two of the three things for which our souls were made are matters of attitude, of relation: adoration and awe. Unless these two are right, the last of the triad, service, won't be right. Unless the whole of your...life is a movement of praise and adoration, unless it is instinct with awe, the work which the life produces won't be much good."

William Stafford's poem, "The Way It Is," contains the following lines—

> There's a thread you follow.
> It goes among the things that change.
> But it doesn't change. ....
> It's hard for others to see.
> While you hold it you can't get lost.

Stafford notes tragedy, hurt, death and aging as what comes with "time's unfolding." He ends with, "You don't ever let go of the thread." It's a useful image for understanding Apostolic Faith. The Apostolic hold onto the thread of Christ and the church. There are expressions of the thread they share in common, but finally each does it in his or her own way. For me it's had two primary sacramental expressions—the liturgy and friendships. Others will have different sacramental threads that hold them in connection with Christ and the church.

Sacramental Faith

They are there on Sunday! They are most of the people in any parish. They are regular in their participation because at some level they understand the notion of sacrament. They behaviorally function as though "outward and visible" things such as the church and the Eucharist can convey inward grace. They may have developed, or be in the process of developing, a sense of their vocation and gifts.

This form of faith has its own phases. One way of expressing this is to think of those gathered on most Sundays as being primarily part of one of five groups: Tentative, Immature, Experimenting, Stable, and Progressing. Apostolic Faith is a sixth group that is present on Sunday. Sacramental faith is a progression toward maturity. It is a movement in which we accept more responsibility for our own spiritual life, a movement in which we see more possibilities, come to understand more about the fit between our personality and resources of spiritual growth, and establish our own spiritual discipline.

The movement within sacramental faith is partly a progression and partly more like a pie chart. Even among the most seemingly stable members there is a hidden tentativeness about faith and practice. We see it when a person who has been very consistent in sacramental practice is challenged by some event in life and withdraws from the parish.

Tentative

Some people are sacramental Christians but are not really sure why they participate so frequently in the parish's life. If asked to say something about their presence they may avoid answering or offer a dismissive or distancing response, e.g., "I needed to visit the 'big guy'," "We all need a spiritual home." They may drift in and out of participation rather easily. They may have a stance that is superficial about faith or the church's place in the life of faith. They may feel anxious about spirituality, or the mention of Christ in worship, or that others know more than they. Whatever the reason, they are off-balance in their relationship with the parish.

A not uncommon form this takes is the desire for faith without the people, or without the institutional realities of the parish. In this way of thinking just attending Mass would be OK, but they find it frustrating to have to put up with being asked to participate in other things, or to deal with people ranting and raving about their political agendas or some "stupid parish issue," or to be asked to contribute financially. All the perceived nonsense of parish life becomes a reason to keep distance, either emotionally or by erratic attendance. Interacting with the parish community is a problem for them. The reverse may also be true, as some would be happy to have the relationships with people but could easily let go of participation in the parish's worship. What we are seeing in these members is either the logic of "believing without belonging" or "belonging without believing."

The "believing without belonging" stance is odd because they do belong. This way of thinking is common among people who talk about being "spiritual but not religious" and among "Vicarious" and "Christmas & Easter" expressions of faith and practice. It can even be something that has been pushed to the back of the mind among people who appear to have a long term "Stable" faith. It's lurking in the background ready to emerge when some event activates it. People with this "believing without belonging" approach may volunteer at a food pantry, attend the early Eucharist frequently, and express an interest in spiritual life or religion, but there is a tentativeness that they carry. In some people this is a reflection of a broader emotional immaturity related to a difficulty in having real connection with others; in others it's more limited and compartmentalized.

The "belonging without believing" people enjoy the parish's community life and related activities. They join in the prayers and hymns more as an expression of community than of faith. Potluck dinners, coffee hour, and the parish's social life may be especially important to them. Or their inclination may be more institutional. The parish is approached as though it were a club or business. The person might then see his or her role as paying dues and attending meetings or as helping the parish be "successful."

Immature

They can come across as childish in matters of faith and their ability to manage their emotions. They may be very sincere, but inclined to a sentimental or legalistic faith. They may place a good bit of value on the traditions they grew up with or the traditions of the parish without having any deeper appreciation of the Church's tradition. This kind of person can slide out of Sacramental Faith over small matters such as changes in worship, the leaving of a priest they liked, or perceived slights by other members or leaders. They may only be at the Eucharist on Sunday if there is something special happening, or they have a specific responsibility, or if there is an activity that they especially enjoy.

Experimenting

This stage is a turning point for many people. For some reason the person "gets religion." They may have just experienced a personal crisis, gone on a silent retreat, read something that touched them, or gone to Cursillo. Or it may have been one of those times in life that invite change. For me it was Patricia. Pat and I dated for a couple of years in my late teens. Her commitment to the Roman Catholic Church and Christian faith set-off a movement in me that brought me to faith. I was seeking a way to give my heart to something. There were many options—America, the Marine Corps, teaching, Pat, civil rights. They were all important, but Christ and the church, specifically the Episcopal Church, most completely caught my heart.

What grabs at the heart of a person will vary from one to another. But once it happens, we are open to changing the way we have understood and practiced the Christian faith. This is an important movement for two reasons. First, it may be the beginning of intentionally allowing oneself to enter more fully into the mystery of God. Second, it may establish a stance toward the spiritual life that is very Anglican—we experiment. We experiment to find a spirituality that fits our own uniqueness while connecting us to a larger community. Experimenting is both a stage and also a necessary aspect of all stages.

It is also a dangerous moment. If the person has gotten excited about a form of faith or spirituality that is narrow (of heart or mind) they may get stuck in that place for some time. Another possibility is that a religious façade emerges in which the person works at appearing "religious." On the surface this may look like Apostolic Faith, but it is only on the surface. Three common Anglican forms of this are the insistent evangelist, the Anglo-Catholic "spike," and the self-righteous social activist. Each may in time develop into a more mature expression as the person gives himself or herself over to a balanced form of Anglican spiritual discipline.

A common distraction from continuing to experiment and grow is when the rector sees someone ready to go deeper and decides to get them involved in the parish's administration and management by giving the person a job. So the person is signed up for a committee or some other task. In and of itself this isn't necessarily a problem. There are some people who find having a way of serving the parish very helpful in its concreteness. It is only a concern if it *takes the place of specific attention to spiritual development*. This stage is an opportunity for experimenting in the spiritual life. The most effective way for that to take place will depend on the person. Some are helped by reading, others by small groups; a retreat or some spiritual direction may be appropriate for others.

This can be an emotionally erratic period with times of insisting upon some "truth" or practice. It is passion trying to find a home. If they are not taken seriously people can slip back into a more immature or tentative faith, even to a Christmas & Easter Faith. Their energy and excitement needs a channel and structure. There is at these times an opportunity for the person to move into a progressing and then Apostolic Faith. Parish clergy have an opportunity to help connect the person to people and activities that can assist in that movement.

Stable

This is a kind of plateau. It may be a productive form of spirituality that nurtures a person for all or much of his or her life, providing a sense of belonging and meaning. It may also be a static condition in which hope is numbed, love is restricted, and faith is conditional. People may find themselves lapsing back into a tentative or immature faith, in need of another phase of experimenting faith to enliven their journey. If during an experimenting phase they did not gain the knowledge and practices needed to take more responsibility for their spiritual life that may need to be addressed before the person can really begin progressing.

Progressing

This is a stage of steady "improvement." The person becomes more consistent in his or her practices and emotional life. The marks of Apostolic Faith can be seen. This stage may be entered into in a sudden and dramatic movement or may be the end of a slow and long journey. Growth in faith, holiness, emerges out of the baptized person's relationship with Jesus Christ. That relationship is nurtured by the totality of life within the church, by the sacraments and by prayer. Three forms of prayer may have a special place in the progressing process: 1) The Daily Office as our participation in the church's daily act of praise, 2) the Scriptures in Lectio and meditation, and 3) some form of disciplined reflection on our experience. These last two can have a significant impact on our self-knowing. It's a decision to progress in the spiritual life when we give ourselves to the inner life, including an increased awareness of ourselves.

Christmas & Easter Faith

These people are there on Christmas and/or Easter, possibly another special occasion or two. People in this stage do not accept "sacramental" faith. They are usually baptized and on the parish rolls. Participation may be sentimental or rooted in family tradition. This is not a place of readiness to advance in faith and practice. They are likely to ignore or resent any action seen as pressure. Others in the parish are ambivalent toward them—we want to be open and welcoming of people at all phases of the journey, we are glad to see the pews filled, but we note, "They are sitting in *my* pew."

Vicarious Faith

People with this approach to faith do not attend worship; they are usually not members, but they may see the parish as "their parish." They may be directly or indirectly influenced by the parish's life. Their connection with the parish is through geography, history, family, friends, or events.

Many of us know of families where one spouse participates in the parish life while the other only shows up for the chicken dinner. On occasion, when the one spouse dies the other begins attending the Eucharist. Or there are the teen-age children or young adults who refuse to attend but seem to get disturbed if their observant parents become less observant. There are those who will show up and help with repairs to the property, come to the pot luck dinner, help in the food pantry, but will not join in the Eucharist.

One parish I served was in an old city neighborhood with brick row houses, narrow streets, and corner stores. While shopping in one of the tiny grocery stores I was moving along the constricted aisles seeking a can of tomato sauce. In the next aisle two women were leaning into one another, whispering. The one said, "He's my priest (a nod toward the aisle I was in), I belong to St. Elisabeth's." I had no idea who she was. What I do know is that the parish had a long-standing link with people in that community. The parish was nearly 100 years old. During the 1920s it had celebrated the Eucharist in Italian. Copies of the Italian 1928 Book of Common Prayer were still in the parish office. During the depression it had used up its endowment to provide heating oil for people in the neighborhood. When there was a parish fair the games for children were conducted on the principle of having every child win a prize every time. The prizes were worth more than the quarter the child paid to play. We lost fifteen cents every time the game was played. We ran a summer day camp for children, sponsored a community education center, and helped form a neighborhood community organization.

Then there were the bells. Some years before I arrived in the parish there had been a dispute in the neighborhood over the electrical bell system in the church tower. For years the bells rang the Angelus at 6:00 a.m., noon, and 6:00 p.m. A couple of newcomers to the area had a scheme for purchasing the old row houses, renovating them and selling the house to young professionals. It was a plan to gentrify the neighborhood and make a lot of money. They decided that they didn't like the bells ringing, especially early in the morning. So, they petitioned the Department of Licenses and Inspections (L&I) to order the church to stop the noise. I guess the bells didn't fit their image of the way the neighborhood needed to be if it was to attract the right people. The response was a flood of letters to L&I, with copies to the parish, about how important the bells were to people. The local paper ran a few articles. The gentrification couple backed off. In time their whole plan was abandoned.

132

These were all occasions of connection that created, sustained or expressed Vicarious Faith.

How Vicarious Faith shows itself will depend on the culture of the parish and the neighborhood. Ethnic identity, education, class, generational cohorts, worship style, and values orientation will influence the specific expression of faith. It will also take on a particular style because of the tradition the parish lives in. Most Episcopal parishes are more or less part of an ethos that values open mindedness, adult spirituality, beauty, and so on. The Episcopal Church has a certain way of living the Christian faith and that will be reflected in the way the Shape of the Parish is expressed.

Nurturing the Faith and Practice of the People of God

Apostolic

This group is usually fed by their participation in well-done liturgy, some use of the Office and personal devotions that are a good fit with their personality or are an appropriate stretching in their devotional life. They may make use of opportunities for individual and group spiritual direction and guidance on a regular or occasional basis. They are usually present at parish silent retreats and quiet days. Participation in EFM (Education for Ministry) and other more advanced studies will appeal to some.

Sacramental

Good liturgy and training and coaching in Eucharistic participation and spirituality usually nurture them. They may be helped by participation in a foundations course, work on gifts and vocational discernment, assistance in creating a rule of life, or help in exploring the relationship of faith to daily life. Progressing faith can be nurtured by participation in the same practices as noted under Apostolic Faith.

Christmas & Easter

Participating in the Christmas and Easter liturgies usually helps this group. Those liturgies need to be well done and adequately traditional. Clergy need to forgo the temptation of scolding sermons, e.g., "how healthy the parish would be if you would all be here every Sunday." Some will value having the priest visit when in the area—briefly. These people do see themselves as connected to the parish. There is little the parish can do that will change the pattern of the C&E people. If it happens, it is because of two factors: 1) an event in the person's life that opens them to a new relationship, and 2) the parish remaining faithful to them by welcoming them when they are present and keeping them on a mailing list or special events e-list.

Vicarious

Parishes have had many ways of connecting to the broader community and in so doing, creating a vicarious group. Many urban churches have basketball courts and summer day camps; others have a labyrinth that is walked daily by people who never attend the Eucharist. I know of rural churches that have a rifle range in the basement or sponsor the town horse show. There are parishes that have a regular art exhibit in the worship space or parish hall. Others have developed a relationship with the jazz community or theater community. In some communities the priest's being visible on the streets and in the neighborhood is important. Parishes have used occasional newsletters to people living near the parish and others who have attended some program. Our approach to pastoral and sacramental matters can be used to develop a vicarious faith relationship with the parish. Family-related liturgies such as baptisms, marriages, burials, and house blessings usually include people with no connection along with the C&E and Vicarious Faith groups. These liturgies are opportunities to expose people to the Christian faith as lived in the Episcopal Church.

General Comments on Nurturing Growth

1. The core pastoral strategy is to **accept** people where they are <u>and</u> to **invite** them to move beyond where they are.
2. Individual growth often comes in leaps (e.g., a person may move quickly from Experimenting to Progressing to Apostolic Faith).
3. Foundations are important. At times there is a desire to grow, or there may be deep feeling about God and/or the church. Such feelings can be the pastor's opening to invite the person into a setting where the needed base is offered. That foundation in spiritual life or knowledge may serve the person ten years later when they are prepared to move more deeply into the relationship with God and the church.
4. Address the gaps that people live in. The gap may be between the person's intentions and the impact of their behavior on others. There may be gaps of understanding more common to some forms of faith than others. The "Believing-Belonging" gaps may be especially strong in people of Vicarious and C&E Faith. The gap between faith and daily life may be common in the phases of Vicarious, C&E and early Sacramental faith.
5. New members need special attention. They may be people transferring from other parishes who already live an Apostolic or Stable Sacramental Faith. They might be C&E or people who for some reason have decided to begin attending. Or they could be people with almost no religious background, without any connection to the parish, who have just decided to "try it." Often these people may come with a good bit of emotional intelligence, a strong longing, and good intentions but lack foundational practices. There is the potential that they might move quickly into a progressing expression of Sacramental faith.

The Emotional Climate

Parishes all have an emotional climate. This isn't about the occasional times of intense happiness at some success or sadness in a member's death. It's about the overall and typical tonality of the parish. Some parishes seem sad, or overwhelmed or tight, while others have a positive energy and resilience in dealing with life.

When the Shape is healthy, the emotional climate is likely to either be healthy or, with minimal intervention, be moved toward health. Parishes can have their Shape distorted by emotions like fear, anger, hate and pride. It's as though the energy of the system becomes obsessed with some issue or mood and it's openness to the movement of the Holy Spirit is weakened. Here are a few examples:

I went church shopping after moving to a new city. I was seeking a parish community. In one parish the clergy were too anxious, in another too faddish, and in another too stiff. It was difficult to find the one that was just right. I'm still not sure about the extent to which this was a matter of discernment or to what extent I was engaged in the Goldilocks syndrome. In time I settled on one.

In my searching I came across a parish that was very angry. In this case their anger was focused on the church's acceptance of women as priests and bishops. Please understand the point here isn't about the issue of gender and ordination. The problem was the anger. It oozed from them. They tried to be welcoming and asked me to a roast beef dinner. I'm sure the food would have been fine, but the risk of choking on rage was significant. The bulletin board had a lot of announcements and letters about things they were angry about or national meetings to attend with other angry people. They were so angry that the senior warden had stopped pledging to the parish, which he loved, because the parish was part of the diocese he was angry at. My hunch is that it was an angry parish well before women were ordained.

In another diocese there was a parish I did some work with that told all visitors a story when they first came to a coffee hour. Someone would happily explain how the parish used to be located in the nearby city but had moved because African Americans were moving into that neighborhood. Visitors were invited to join in the hate and fear of black people. There was no significant spiritual growth happening in that parish.

We may all have examples of places where an excessive pride is interfering with a parish's health. I've seen this kind of pride around beautiful liturgy, or how casual our worship is, or all our programs, or our wealth. Recently I came across a web site that wanted me to know how successful the parish was. It had grown in members, it was going to build a wonderful church building, and its pledging was just grand. It gave me the creeps.

Little energy will be available for spiritual growth when a parish is caught up in fear or anger, hate or pride. One of the most common forms of this distortion in the church today is the anger being generated on the left and the right about who is correct on a variety of social and theological issues. The Episcopal Church faces the danger of losing its tradition of generous orthodoxy. Alan K. Simpson, an Episcopalian and the former Republican senator from Wyoming, was a member of the Baker – Hamilton Committee that studied the Iraq War. In a news conference on that report he made a comment about the kind of people who create an angry tonality in our nation's common life, "And the sad part to me is that, you know, you see people in this who are 'hundred percenters' in America. A 'hundred percenter' is a person you don't want to be around. … They're not seekers. They're not seekers, they're seethers."

The role of leader involves shaping a constructive climate, including not allowing the "seethers" to have much impact on that climate.

Membership Growth

The Pure Land school of Buddhism hasn't had the same success in attracting Americans as other Buddhist groups because it has not included meditation among its practices. Americans who were going to be Buddhists expected meditation. Even though Pure Land was one of the most widespread forms of the religion in the world, especially in Japan, it was not growing in the United States, while Zen and Tibetan traditions were. So, they changed their practices and included meditation to attract Americans.

This is an example of adapting an organizational culture to fit a different social culture. It's how organizations survive and possibly grow when the circumstances around them change. You can add to or revise ways in which you function in order to attract people or better fulfill your mission.

Theorists on organizational culture talk about a tension between adaptation and organizational integrity and integration. There are times when if you don't adapt, you will die. There is also the danger that you will adapt so much that you "lose your soul." In recent years Pure Land has lost two-thirds of its membership in America. There was a clear survival issue. So, for the Pure Land Buddhists, and for many other religious traditions, the trick is to adapt in a manner that brings people into the tradition without confusing them about the tradition, misleading them, or giving away what is central to the tradition.

The BBC.com religion and ethics section describes Pure Land Buddhism this way.

> [It] offers a way to enlightenment for people who can't handle the subtleties of meditation, endure long rituals, or just live especially good lives. The essential practice in Pure Land Buddhism is the chanting of the name of Amitabha Buddha with total concentration, trusting that one will be reborn in the Pure Land, a place where it is much easier for a being to work towards enlightenment.

> Pure Land Buddhism adds mystical elements to the basic Buddhist teachings which make those teachings easier (and more comforting) to work with. These elements include faith and trust and a personal relationship with Amitabha Buddha, who is regarded by Pure Land Buddhists as a sort of saviour; and belief in the Pure Land, a place which provides a stepping stone towards enlightenment and liberation.

A *New York Times* (6/19/06) story on the Pure Land Buddhists explained that this group had not had meditation as a practice because it assumed it was irrelevant to the journey. The article said, "Colin Anderson, 47, a regular participant in New York Buddhist Church's class, drops in on meditation centers all over the city. 'I don't see it as a religion,' he said. 'I see it as more of a science of the mind.' The concept that is taught at many meditation centers—that controlling one's mind can lead to better controlling one's actions—which might lead to being reborn into a better life, makes sense to him. 'You're in control of your own life with your own karma,' he said. But that idea directly contradicts what Shinran, the founder of Shin Buddhism, taught some 800 years ago. Shinran came to Pure Land after growing frustrated with meditation and other practices taught by other Buddhist schools. He advocated that believers not pursue any specific practice but instead trust in the Amida Buddha's infinite wisdom and compassion for liberation from the endless cycle of life, death and rebirth."

So, for some followers of Pure Land the incorporation of meditation into the tradition is a loss of organizational integrity. It can also be seen as a loss of organizational integration because it introduces a practice that does not fit the traditional course of formation. In fact it may serve to undermine much that the tradition offers.

Episcopalians face the same issues of organizational integrity and integration when they explore changes in worship and spiritual disciplines. Some have claimed that to appeal to one segment of the population we need to have "user-friendly" worship with rock bands and hymns on a screen. More recently some of us have been looking at the potential for the Episcopal Church among younger people interested in the approaches labeled "ancient – modern" and the emerging church.

What do we need to consider in making these decisions?

- Will it result in a sustainable increase in members? One Buddhist leader said, "Just because we have meditation doesn't mean these people are going to stay … They're driven by this Hollywood aura of meditation. They're supermarket shopping." The closer the fit between the common culture of the Episcopal Church and what the "target group" is seeking, the more likely that any growth will be sustained. The closer fit allows an easier integration of practices and is less likely to cause conflict over questions related to organizational integrity.

- From the perspective of an organizational culture analysis the situation might raise these questions.

   What problems do you create when you make use of artifacts (behaviors and objects) that affirm one element of your espoused values but undercut others and are inconsistent with the deeper underlying assumptions of your organizational culture? Or to put it in specific terms, what can we expect if we use worship styles that are directed toward the values of membership growth and welcoming but appear to be inconsistent with our values about beauty and flow in liturgy and adult formation?

   Do we decide to hold a deeper underlying assumption about growth, such as the fact that the Episcopal Church has a history of attracting new members because of its rich liturgy and that there are a significant number of people in the society who are inclined to be attracted to that, if only we did a better job of communicating outside ourselves? Or, do we operate on a deeper assumption that those people don't exist, or we can't attract them, or that the formation power of graceful and rich liturgy is not real?

- Do we end up moving away from long standing assumptions about liturgy, formation and pastoral theology by using worship styles that contradict those assumptions?

How does the Shape of the Parish Model speak to the question of membership growth as seen in the above? As a starting point, I assume that there is value in bringing people into the Christian faith as experienced in the Episcopal Church, that there is something special about that particular way of being a Christian. I assume that the world is a better place when it contains more people with this kind of formation. I also assume that the way into that formation experience needs to be the experience itself, not some other experience that is easier for some to manage.

It is a mistake to pursue an approach that seeks to draw people who are not naturally attracted to liturgy, rather than all those out there who *are* drawn to beauty and grace in life and worship.

We know that many people become members because they love the liturgy. It's the single most offered reason for coming to an Episcopal Church along with the desire for community and relationships. It's what has worked for us as a method of membership growth. Everything we have learned about appreciative processes in systems, not to mention Marketing 101, suggests we need to stay with and enhance what we are good at.

Using the Shape of the Parish Model we might approach the issue this way. We can trust that significant numbers of people will be attracted 1) to a parish where those of Apostolic Faith and Practice are enough of a critical mass that they are setting the tone and in which their reflection of God's love and beauty is part of the climate; and 2) to a parish with a climate of prayer, hospitality and humility.

Yes, some will be put off by that energy, but that will be true no matter what we do. Whatever we do to bring some groups of people into the church will repel others. Some will fear an expression of faith and spiritual life that is mature, that provides space for people in all the places along the journey's way and that expresses a generous orthodoxy. Others will not be drawn to our way of being Christians. So, we might as well offer what we do best when we are at our best. This suggests an approach that offers an apostolic climate and practice with beautiful liturgy and resources for spiritual life. We need to avoid dumbing down in a manner that may end up neither attracting people in a sustainable manner nor working effectively in the formation of people.

Distortions of the Shape

The Parish as "Cult"

This is what happens when the Shape created is based on an assumption that to be a real member of the parish you must be a person of Apostolic Faith or that you must conform to some particular definition of Apostolic Faith. In my experience these attempts to over-define Apostolic Faith create a distortion. They draw a hard line around the apostolic ring. This pattern is usually seen in parishes that are uncomfortable with the core tradition of Episcopal spirituality, especially those aspects of the tradition that invite openness and an acceptance of ambiguity and paradox.

An example of such a parish was in a New England diocese where the bishop was scheduled to make a visitation and preside at the Eucharist. The bishop told his staff that parish leaders informed him that all members of the parish had to speak in tongues. They saw it as "scriptural." The message delivered was that it would not be appropriate for someone to preside at the Eucharist who was not a complete Christian, which meant that the rector was inviting the bishop for coffee but not to preside at the Eucharist. The staff's laughter went on for some time. The bishop subsequently had a "come to the bishop" dialogue with the rector and wardens, and the bishop presided at the Eucharist.

Unless such a parish is unusually small it's likely that there is a great deal of pretending going on. People will say or do what is accepted because they want to attend the parish for a variety of reasons.

It's also possible for this to take a more subtle form in which the dominant culture of the parish so matches the dominant culture of the region that there is little sense of how narrow we have become. This can be true for conservative parishes in the Deep South as well as more liberal parishes in Manhattan or Seattle.

The Parish Without Shape

This is the illusion promoted in some parishes that "we are all the same." It reflects an unwillingness to acknowledge that people differ in where they are on the journey. The intention may be kind, but the effect is not. The potential of people is usually valued but the climate and processes by which that potential is nurtured are absent. This resistance to acknowledge differences is often rooted in valuing human dignity and the democratization of the parish. It may also be related to a fear that people will be uncomfortable or feel judged if differences are acknowledged. This can plug into a leader's anxiety of not being skilled enough to make use of the dynamics set loose in the service of formation.

Inversion of the Shape

There are some parishes where the least mature people in the Sacramental ring are in control of the climate. The first parish where I was asked to be priest-in-charge was Church of the Epiphany in West Philadelphia. The bishop asked me and another priest, Mike, if we would tend it on Sundays for a year. The bishop assumed that he would close the parish in the next few years. The two of us had other jobs that tied us up for most of the week, so there were limits to the time we had available.

The lay leadership was in the hands of a few men. They included a senior warden who usually left the Eucharist at the offertory with the collection so he could count it before the coffee was served, and a treasurer who made a yearly report on Christmas Eve because that was the only day he would attend. Even with the limited time Mike and I could offer, there began to be some membership growth.

The new members were mostly younger African American women with children. They brought new energy and a willingness to work. They joined with the clergy on projects but the existing leaders closed the door on their participation in broader decision-making. It was clear that with just a little effort the parish could attract new members. But the bishop didn't have much imagination about such things or the commitment that would have been necessary to back the two very young, and occasionally clueless, priests in a way that would shift the emotional control from the small group of men to the clergy and the new members. When our year was up, we left. In another couple of years the diocese closed the parish.

Another case was the parish that had developed a self-definition around how it had escaped from the city and black people. Along with their racism some of the key leaders carried a lot of bitterness and resentment about life in general. At times there was an undertone of potential violence. Emotional outbursts and threats were common. Their skills for dealing with disagreement and conflict were very limited.

Instead of the center ring being filled with people of Apostolic Faith it was filled with people of immature and tentative faith. Attempts to create a healthier situation were met with strong and stubborn resistance. In time the parish was brought to a healthy shape by the persistence and competence on the part of the diocese and the effective oversight of two vicars. The vicars received a significant amount of congregational development training and the parish was assisted by well-trained consultants and special attention by the bishop's office. It took six years before the new shape was firmly in place.

"People like a superficial religion," was the comment of a Pentecostal minister in a 2007 *New York Times* report on Hispanics and religion. There are a significant number of people in any church who are of a tentative or immature Sacramental Faith. That's as it "is" and in some sense as it should be. This is part of the picture of how sanctification functions in a parish where the "Shape" is healthy.

This fact that many people prefer a superficial religion becomes a parish development problem when inversion of the shape occurs. There are three common ways that happens. The first is in the creation of the parish. A mix of property obsession and jazzed-up programming, without a strong emphasis on spiritual discipline and formation, can mean that a parish starts out with the inversion and never moves beyond it. The second is by drift. Over time, especially in periods of stagnation or decline, the leadership and energy shifts to the less mature. A third is when parish leaders play to the immaturity by an excessive emphasis on people's comfort and safety. This can emerge from the leader's anxiety about keeping people happy or membership growth.

The Dynamic of the Shape

The story of every parish should be a love story…One possible definition for a parish is that it is God's way of meeting the problems of the unloved. This meeting between God and the unloved, the unwanted, takes place in the preaching of the Word, in the Sacraments, in the social life of the parish made possible by the climate of acceptance which is engendered by those who have been baptized and confirmed in the Catholic faith. One of the main tasks of the parish priest is to train the militant core of his parishioners in such a way that they understand as fully as possible the true nature of a Christian parish. Kilmer Myers in *Light the Dark Streets*

Drawing People Deeper

When a parish has a healthy and productive Shape you see a definite movement. People are drawn into a deeper relationship with God and the church. There is a sense of spiritual movement in the parish. The Apostolic Faith percentage increases. Those of Apostolic Faith serve others by the example of their prayerfulness, humility, and openness. The sacramental and apostolic life of the parish draws the C&E and Vicarious. This process of drawing is evangelization.

What this is not, but can be mistaken for, is the spirituality seen in some parishes that is really an outburst of experimenting Sacramental Faith. The parish seems full of energy. There's a lot of motion but if you look closely there's little personal and spiritual growth. Some parishes get caught up in multiple service projects, others in looking for behaviors that appear joyful, warm, and friendly, and others in signs of common agreement to a political version of faith.

What's happening in these situations can end up being either a distraction from the primary task or a chance to grow. In group-process terms this particular form of energy happens when a group has achieved some success together, has worked out some of the early tensions about inclusion and control, and is now excited about being a group. It is a stage of development that can happen again and again in the life of a group and therefore in a congregation.

The group can get stuck and fail to move toward a higher level of development. The good feeling feels so good that the group unconsciously wants to stay in that place. Possibly like Peter, James and John with Jesus on top of the mountain.

These moments are also an opportunity. These occasions of excited experimenting faith can be used to move individuals and the whole parish to increased maturity. A priest and a few lay leaders with the wisdom to see things as they are will use this as a way of inviting people to a new depth. The alternative is to enter the illusion of the moment and build the booths. The task is to invite people to go deeper in prayer and study and love.

Something else we know from group development theories is that during this stage people will resist going to a new place. Leaders will need to skillfully engage the resistance by listening to the concerns and revising elements of the direction as needed, teaching the competencies needed for the next step, and staying on course. If the leaders can help the parish make this transition the parish is likely to become a healthier community. If they fail to facilitate the transition, the parish may either settle into a facade of Apostolic Faith or move to the safety of "Episcopal lite."

The dynamic of people being drawn to a new depth is the measure to look for when trying to assess health according to this model. In the end there's not some mathematical formula of a certain percentage of people of Apostolic Faith and a certain number of Sacramental Faith. What we want to see is a dynamic in play. Something is happening within the processes of parish life that moves people further into the life of faith.

All parishes are places in which saints are formed. All parishes are microcosms of the Body of Christ, and so all parishes are communities of grace. Even the most pathetic parish may be a source of sanctification as the sacraments are offered and the Word read and preached. Some parishes are places of deep prayer, some become truly holy places, and those parishes are likely to form more of the saints among us.

Setting Loose the Dynamic

Among the central factors in "setting loose the dynamic" is parish leaders establishing the processes, structures and climate that facilitate that shape.

It is possible for a parish to have people of Apostolic Faith without that fact having much "drawing" effect. They are present but the impact of their presence is minimal. So, what sets loose the dynamic we seek?

In all cases what sets it loose is a combination of the Holy Spirit's movement within a parish and that parish's having arranged its life so that the "power from on high" can have its impact. The Spirit acts; we cooperate and accept responsibility. What is that arrangement, what is it to put ourselves in the places where the Spirit's gifts might come to us? We need to take care in our thinking about this to avoid the idea that this is some magical incantation: get the formula right and the Spirit will do what we want.

Things that parishes can do to set loose the dynamic include attention to the Sunday morning experience, parish leadership, the total rhythm of prayer, and more formal kinds of adult Christian formation.

The Sunday Morning Experience

The Sunday morning climate needs to be adult, as well as Apostolic—an adult environment that includes children. This includes worship that expects adult participation and responsibility. It means facing the challenge of ending practices that reinforce a damaging dependency and establishing practices that call for competence and commitment. Teach people how to participate, how to put the Prayer Book down for most of the liturgy, and how to use their body in worship. Stop giving instructions about page numbers, posture, and the meaning of the reading or creed. Gently move away from allowing self-administration of the sacrament (self-intinction). When you are really feeling brave, move the announcements out of the Eucharist and to coffee hour. Allow the "town meeting" feeling to take place where it fits the occasion and can have its full expression while also preserving the grace of Liturgy. This is a shift from unhealthy dependency to the interplay of creative dependency and human responsibility.

Among the purposes of the Sunday Eucharist is formation. We undermine the formation process if we tilt things toward the comfort of visitors. Excessive anxiety about the relationship between worship and membership growth often ends up distorting both processes. Try approaching this as a polarity to manage. We want graceful, rich liturgy, *and* we want hospitality. We want people to experience a liturgy that is Apostolic with the power to form our hearts and minds *and* we want to make that liturgy adequately accessible. We get better solutions once we see it as a polarity in which we want to do both/and.

Attend to the hospitality need by making the information in the bulletin easy to follow. Have statements in the bulletin about how visitors might want to allow themselves to be carried by the congregation in the liturgy and about how to receive communion. Instruct members about sensitivity to the needs of visitors. Show them how to notice the signals from people about being willing to receive assistance. Some are willing to receive a Hymnal open to the hymn being sung; others would rather be left alone. Find ways to nudge visitors toward coffee hour and make sure they are neither overwhelmed nor abandoned once there.

Another part of what creates the dynamic is what Kilmer Myers called "the climate of acceptance which is engendered by those who have been baptized and confirmed in the Catholic faith." People are accepted as they present themselves. You come as extravert or introvert, as gay or straight, as single or married and we exchange the Peace with you. You come with whatever maturity of faith and emotional life as circumstances, grace, and effort have brought you to, and we share communion and coffee with you. The starting place, and the ongoing ground, for life in the parish is that we are loved and accepted.

Along with the acceptance will come challenge. The invitation to become more of what you are is one reason why people need to have an apostolic experience on their first Sunday. The liturgy and the climate of acceptance may confront something in the person that suggests they have more potential than they yet see, that there is more glory in this person than they yet know. If on that first Sunday and the weeks that follow visitors are touched by God's glory and beauty then some will run from it and others will be drawn into God's enchantment, be delighted and make this their home. In the years that follow people will also experience the challenge dimension in other ways. There will be the disappointment of finding that the parish is not all love and magic, there will be tensions around inclusion and influence, and there will be personal confrontations. In each, the person will advance in faith or retreat for the time being.

Leadership

The progression to a healthier Shape includes a shift in leadership. People of Apostolic Faith are playing a stronger leadership role, new leaders are more likely to come from those of Apostolic Faith, and some existing leaders become people of Apostolic Faith. Parish leaders need to actively make use of the presence of these members for the desired dynamics to take place. Some should be on the vestry. The rector should be listening closely to those of Apostolic Faith.

Ideally a vestry would be people of Apostolic or Progressing Sacramental Faith who have an ability to work with others as part of a team and the availability and energy to fully participate. While the make up of the parish reflects the whole church's diversity of faith and practice, *the leadership needs to consist of people who understand and live the life*. This is true for any organization. The leaders need to understand the purpose and nature of the enterprise if that organization is to be faithful to its reason for being and effective in its work. A vestry that is half people of Tentative or Immature Sacramental Faith will shape a parish that is limited in its living of the Christian life.

The process of getting to such a vestry usually needs to be a gradual one. Clergy would be wise to imagine they'll need two or three years to accomplish it. Build the vestry by encouraging Apostolic and progressing Sacramental Faith people to consider serving, actively recruit, teach and preach about the nature and mission of the church and what that suggests about parish leadership. Offer examples of the characteristics needed in a vestry member, and develop an apostolic parish climate.

The Rhythm of Prayer

The rhythm of prayer, the ascetical system of the parish, is more than what happens on Sunday. Four members who pray the Office on most days contribute more to the dynamic of the Shape of the Parish than adding another fifty people to Sunday attendance. It doesn't really matter if they say the Office at home on their own or together in the parish chapel. Nor does it finally matter if others are aware of the Office being offered. It is the fact that it is offered that is important. Some parishes get known as places of prayer. Most of us have heard of parishes where the "walls are soaked in the prayers of generations." That's about a parish in which the Renewal-Apostolate rhythm is effective and efficient, in which there are people of Apostolic Faith maintaining a spiritual discipline grounded in the Rule of the Church. Without these real, concrete things taking place, it is mere sentimentality.

The exchanges that take place in the day-by-day life of the parish are occasions of acceptance and challenge, of grace and judgment. Those exchanges change both the people directly involved and others in the parish in a ripple effect. The small courtesies of the Body nurture hospitality and kindness. The occasional confrontations with the over-controlling vestry member or the chronic grumbler may create boundaries and protect the unity of the parish.

Adult Formation

A more formal kind of adult Christian formation is essential in most parishes. There are examples of Foundations Courses in the "Resources" section and a brief description in the Oversight discussion in the Christian Life Model.

The Social Life of the Parish

Kilmer Myers saw the social life of the parish as one of the ways in which we meet God; in which the parish's story becomes a love story. For him it stood alongside Word and Sacrament

There are three things that for me mark a healthy parish social life.

The first is that there are occasions of coming together as a whole community and in sub groups (cliques if you like). How that happens will depend on the social culture of the people who make up the parish. There will of course be a Sunday coffee hour. Beyond that in some congregations it will be pot-luck suppers, for others breakfast out after the early Eucharist, and still others will have people in their homes for drinks and dinner.

The second is that a significant number of people develop particular friendships. It will just happen if the parish hasn't developed a restricted culture that interferes with the process of friendships emerging. The church has had a history of suspicion about "particular friendships." It has often focused on the fear that such friendships would lead to sexual activity. In some monastic communities it was really about a fear of gay relationships. There is something of this fear within the safe church effort. The absolutely essential work of protecting people from pedophiles and predators has, in some places, had tacked onto it an anxiety about all close relationships, especially between priest and parishioner.

The broader issue facing the parish, and other communities, is how we maintain the unity and harmony of the larger community and also allow for close friendships. Here's another situation where polarity management might be useful. We are probably being more realistic and honest if we approach this as something to responsibly manage verses something to avoid.

"Pairing up" behavior can be a threat to the work and concord of a group. Close friends, couples, or family members can, and will, join together in coalitions that may upset others. This has lead in some parishes to rules against a couple serving on the vestry at the same time or a rector trying to forbid a spouse from having friendships in the parish. So we end up losing the services of dedicated people and spouses who stop attending or leave for other parishes. Instead of trying to solve such matters with rules and attempts at controlling others we might end up with a healthier church if we focused our attention on building the emotional intelligence of members and leaders.

"Create bonds of affection that fly in the face of conventional wisdom." That's a line from a sermon given by Paul Collins at Trinity, Seattle. It's also my third sign of health. Paul was exploring the Naomi – Ruth story. "All of Ruth's world, both economic and emotional, has been destroyed. She must return to her clan far away and beg for help--Naomi could do the same thing with her own people. But Ruth refuses to leave Naomi: 'Where you go, I go.' " Father Collins saw Ruth and Naomi as representing the best of our humanity.

When I heard Paul's words I initially thought he was speaking directly to me and addressing my friendships that crossed gender and age differences (something we had discussed). But as he went on I looked around the congregation and I saw other "bonds of affection that fly in the face of conventional wisdom." There were interracial and gay couples; there were friendships among people of vastly different ages, gender and economic status.

Leadership and the Shape of the Parish

There are broad objectives that make up a strategy for shaping the parish.

1. **Nurture the Shape.** If there are no people of Apostolic Faith, seek ways to establish a core of people in the parish community; if there is no Vicarious ring, build relationships with other communities of people. Assume that it will take years to do these things.
2. **Accept and Invite.** Take a stance in which you *accept* people wherever they are in the journey and *invite* them to go deeper. Include people in a manner that respects and loves them for who they are now while also seeking opportunities to offer new ways and new life.
3. **Set Loose the Dynamic.** Root the overall climate of the parish in Apostolic Faith and set loose the dynamic by building the appropriate culture.

Leadership and Power in the Process of Shaping the Parish

Those trying to "shape the parish" need to pay attention to the political realties of the parish. There is something of a chicken and egg dynamic in creating a state in which a significant portion of the formal and informal leaders are of Apostolic or progressing Sacramental Faith and are also collaborating with efforts to appropriately shape the parish. It's a slow building process in which, bit-by-bit, those of a more mature faith become the emotional and spiritual center of the parish.

When we jump past this gradual process by establishing high standards on paper, or putting pressure on people to change, it's likely to backfire and increase the resistance. Even when well done, attempts to introduce new ways will usually bring resistance.

In a large New England parish there was a change in leadership in the Episcopal Church Women (ECW). The new president was considerably younger than the previous president (early 40s vs. mid 60s). She had an active career, which most other members did not have. The new president set out to make changes that she believed would attract some of the younger women in the parish while retaining the current members. She explored having meetings at different times, asked younger members to accept responsibilities that had been the "turf" of others, changed the climate of the meetings, and broadened the topics and activities of the group. She was gracious toward the previous president while skillfully leading the group into a new way of doing things. There was some resistance, but all in all, not as much as might have been anticipated. That was true until she decided to schedule a weekend silent retreat for members. In a public meeting of the group, the previous president, joined by several other members, made it clear that the retreat idea was going "too far." One memorable phrase was, "That's not the way we do things at St. Phillip's"

The new leader wanted to introduce the silent retreat and an occasional quiet day in an effort to nurture a deeper spiritual life in the group. That produced active resistance on the part of a number of former leaders. Efforts to explore the resistance were met by an angry silence or restatements of, "That's not how we do things." The fact that the retreat would be an optional offering seemed to do little to calm those most agitated. What became clear is that the resistance was rooted in a fear that offering a silent retreat carried with it two implications: First, that the previous leaders had not done things they "should" have done; and second, that there existed a deeper spirituality than many in the group had experienced.

In another parish the priest was working to shape the parish by establishing a liturgy that had more grace, beauty and flow than had been the case. The congregation was being helped to increase its competency for participation. They began to "know that they knew" how to participate as adults. Chalice bearers and acolytes were trained to move with more grace and dignity, and so on. The changes were generally well received. A number of members had desired it for some time; others for whom it was a new experience found themselves saying things like, "I feel like I've really been to church," and, "This place is becoming a real parish church." So, how did the resistance show itself? It wasn't anything organized but occasionally one or the other of those feeling disturbed by the changes would use coffee hour to conduct informal polls. They would go from person to person fishing for unhappiness. "What do you think of all the changes in worship?" When they found support for the changes they would move on. When they found someone who was also concerned (or ambivalent) about the changes, they would invite negative comments.

Resistance may come from the formal leadership or may show itself in small acts of sabotage by people with some influence with others. Either can block or slow the process of "shaping" the parish.

A common mistake in making this shift happens when the clergy put their energy in the wrong place. There are two forms this usually takes.

One is when the priest tries to "convert" the current leaders and influential people to Progressing Sacramental or Apostolic Faith. There is usually an expectation that this can, or should, happen quickly. Sermons and teaching take on an insistent tone. There may be attempts to craft mission statements or standards for vestry members that move well beyond what the current leaders can absorb. Vestry meetings are redesigned to include more prayer or Bible study. People are rarely moved by such an approach, and what is worse, they may take on a façade of having a deeper faith.

The other common waste of energy is when the priest, sometimes in collaboration with a few lay leaders, decides to change the behavior of a particular influential person. This is often someone the priest finds especially annoying or frustrating. A struggle of wills can begin that absorbs a lot of the priest's energy and attention. The priest may talk about trying to "get through" to the person but all too frequently what is really happening as an attempt to "get rid of" the person.

Both cases fail to recognize the ways of sanctification and parish politics. We are usually more effective when we begin with those in the congregation who seem ready to move deeper and create an apostolic climate in liturgy, spirituality and parish social life. Let the leadership become more Apostolic in the process of sanctification that we cooperate with by skillful politics and sound formation.

Accepting the Human and the Symbol

We accept the Incarnation when we accept the sacramental reality of "human and symbol," of human and divine. The sacramental principle is that outward and visible things convey inward and spiritual power. Each of the baptized is a person and is the light of Christ. The priest is "just human" and also a holy being. The parish itself is an institution like any other and is also the one, holy, catholic and apostolic church. The priest, the parish itself, and the individual

Christian are both human and a symbol. It's the sacramental principle seen again and again. The outward and visible, the inward and spiritual, both are real, each require their own acceptance.

There is always the temptation to diminish existence by collapsing reality. The desire to oversimplify, and thereby destroy reality, is always with us. Christ is just a man, he is God and not human, versus he is the Word made Flesh, true man and true God. It is just bread and wine, it is the body and blood of Christ and no longer real bread and wine, or it is the Body of Christ, the Bread of Heaven. We are only human, we are gods, or we share in the very life of God. Accepting the sacramental nature of our existence has always been difficult.

	Baptized Christian	Parish	Priest
Human	A person with all the potential and limitations.	An association of people	A person with all the potential and limitations.
Symbol	A child of God; the light of Christ to the world; an instrument of God's love	A microcosm of the Body of Christ, a wonderful and sacred mystery; an extension of the Incarnation	A bridge between humanity and God; the light of Christ for the parish.

A sign of a parish's maturity is that there is a high degree of acceptance of the sacramental principle. The acceptance is seen in practice and theory.

In some parishes there are liturgical traditions of reverence that mirror the sacramental principle. For example, there are parishes where a solemn bow between altar party and the congregation at the beginning and end of the Eucharist, and between the deacon and people during the offertory censing extend the practice of showing reverence for the Blessed Sacrament by genuflecting or a solemn bow. A few members also continue the tradition of a bow when the celebrant passes in procession.

The "Episcopal Lite" parish avoids its own deep life, there is little attention to spiritual life, and language about the nature and mission of the church may be used in a formal manner but is not understood. Frequently, but not always, this "lite" culture is mirrored in the superficialness of relationships among people.

Clergy often see it in their first months in a parish. There are those who seem desperate to be your friend, and others to keep you distant and high. There are those who can only call you Jane, and others who can only call you Mother Smith.

Urban Holmes use to speak of the role of the priest as that of "enchanter." In *The Priest in Community* he wrote "keep in mind that the power of the priestly symbol lies in its ability to evoke a mythic and symbolic meaning latent within the members of the community who recognize the person as priest." There is a relationship between our acceptance of the priest as person and symbol and the priest's capacity to be an instrument in which we see the fullness and depth of the parish and of our own selves.

In 1974 - 75 there was a survey of parish calling committees about what people valued most in a potential rector. The overwhelming response had to do with spiritual depth and preaching skill. According to Holmes they "both are aspects of being a living symbol" and "are means of illuminating Christ." We still hear the same longings from people toward their priests. Holmes also reported the resistance among many priests to the findings. He acknowledged the "frightening demand" that was being placed upon the priest. Many priests have come to understand that leadership is part of the vocation. The more ancient idea that the priest is a living sacrament comes as the greater challenge for many.

Holmes reports on the strength of one lay leader's feelings about this. When he mentioned the resistance of many clergy to a woman who was chair of a search committee, "Suddenly she bristled and said firmly, 'You tell those bastards we mean it!' " Clergy are often surprised by the strength of longing and feeling that many lay people have about this.

The woman was expressing a common desire among many baptized people. They want clergy to be interested in their spiritual life. The expectation may be strongest among those of Experimenting, Progressing and Apostolic Faith. They aren't seeking an interrogation ("Do you pray?") but a sense of curiosity and an openness to listen. "Tell me about your spiritual life," "I'd love to hear something about who the people were and are in your life who have helped you in your spiritual life." In the Resources section there is the "Three Interview Process" used by participants in the Church Development Institute (CDI) to explore spiritual life with others in the parish. It's been used by hundreds of laity and clergy to provide a sense of safety for what is usually a very important conversation for both parties.

While I do run into the occasional priest who seems stuck in a supernatural role, my more common experience is of clergy who fear being anything other than just one of the folks. The symbolic role and the responsibility for leadership are, as Holmes noted, a "frightening demand." Some clergy have reported that it was working through this issue, in spiritual direction or a program like the CDI that allowed them to settle into their vocation.

In *The Purpose and Meaning of the Church*, H. Richard Niebuhr wrote about the two-fold reality of the church in this way: "The church is never only a function of a culture nor ever only a supercultural community." The faith crisis for many people isn't about God, or Christ, it's about the church. It's especially about the church when they see our hypocrisy, our corruption and our blindness. In other words it's about having to deal with the church being made up of human beings. If they can approach it at a distance, as a universal system or in a broad historical sweep, the image of being Christ's Body might be possible. But it may be difficult to look at their all too human parish church and see the Body of Christ. These thought patterns of spiritualizing and idealizing are part of what keeps people trapped in a tentative or immature form of Sacramental Faith.

A small but symbolically important action related to leadership is about titles for clergy. Clergy that are new to a parish have all heard the question, "what shall we call you?" It's usually a person's desire to be courteous to the priest by learning about her or his preferences. Occasionally, the person is coming with the question with a right answer in mind and prepared to make a judgment about the priest. It's a mistake for the priest to answer the question with his or her own preference. Worse yet would be to make a joke out if it, turn it into an opportunity to slam the preferences of other clergy, or make it into a grammar lesson.

We need to leave people with the freedom to work this out for themselves. They need to be able to call their priest Father or Mother at times and Sarah or Paul at other times. They need to be able to move into a healthy dependency when that is necessary for spiritual growth and into peer and friendly relationship when that is called for. So, when the question is asked I'd suggest that clergy respond along these lines. "There are several ways that people approach this. You can use the traditional titles of Father or Mother if that appeals to you some or all the time. You can also use my first name. Do what seems right to you at the time." This isn't about our preferences as individual priests; it's about the mystery of how Christ uses us in the process of sanctification.

We are a Holy People and we are just people, Mark is just Mark and he is Father Smith. There is a process of growth in which people come to see themselves, their parish and their priest in this paradoxical way, as human and as symbol. It's one of the ways in which an apostolic culture develops in the parish.

Aligning Leadership Style with the Maturity of the Parish

The style and behavior of parish leaders needs to be appropriate to several factors that make up an assessment of parish maturity and health. Leaders often need to be more assertive and play the primary role in setting direction in a less mature parish. In very immature parishes this may fall to the priest alone. In parishes moving into serious decline it will usually require diocesan intervention.

In more mature parishes the leaders will make use of a broader range of styles and skills. There may be a tilting toward participation and empowerment but there is also a readiness and ability to use other leadership styles as the situation requires.

The "Situational Leadership" approach of Hersey, Blanchard, and Johnson suggests that what the leader needs to do is fit his or her leadership style to the competence and commitment of the person or group. This has been a very useful tool in organizations trying to empower employees and members. The idea is that if a team has a high degree of competence and commitment for their work then they can be more self-managing of the task and the relationships in the team. In such a group the leader might delegate tasks, make very selective interventions, help the team stay connected with the big picture of the organization, and be available when needed. The leader would avoid abandoning the team or dumping work on the team. On the other hand if a team had low competence and commitment the leader would provide specific direction about the details of the task, make the decisions, and provide close supervision and accountability. Depending on a number of factors the leader might work to increase the group's competence and commitment so the range of self management could be increased.

Is there something comparable to be said about leadership in relationship to the Shape of the parish? What kind of leadership is needed given the current Shape of the parish? A starting place may be to modify and use the ideas of Situational Leadership. On the next page is a description based on that model.

The reader can use this in a two-step process: 1) Assess the Shape of the parish. Select the description that is most like what you see in your parish. 2) Then look at what would be involved in applying a leadership style that fits that Shape.

Assessing the Shape—The Readiness Level

You can use the descriptions below to assess your parish. Which comes closest to the characteristics of your parish? The focus here would be on the existence of a critical mass of people of Apostolic Faith and the extent to which the dynamics of the "shape" have been set loose.

"Episcopal Lite"

Some indicators:
- If there are people of Apostolic Faith they look outside the parish for guidance and development in their spiritual life
- There may not be people of Apostolic Faith in the parish
- People seem intimidated or resistant to any work on the spiritual life.
- A number of people claim confusion when there are attempts to help the congregation function competently in the Eucharist
- Asking the same questions over and over about a task to be preformed; or asking questions when they really know the answer
- The climate is one of superficial congeniality
- On the whole people are incompetent in the spiritual life and do not accept responsibility for their own spiritual life
- General pressure about "taking care of people" around things that people are capable of dealing with on their own

Ready But Not Competent

Some indicators:
- There is noticeable interest and responsiveness toward spiritual growth
- A number of people show moderate ability in their prayer life and spiritual discipline
- They are receptive to coaching and guidance
- This is new for people, there is little experience to draw upon
- Few or no people of Apostolic Faith; they look outside the parish for guidance and development in their spiritual life

Developing

Some indicators:
- There are a number of people of a Progressing or Apostolic Faith with a stable spiritual discipline
- They appear to have a sense of hesitation or confusion about their role and impact in the parish, or
- There is an active resistance or suspicion toward Apostolic Faith by a number of people
- There are not many people of Apostolic Faith in key leadership positions

Mature, Healthy Shape

Some indicators:
- A critical mass of people of Apostolic Faith are in the parish (15 – 20% of Sunday attendees might be a rule of thumb but will depend on other factors)
- They are able to maintain their spiritual discipline without a lot of guidance or encouragement; they are aware that they are proficient in the spiritual life
- The overall climate and culture of the parish is Apostolic

- The structures and processes that undergird a healthy Shape are present. For example, the Office is said on most days by several people; there is an adult foundations program; spiritual guidance is available.
- The parish is resilient and open to exploring change.
- The dynamic of a healthy Shape is in play, people are progressing, and there is a stable energy present.

In making an assessment it's common for leaders to realize how complex this process is. For example, a parish may have a spiritual life that seems to fit the "Mature, Healthy Shape" category while being unable to make difficult decisions to balance the budget by making needed staff cuts. Some elements of emotional maturity may be weak. Or a parish could consist of people who show a great deal of emotional and social intelligence while maintaining liturgical and spiritual practices that suggest immaturity.

Pastoral Oversight Style

Once you have located your parish, more or less, you can consider what leadership style is needed to fit the situation. The assumption is that if you fit your style to the level of readiness you will get better results. In the early stages this is more about the leadership of the clergy. You don't want to approach this literally—if other dynamics and issues come to mind take them into account.

"Episcopal Lite"—Not Ready or Competent

- Identify those in the parish who seem most ready to have the priest engage them in an adult way. Get to know them. Have coffee and drinks with individuals or a small group every few weeks. Find out about their life and interests. Avoid spending a lot of time with the neediest people.
- Offer a class on "Episcopal/Anglican Spirituality" or on "How We Grow in the Spiritual Life" or "How to Pray the Bible." Focus on classes in which people will learn a few skills for the spiritual life, explore a few core ideas, and get to be with others. Do enough that it will have an impact and require some initial commitment (three sessions?). In the sessions provide specific direction about what you are asking them to try. Don't provide a lot of open discussion time. Focus the time and the discussion on their learning—something new that they can use. Avoid the conventional, such as general Bible study groups, or the non-threatening such as a PowerPoint presentation on the Bible.
- Improve people's competence for Eucharistic participation. Develop a plan that moves each congregation in the parish to competence.
- Use sermons to teach about the spiritual life.
- Avoid the temptation to attack or discount people. Don't tell them that they are incompetent or "Episcopal Lite." Let them come to it themselves as they experience a gap between what is possible in their lives versus where they are now. Speak about development and how we are all growing. Don't get into a demanding and insistent tone. Be persistent, firm and gentle.
- Practice self-care. Maintain a spiritual discipline and grow in your own spiritual life. Pay attention to your own spiritual growth. Stay very connected to the wider church.

Ready But Not Competent

- Build the Apostolic Faith ring. Actively recruit people into the Foundations Course; teach the spiritual life in sermons; have inserts in the bulletin on spiritual life and competencies.
- Notice when members suddenly are in an Experimenting faith stage. Take initiative with them. Encourage them and guide them to focus on continued growth. If possible you want them to have a chance to move into a Progressing faith stage. The danger is that you will allow them to get

involved in institutional housekeeping or teaching church school. If that happens they may plateau into a Stable Sacramental Faith and stay there for years.

- Provide opportunities for give and take, both informally and in classes.
- Accept that this is a time when allowing people to be dependent on you is appropriate. You are the one with knowledge and skills they need but lack. This is a form of healthy dependency.
- This is a stage to persuade and make the case about spiritual life and discipline. Use one-on-one meetings, classes, sermons, the parish website, and printed material. Engage in a lot of two-way communication to clarify abilities and reinforce small improvements
- Avoid the temptation to manipulate people into a class or a retreat. Don't defend the emphasis on the spiritual life. Listen but be persistent and patient when some in the parish grumble about things changing.

Developing

- Bring those of Apostolic Faith and those Progressing together at times to pray and talk about their experiences. You are working to help them overcome their own uncertainty and confusion.
- Participate in groups with them, share your own spiritual journey and struggles.
- Encourage experimentation, listen a lot, be selective about suggestions.
- Acknowledge and affirm people's progress. Avoid anything that looks like you are patronizing their attempts.
- Begin to invite Apostolic Faith and Progressing people into leadership positions. Be sure they have the necessary gifts for leadership and working with others.
- Continue to build the Apostolic Faith ring, as in "Ready but Not Competent" Style of Oversight.
- Manage the need to both give a lot of time to developing the Shape of the parish while also needing to attend to the measures of health that are distorted but still powerful among some members.
- Practice self-care. Maintain your own spiritual discipline. Take care with feelings of frustration and impatience in people's growth or anger toward those who are trying to take the parish back to the old way.

Mature, Healthy Shape

- Maintain and protect the core structures, processes and climate. Make sure that it functions— liturgies are well done, Daily Office rota is maintained.
- Give special attention to those of Apostolic Faith. Have retreats and quiet days, schedule times for confession to be heard at least in Advent and Lent, make it easy for them to receive spiritual guidance (with you, in self directed groups).
- Create some occasions so people of Apostolic Faith can gather to explore the spiritual life. Protect those gatherings from people of Experimenting faith who may be inclined to attend (their presence would dumb down the group's work).
- Invite those Apostolic Faith people with the gifts into leadership. Move toward the key leaders being a third to half Apostolic Faith, and all others of Progressing or Stable Sacramental Faith
- Watch out for any withdrawing of attention from Apostolic Faith, those Progressing, and the needed undergirding structures and climate
- Fewer meetings in the parish about institutional life. Reduce the number of groups dealing with institutional matters. Use goal focused working groups instead of standing committees
- Practice self-care. Maintain a spiritual discipline and grow in your own spiritual life.

Use of Processes, Structures, Standards and Norms: Creating a Climate

The process of shaping the parish involves opening up pathways for people to experiment with, and explore, deeper expressions of faith and practice. In organization development terms this involves establishing the processes, structures, norms and climate that are consistent with the objectives in the strategy for shaping a parish.

The process of shaping the parish is about wisdom and good judgment. Even for the wisest of leaders it's not always apparent how to facilitate the Shape without doing things in a way that jumps past the congregation's readiness.

Common interventions include:

- Improve the Sunday Eucharist at several levels: 1) The competent action of the presider and those assisting in the Liturgy; 2) The competent participation of a critical mass of the congregation; and 3) The development of a Eucharistic spirituality among a critical mass.
- Train those willing in the use of the Daily Office and a process of experimenting with Personal Devotions.
- Establish a foundations course and maintain it year after year.
- Work with standards that are in the BCP and/or canon law. On the whole these standards fall firmly within Sacramental Faith practices.
- Coach people. Actively work with leaders, servers, catechists, officiants, those who shape social events and everyone who influences the climate.
- Make full use of the BCP: Holy Week Liturgies, Easter Vigil, Reconciliation, etc.

Avoid establishing rules and policies that create a façade. An example of this is when the rector pushes the parish or vestry to adopt standards for vestry membership that move beyond what is really already present. Examples: "All vestry members say some form of the Daily Office." "All vestry members contribute financially to the parish by giving proportionately." Vestries have been known to adopt such standards out of some misguided sense of what we *should* be doing.

It is quite another thing for processes and structures to emerge as the parish takes Shape. At a point when almost all members of the vestry are already living the practice, and there are a significant number of members also living the practice, then it may be time to establish it as a formal standard.

You don't want a façade. You do want something that is sustainable.

There is an understanding in the field of organization development that organizations usually cannot attend to growth and maturity at the same time. In times of size transition, starting a new parish, crisis and construction, so much of the leadership and members' attention is drawn into these efforts that the deeper issues of development are set on the back burner. This is an inevitable process. There is no sense in pretending it will not happen to us. At the same time there are things that can be done during these periods that make the parish ready for the deeper work.

- In these parishes we can take care to select clergy leadership firm in its loyalty to the Episcopal Church (too many new starts have a tone that is judgmental of the rest of the church and have leaders hostile to the church). We can seek clergy whose spiritual life is grounded in the Anglican tradition and the Prayer Book. We can look for emotional intelligence, specifically an awareness of and ability to cope with power.
- The bishop's office can insist on three-party agreements (clergy, lay leaders, bishop) that establish shared direction and accountability. The use of a skilled consultant might be a useful part of such an agreement.
- Maintain the basics: do the Eucharist well, offer the threefold rule of prayer, and have a foundations course.

A movement toward real life and engagement with an energy not our own

Leaders are establishing two dynamics at the center in shaping the parish. They are the deep underlying assumptions that provide the base for a healthy parish culture. The parish church is about forming people for "real life;" for maturity in Christ. It is developing in women and men a taste for life in what John Macquarrie saw as "a commonwealth of free, responsible beings united in love." Secondly, the parish is about engaging "an energy not its own." Formation isn't about creating perfect, sinless people. It is about connecting us to the power of the Holy Spirit.

The parish is a community of becoming and connecting. It will also be a place of suffering and joy. What is it like living in such a parish? What is the process of growth like?

"Does it hurt?" asked the Rabbit.
"Sometimes," said the Skin Horse, for he was always truthful.
"When you are Real, you don't mind being hurt."

"Does it happen all at once, like being wound up," he asked, "or just bit by bit?"

"It doesn't happen all at once," said the Skin Horse. "You become. It takes a long time. That's why it doesn't often happen to people who break easily, or have sharp edges, or who have to be carefully kept.

"Generally, by the time you are Real, most of your hair has been loved off, and your eyes drop out and you get loose in the joints and very shabby.

"But these things don't matter at all, because once you are Real, you can't be ugly, except to people who don't understand." (from The Velveteen Rabbit)

Other Models

The Theology of the Remnant

Martin Thornton in *Pastoral Theology: A Reorientation* and later republished as *The Heart of the Parish: A Theology of the Remnant*

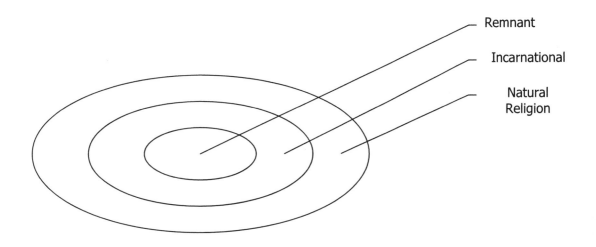

The parish is "a sacramental organism"
The Remnant – "The Body of Christ recapitulated in place;" keep the Rule of the Church (Mass on Sundays and Red Letter Days, Office, Private Prayer under direction)
Incarnational Religion – Those progressing toward the fullness of the Church's Rule, ... "babes in Christ" who are immature but truly "in Christ"; includes the occasional church attendee
Natural Religion – Natural but not incarnational religion; sub-Christian

John Westerhoff

In *Will Our Children Have Faith?*

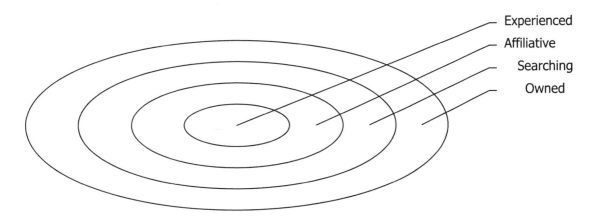

Faith grows like the rings of a tree, with each ring adding to and changing the tree somewhat, yet building on that which has grown before.

Experienced Faith – The faith experienced when young (also possibly with a major reorientation of belief). We receive this faith from others who nurture us and whom we trust. such as during early childhood.

Affiliative Faith – Faith that is concerned with belonging and identity related to belonging. Usually first expressed during adolescent years.

Searching Faith – A faith related to finding oneself. It's part of self-differentiating from ones families and peers.. There may be a good bit of experimentation.

Owned Faith – Accepting ownership of and responsibility for one's beliefs and practices.

Westerhoff revised his system later to three stages: Affiliative, Searching, and Mature

Critical Mass Theory

Robert A. Gallagher, 1998

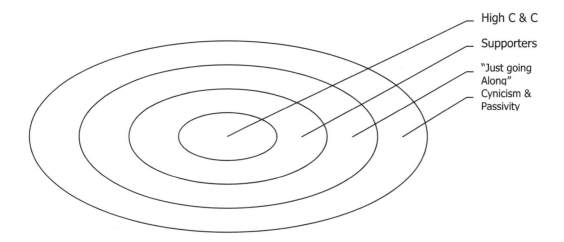

High competence and commitment—People invested in all aspects of the organization's life high degree of emotional maturity, competence and commitment

Supporters—Want to help be productive and healthy

"Just Going Along"—May have mixed feelings regarding commitment; may want to "just do my job;" competence may be in limited areas; may "go along" with health or non-health at the center.

Stances of Cynicism, Counter-dependency, Passivity—Most organizations have people that are not able or willing to take a healthy and productive stance. This may be a stance that the person typically takes or may be situational.

STRATEGY: In most organizations—build a "critical mass" of people with a stance of *High Commitment & Competence* and *Supporters*. Develop organizational processes, values and norms that reinforce a productive, empowering, and humane culture. Accept people in the stance they have taken; invite them to develop their abilities and willingness to invest themselves more broadly and deeply. Place boundaries on behavior that is undermining the well being of the organization's culture.

The New Self, on the New Way

In *He Came Down from Heaven*, Charles Williams wrote, "The Church (it was early decided) was not an organization of sinless men but of sinful, not a union of adepts but of less than neophytes, not illuminati but of those that sat in darkness. Nevertheless, it carried within it an energy not its own, and it knew what it believed about that energy."

He went on to write about the need for both a new self and a new way.

There are always three degrees of consciousness, all infinitely divisible:
The old self on the old way
The old self on the new way
The new self on the new way.

The second group is always the largest, at all times and in all places. ... It forms, at any one moment, the greatest part of the visibility of the church, and, at most moments, practically all of oneself that one can know, for the new self does not know itself.

V. Related Resources

Renewal—What Kind of Person is Being Formed?

(God) said that we were "gods" and He is going to make good His words. If we let Him—for we can prevent Him if we choose—He will make the feeblest and filthiest of us into a god or goddess, dazzling, radiant, immortal creature, pulsating all through with such energy and joy and wisdom and love as we cannot now imagine, a bright stainless mirror which reflects back to God perfectly (though, of course, on a smaller scale) His own boundless power and delight and goodness. The process will be long and in parts very painful; but that is what we are in for.
-C. S. Lewis, *Mere Christianity*, p 174-5

One diocese I worked with saw congregational development as being about creating communities of Christian formation. This was an approach that helped focus parish and diocesan energy and resources around something people cared about. It started with clarity about the end result we were seeking. What did we hope would happen to people as a result of being part of a parish church? What does it mean to grow into the fullness of your baptism, to be an apostolic Christian, to "be renewed in the spirit of your minds...to put on the new nature?"

The parish is in the business of formation. The formation of people is an aspect of everything that happens in a parish—liturgy, social life, spiritual guidance, education and Christian action. A related leadership task is to help people accept responsibility for their own spiritual life, for how they manage their Renewal-Apostolate Cycle. We do that best by establishing the climate, structures and processes that make up an environment in which people can grow in the Christian life.

It is useful when a parish regularly holds up two or three ways of describing the kind of person being formed. There are, of course, more ways than just two or three. Over time we want to expose parishioners to a wide range of models. But during any one-time period it's useful to focus on a limited number of ways. At the same time we want to avoid offering just one language system with its danger of creating literalists among our more immature and experimenting members. Here are a few possibilities for describing what we are seeking.

One Baptized into the Body of Christ

A new person in Christ; becoming salt, light and leaven; growing up in Christ. " Buried with Christ in his death...share in his resurrection...reborn by the Holy Spirit." "An inquiring and discerning heart, the courage to will and to persevere, a spirit to know and to love you, and the gift of joy and wonder in all your works." A believer in God—Father, Son and Holy Spirit; called to "persevere in resisting evil, and, whenever you fall into sin, repent and return...proclaim by word and example the Good News...seek and serve Christ in all persons...strive for justice and peace among all people, and respect the dignity of every human being."

An Ordinary Life – A Holy Life – A Heroic Life

Having what Augustine called "a real life." A life reflecting the glory of God; process of formation in which we develop the longings and hungers that change us and change the world.

160

The longing for justice and mercy, a hunger for life with others in community, a longing for wonder and awe, and the humility to seek just an ordinary life, a life without great trials and without having to face great evils.

In *A Man For All Seasons*, Robert Bolt pictures Thomas Moore as a man given to both humility and integrity "God made the angels to show Him splendour — as He made animals for innocence and plants for their simplicity. But Man He made to serve Him wittily, in the tangle of his mind. If He suffers us to fall to such a case that there is no scaping, then we may stand our tackle as best we can, and yes Will, then we may clamour like champions – if we have the spittle for it. And no doubt it delights God to see splendour where He only looked for complexity. But it's God's part, not our own, to being us to that extremity. Our natural business lies in escaping .." Moore wants his life with Meg and their children but he wants that to be part of a "real life." And that longing finally doesn't permit the escape he hoped for. If God brings us to the cross that is God's awful business.

We each have different ways into this ordinary, holy, heroic life. For me one way has been the work of the angels. The angels are about our moments and seasons of wonder and awe. These moments are, for me, times when I'm not quite tuned in, or when I am half awake, just beginning to stir from sleep, or drifting off over the computer, and see and feel an experience, another person, or my own life, in some new way. I see something of the glory, beauty and terror present.

On occasion, the moments are more immediate. In sitting at a bar, looking at a friend and knowing that it is a holy moment, a meeting connected to the ways of eternity. Or, of glancing across the aisle during Mass and realizing that the person you find most annoying is oddly beautiful. You don't want to get too worried about these moments. Soon enough you'll return to your usual state of blindness and annoyance.

There are also seasons of wonder and awe—months and even years in our life, or the life of a people, when glory breaks loose. These are the times of being fully alive, times of rich and deep relationships, times of struggle in which all might be lost except that solidarity with others who also are in the battle.

The angels allow us to see that *greater things* are happening within, among and around us. They bring the deepest and best parts of us into view – so we can know wonder and awe.

The story of Mary and Martha is all too frequently twisted by preachers to avoid making us uncomfortable. They offer the ways of Mary and Martha as equally valid paths. But that's not the story. Our Lord gives us a challenge — *"Mary has chosen the better part."* To receive the challenge, and the grace that accompanies it, is to enter into our own life in a new way. We come to see and understand that the Eucharist is not only about us being fed so we might feed others; Eucharist is an end in itself. Just being with one another and God in communion is the purpose and completion of life. We come to understand that sitting on a porch drinking fine Scotch or cheap beer is not just a break from the struggles of life, but is a taste of eternity.

The Full Stature of Christ

There is, of course, Paul's understanding of what God is doing in our lives, e.g. in Ephesians that we are to grow into the full stature of Christ; that the graces and practices necessary for that growth are humility, gentleness, patience, forbearance born of love, eagerness to maintain unity in the bond of peace, truthfulness mediated in love, mutual kindness, tenderheartedness and forgiveness; and in Galatians that the fruit of the spirit is love, joy, peace, patience, kindness, generosity, faithfulness, gentleness and self-control.

Seven Deadly Sins

A definition of sin offered by Richard Holloway (one-time Presiding Bishop of Scotland) is "a wrongly directed effort; a good drive that fails to find the right object; a good thing in itself that is done to excess." (*Seven to Flee, Seven to Follow*, 1986). This fits Newman's understanding that, "Evil has no substance of its own, but is only the defect, excess, perversion, or corruption of that which has substance." Martin Smith, in his book on reconciliation, urges, "Fix your mind on the positive virtues, of which sins are the shadow." In a related understanding, Martin Thornton viewed the purpose of self-examination as aiming at "*tranquillitas*; not the suppression of desire, not *apatheia*, but harmony between the elements of personality." So, in all this we are dealing with health and wholeness rather than simply avoidance and self-protection.

In some of the material below I'm drawing on Holloway's work.

- **Pride**. Self esteem raised to an inordinate level, so that all sense of proportion is lost
- **Envy (jealousy)**. "Sorrow for another's good," "Satisfaction at the misfortunes of our friends." A characteristic of envy is that it offers no real pleasure, it is without fun; other sins offer some gratification. Symptoms include malice, being good at noticing the defects in others, hypocrisy, dejection. Envy may lead into the third sin.
- **Covetousness (avarice).** "Itching hunger for the good things of life" (success, possessions, popularity). It shows itself in conspicuous consumption of things or people, fear of aging. [Note: pride and envy are rooted in a sense of inadequacy. There is in us a "deep longing to be accepted and appreciated; the need is to know that we are loved as we are."]
- **Anger.** A disproportionate response to danger; phases that are destructive—impatience, retaliation, lack of control, resentment. The antidotes are to give ourselves to systematically willing another person's good and to act quickly as anger breaks out to minimize the damage.
- **Lust.** A distorted instinct that is good in itself. It is rooted in a pursuit of pleasure that gives permission for exploitation, even if mutually agreed upon. There is a danger of moving into an addictive cycle and diminishing ones capacity for committed, joyful relationships. C.S. Lewis saw this as the least significant of the sins.
- **Gluttony**. Much the same as the above in its dynamics. The person is driven to a pursuit of satisfying appetites—too much drink, food, smoking, talk; compulsive behavior. They are natural instincts that are allowed to play a disproportionate role and can end up dominating the personality. An approach to lust and gluttony is learning self discipline and redirect the instincts toward "the good."
- **Sloth**. "The instinct for rest and creative idling taken and distorted into an unattractive passivity," "everything is too much trouble." It is a disease of the will, it numbs the will. Instead of taking our life in our own hand we drift along, not really being bad people (we don't have the energy for it). Sloth does create the conditions under which evil takes hold in society. It may be related to why people seem to resist "giving themselves" to another, to their work, and to civic life.

Seven Gifts of the Holy Spirit

- **Fear (awe).** I'd understand it as fear that you will not have the life you could have; the life God wants for you. It is as opposed to a life that is not for "the good" or that is trivial. This is the "fear that establishes proportions and recognizes consequences" and may lead "to a realistic, rueful ... almost humorous awareness of our true state."
- **Piety (affection).** "A kind of fondness or love, a recognition of what you owe the land that bred you," gratitude for the love, forgiveness and understanding one receives
- **Knowledge.** A capacity to accept paradox, to hold things in balance, to see more completely. It is the knowledge of God and the dynamics of awe and affection.
- **Courage (fortitude).** Closing the gap between belief and action "by reaching beyond themselves to Christ," rather than "by pulling Christ towards them and adapting him to their own uses." Standing fast even though you want to run. Especially needed in moral life, the world of ideas, and in personal relations.
- **Counsel (guidance).** An openness to the Holy Spirit; openness to an energy for good that comes from beyond ourselves. It is related to developing a capacity for listening and an inner silence.
- **Understanding.** The gift of balance, an awareness of the situation. It is "knowing when to celebrate and when to lament." This is self knowledge. It is seeing the world rightly -- that the creation is good, that God is encountered through it.
- **Wisdom.** The coming together of the other six gifts; wholeness. Most contemporary books on the spiritual life speak of spiritual maturity.

Four Cardinal Virtues

The four are interdependent; if you don't adequately possess one of them, the others are distorted in some fashion.

- **Prudence.** In the most down-to-earth meaning we are speaking of having good sense; the capacity for practical judgment. The virtue of it is in being grounded in reality and directed toward what is good. It assumes openness to reality. This is not the same thing as excess caution and a withholding spirit.
- **Justice.** The virtue is rooted in the assumption that we live with one another. That then presents us with several issues to address, including -- what we as individuals owe society; what we own other individuals; what society owns individuals.
- **Fortitude.** This is about removing barriers to justice. A central element is perseverance. Justice is only possible when we stay with the work before us. It is not the same as stubbornness.
- **Temperance.** Self-awareness and self-control are needed if we are to enjoy life and at the same time be good people. The work that has been done in recent decades on emotional and social intelligence is a resource.

Episcopal Spirituality

The parish is forming a baptized person for living the Christian life as expressed in the Anglican tradition.

The Christian life is a life lived within a particular tradition. We all live someplace, in some tradition of the church, which means that the parish is not just concerned with the formation of "a Christian" but of a Christian in the Episcopal tradition of spirituality. This is a certain way of being "Christian." We need to avoid the artificial logic that says, "I am a Christian first, and a particular religious denomination, second. God does not call us to be Episcopalians, he calls us to be Christians." I'd suggest that God does call us to live as Christians within particular traditions, communions and families. The different ways of being a Christian are not some mistake, or secondary concern, but are at least ways of addressing the diversity of spiritual temperament found among people. Many of us also think that some ways are better than others; that some spiritualities are more likely to result in adults who are more grounded in the life of God, more self aware, and more inclined to responsibility in daily life.

The Episcopal Church has developed a form of Christian spirituality that has emerged from its roots in Anglicanism and in the American experience. That spirit can be found in most parishes and dioceses of the church. A way of expressing the elements of that spirituality is to say that it is: Christian, balanced—holistic, world-embracing, adult, organic, open-minded, and a spirituality of beauty.

Other frameworks for thinking about the formation of Christians in the Episcopal Church's tradition include:
- Jim Fenhagan in *The Anglican Way*—holy worldliness, personal holiness, and comprehensiveness.
- John Westerhoff in *A People Called Episcopalians*—explores characteristics such as liturgical/biblical, communal, sacramental, and pastoral.
- The Christian Life Model—developing a strong life of worship, doctrine and action.
- Benedictine Spirituality—living in the dynamics of the Promise: Obedience, Stability and Conversion of Life.

A Christian Spirituality

Grounded in the love of God for humanity as seen in the incarnation of Jesus Christ, Christian Life is life lived in Christ: "Christ in us and we in him." Worship, doctrine and action are the means by which we participate in the life of Christ's Body, the Church; in her unity, holiness, catholicity and apostolicity. They are the means by which we participate in the Church's mission "to restore all people to unity with God and each other in Christ." We are restored to unity as we are drawn into the prayer of Christ, the mind of Christ, and the work of Christ. In prayer, study, and work we become instruments of God's holy mission.

A Spirituality of Beauty

We tend to take delight in the natural rhythm of life. We rejoice in the beauty of creation and have a strong commitment to environmental protection. Our worship strives for good music, a sense of flow and grace, and poetry and drama. We seek beauty in our worship space using artists, live flowers, and real candles in creating an appropriate climate.

An Adult Spirituality

We value **personal responsibility and freedom** in the process of shaping and living life as a Christian. Adults are invited to **explore and experiment with** the resources of Christian and Anglican spirituality to discover ways that best nurture them in the Christian life. We understand that what feeds one person may not feed another. We each work out our relationship with God, each other, creation and self in unique ways. The adult Christian shapes a spiritual life that fits his or her personality and circumstances. Please note -- this isn't about whether children are included (they are) but about what kind of adults we hope children will become.

A World-Embracing Spirituality

Our tendency is to **affirm life and this world**. Those things in life that give us pleasure are understood as being fundamentally good. Fun, our bodies, material things, good food are all accepted as part of living a full life. Our call to faith is linked to hope and love rather than fear and guilt.

For most of us the **Christian life is lived in the context of our family, friendships, work and civic life**. Those are the places in which the love of Christ may flow through us to offer light and hope in the world. We generally see that process as organic rather than planned. To the extent we have been touched by the love of God we will show that love in our daily life.

We see Christian faith as **having political implications**. Episcopalians have a long history of involvement in the civic life of communities and the nation. The individual Christian is called to both inform and act on their conscience. The church doesn't usually ask its members to accept particular political views but it does ask members to consider in their thinking and decision making what might be understood from the Scriptures, what the church has learned over the centuries (as seen in the Tradition and the contemporary councils of the church) and in their own Reason. As a church we take positions on public issues. While these positions are often on what is seen as the more liberal side of the political spectrum; they frequently exhibit an Anglican comprehensiveness in affirming the complexity of a situation.

A Balanced—Holistic Spirituality

We are moderate, seeking a balanced, reasonable approach to life. It is a life in which prayer, work, study and play have a rhythm. We seek to take into account the whole of experience, ambiguity and all. We attend to the whole and the interdependence of its parts in how we live as people and parish communities. We are interested in the whole person—mind, body and spirit—and the whole of faith, in all its complexity and with all its paradox.

An Organic Spirituality

We understand individual spiritual development to be rooted in communal daily prayer that shapes our relationship to God. Decisions are made in the context of common prayer so the Holy Spirit fills and enfolds us. We are sacramental—"outward and visible signs of inward and spiritual grace." As Christ was the sacrament of God, the church is the sacrament of Christ in the world. Martin Thornton put it this way: "The prayer and life of each member is wholly dependent on the health of the total organism." It's a very radical statement about the holiness of the church.

An Open–Minded Spirituality

Our way has stressed **an open-minded, searching approach** to faith. Engagement with God and the church is intended to open us to the mystery that is God. So doubt, questioning, exploration and openness to new insights is a path to God and wholeness of life. This involves being open to what may be learned: from studying and praying the Scriptures, from the wisdom gained as the church has struggled with life's issues in the past, from the councils of the church today, from the insights and views of other people, and from the application of our own reason and what we have learned from our experience.

We see value in **comprehensiveness and ambiguity**. Our way includes holding opposites in tension, appreciating paradoxical thinking, assuming that what appears to be irreconcilable differences may contain a balanced truth, allowing a certain messiness and grayness in our theological and ethical thinking. Living in this way means developing a tolerance of differences in thinking and practice. It also calls for a capacity to listen deeply and respectfully, to have courage in expressing one's own understanding, to wait on God in silence and with patience. Our unity is not the unity of sameness of thought but a unity of trust in God and God's wisdom. It's the unity of the Eucharist and a shared life. This makes for a roomy church with space for many (as long as they will accept allowing space for others).

The Church's Influence in Society

This book focuses on the dynamics and vocation of the parish church. Within that arena the primary way in which the church influences society is through the lives of the baptized as they play their roles in families, with friends, in the workplace and in civic life. To a lesser extent a parish may also have an impact as an institution by how it invests its funds, uses its purchasing power, and educates its members, and engages in corporate ministries of service.

The wider church, in convention, frequently takes positions on issues facing the region and nation and may form vehicles to act in support of those positions. What are some of the principles upon which the church might base those statements as it attempts to influence government and other institutions? Here's a sampling from a few Anglican thinkers.

In *Christianity and Social Order*, in 1942 William Temple wrote that what he was offering were not "an expression of a purely personal point of view but represent the main trend of Christian social teaching." He suggested considerations such as these:

- The world...results from His love; creation is a kind of overflow of the divine love."
- "The aim of a Christian social order is the fullest possible development of individual personality in the widest and deepest possible fellowship."
- In a chapter on "How Should the Church Interfere?" he began with an affirmation of the lay apostolate. "Nine-tenths of the work of the Church in the world is done by Christian people fulfilling responsibilities and performing tasks which in themselves are not part of he official system of the Church at all." In a later work, Temple wrote of the organic reality of the Body, "the stream of redemptive power flows out from the church through the lives of its members into the society which they influence." (*What Christians Stand for in the Secular World*)
- "It is of crucial importance that the Church acting corporately should not commit itself to any particular policy. A policy always depends on technical decisions concerning the actual relations of cause and effect in the political and economic world; about these the Christian has no more reliable judgment than an atheist…"
- His answer to how the church should interfere had three parts: 1) through its members fulfilling "their moral responsibilities and functions in a Christian spirit;" 2) its members exercising their civic rights in a Christian spirit; and 3) offering its members "a systematic statement of principles" to guide the first two.
- Cautious about utopian approaches. "...no one really wants to live in the ideal state as depicted by anyone else."
- "The art of government in fact is the art of so ordering life that self-interest prompts what justice demands."
- Every child should "find itself a member of a family housed with decency and dignity" without having to face lack of food or conditions that are overcrowded, dirty or drab, and "have the opportunity of an education…as to allow for his peculiar aptitudes and make possible their full development." Every citizen should have an income to "enable him to maintain a home and bring up children," "have a voice in the conduct of the business or industry which is carried on by means of his labor," "have sufficient daily leisure with two days rest in seven," "have assured liberty in the forms of freedom of worship, of speech, of assembly." "The resources of the earth should be used as God's gifts to the whole human race, and used with due consideration for the needs of the present and future generations."

In *The Christian Moral Vision* (1979), Earl Brill offered these comments on influencing public policy

- "It is difficult to talk about 'Christian' public policy because there is no one Christian way to run a country. There is no political program which all the faithful ought to support."
- "There are, however, some Christian presumptions concerning public policy. They would include a concern for social justice; a bias in favor of the poor, the oppressed, the outsider; a commitment to the solidarity of the whole human family; an investment in the freedom of individuals to develop their own gifts and interests; and a commitment to equal treatment under the law."
- On work – ".. all God's children should have a chance to work ... society itself has an obligation to provide work for everyone.". Work can be seen as vocation with its opportunities to serve others and " can enable us to express that creative urge within ourselves that is the image of God." Leisure – "... leisure is also good. It also affords an opportunity to express our creativity. In leisure we also imitate God, who, after he had created the 'world, rested on the seventh day." Labor unions – "represent legitimate expressions of the corporate concerns of American workers. ... They have conferred a measure of dignity upon the worker who can assert, through the union, the right to bargain on equal terms with the employer."

In the *Christian Social Witness* (2001) by Harold Lewis
- "Does not God want us to show the same love and compassion for others that he has shown to us? ... The concept that we call 'human rights' is basically grounded in our belief that God places value on each person. The recognition of one another's human rights is the cornerstone of justice, which in turn is grounded in love. We are, therefore, called upon to as Christians to uphold and execute justice as an expression of the love that God holds for all of us."
- He raises a concern about a dynamic within the Episcopal Church that seems to undermine our social witness. "A glance at General Convention resolutions over the past two or three decades revels that the church has flitted from one concern to another."
- A commitment to social justice has always been a hallmark of Anglicanism. . ." (p. 33).

The Daily Office

A Philadelphia attorney gets up each morning at six, puts on his robe and wanders to the kitchen. He starts the coffee, finds the half-and-half in the refrigerator and places it on the pine table next to the prayer book. When the coffee is ready he sits, sips the coffee, and opens the book. In a very low voice he begins – "Lord, open our lips." By 6:30 he is in the shower.

In Seattle, a woman who plays with a rock band sits in the chapel wearing a black cassock. Behind the altar there are six candles that have been lit. It's 5:30 p.m. on Wednesday night. This is her first time officiating at Evening Prayer. She rings a small bell, the eight people that have gathered are still and silent for two minutes; she rings the bell again. Once the sound of the bell has faded she and they stand. She prays – "O God, make speed to save us."

The Daily Office is the church's daily offering of praise to God. Whether said in a group in a parish church or as an individual with morning coffee, the Office is our participation in the Church's daily praise of God

Why do people say the Office?

Here are the comments of several people about why they participate in Evening Prayer.

"So much of my time is spent working, being places and being 'productive,' evening prayer is a way for me to slow down; it is a kind of spiritual 'me time' that I look forward to. For me evening prayer is not time spent in being 'productive' but waiting and trusting, giving up the sense of the ability to control everything and relax. What is also great is that I can just show up as I am." Denise Crawford

"The reason I participate in Evening Prayer is for the opportunity to immerse myself in the mystery, to explore the silences, and to be alone with other people in the presence of God." Robin Allan Jones

"Officiating is a discipline to ensure I attend. On Saturdays we are privileged to read from Julian of Norwich, a deep education in why and how to pray. Thanks be to God." Robert Kluckhohn

"It was also a way of making a small commitment which was something that I needed to do. Since Lee's death, I have been very uneasy about making any promises. I saw this as a way to overcome that or start to. I found as I became more comfortable with the service, that it gave me a good feeling and a feeling of belonging to a larger group." Joseph Tafelski

"Gail Ramshaw, a liturgical-language scholar and a favorite writer of mine, says something with which I heartily agree (these are my words, but drawn from her idea): that my own little made-up prayers fall short, that my own poetry and prose just doesn't cut it, that I'm better off saying the words that have been said time out of mind, by Christians living and dead. 'Soloists perform, but choristers praise', says Ramshaw. History does not begin (or end) with me. ....
Most mornings (nearly all weekday mornings) I take our little dog Stella on a two-mile walk. In June, the sun pours over the landscape, even as early as 5:30 a.m. In November, darkness and clammy mist cover Puget Sound. In all seasons, Stella and I reach Sunset Hill, a grand but small park with a magnificent scenic overlook, and I find myself saying, 'Lord, open my lips, and my mouth will proclaim your praise.' All the hosts are gathered round." Stephen Crippen

"Praying the Daily Office grounds my life in time—the rhythm of day/night—and sanctifies my ordinary, daily, temporal existence by offering God praise and thanks. This pattern of daily prayer is incomparable richer when offered up as part of a community, as opposed to by myself." Mark Lloyd Taylor

"When I am not feeling especially grateful, or especially dependent on God, or especially inclined to pray—or when I am feeling overwhelmingly so—in all cases my feelings can easily become either a substitute for prayer or a reason to not pray. The most important thing the Office does for me is to pry me out of my own agenda, not by helping me ignore my feelings, whatever they might be, but by giving me a place to put them." Bryan Carr

"You asked about what draws me to the daily office—simply, it is the prayer that engages my mind *and* forms my heart with very little effort on my part. I just need to show up and don't have to manufacture some deep 'spiritual' feeling. This is glorious freedom and grace for me who has often felt much guilt around prayer. Much like *lectio divina* — I come to the text where I am at, and just by virtue of engaging with it (reading it), the Spirit works, often invisibly, sometimes visibly. I love that it can be done anywhere — on a train, at work, on a park bench, in the midst of lots of people — without the need for extra trappings, solitude, or even silence — or in full glory with incense and chant and beautiful liturgy. More and more, the communal nature of the office has become important to me—that it not just 'my' prayer, but the prayer of the Church, offered in a particular locale, by me or a group, yet with and for the larger Body of Christ (past, present, and future). I can say more, but this pretty much captures it." Susan Forshey

The Place of the Office in Congregational Development

The public offering of the Office, and/or the persistent training and coaching of individuals in how to use the Office, have three primary congregational development impacts.

Nurturing Spiritual Life and Growth - It can nurture people of Apostolic Faith; which can also help them play a vicarious role in grounding the parish. It offers may people a time of renewal. It can become a way of nurturing our connectedness with God and others; a way of nurturing listening and empathy. It suggests to the whole parish that there is a deeper place to move to in their spiritual life. This offers people who are ready to progress in their spiritual life a concrete way.

Parish Identity - It helps the parish take on an identity of being a place of deep prayer.
It is part of what creates a place soaked in prayer. Such places become holy places. Such an identity both attracts and frightens people.

Connection - It connects us to something bigger than ourselves. The parish plays its role in offering the prayer of the whole church and in doing that reinforces its connection with the whole communion of saints.

Strengthen the Daily Office

One place to begin is by equipping members of the parish to offer the Office on their own. Part of that equipping might include:

- Learn the mechanics – Going through the Office in the BCP, how to use the Office lectionary, where to find it on the internet
- The parish might create several resources that individuals could use - a card with short forms of the Office, a sheet with parts of the Office that are easily memorized (e.g., "In the tender compassion of our God the dawn from on high shall break upon us" …").
- Explore the spirituality of the Office – Its role in a balanced spirituality; its function as a heartbeat for the Body of Christ, its detachment from our passing feelings and engagement of a duty
- Facilitate a thinking through of the logistics of how this particular person can make it part of the day's routine – Where and when will it usually be done?, What forms used?, What is the optimal use of the Office for this person, something less than optimal, and finally a bare minimum of participation by in a daily saying of the Lord's Prayer of a phrase such as "Guide us walking .." from Compline.
- Connect the Office to people's hearts and minds. Look for resources that interpret and enliven the Office. For example, the story of Jonathan Daniels use of Evening Prayer or a poem by Amy Hunter on her experience of the Office that includes this –
    these prayers are not woven by angels
    but are built
        every day every office anew
    by human voice and hunger
    the work of a people
    who have been doing this
    a long time
    (The whole poem is below.)

This offering by individuals of the church's daily offering of prayer may be the primary way a parish church engages the Office. In parishes where the Office is not on the parish schedule it is appropriate to have a statement on the web site in the section of worship that might read something like this, "St. Mary's Church participates in the offering of the church's daily prayer as its members pray the Daily Office at home and workplace. This pattern of reading the appointed psalms and scripture, and saying the prayers, grounds us all in the life of God and connects us to the prayer of the whole church, living and dead."

Many parish churches are able to schedule the Office. It is relatively easy for a large parish to schedule the Office. How might smaller and middle-sized parishes do it?
- Make it easy - What time of the day is most convenient for people to attend? (e.g., A business district might find that offering Noonday Prayers that makes use of one of the appointed psalms and readings will work; other places have timed Evening Prayer for people on their way home from work. When is the best time for people willing to be officiants? Do a survey to find out.
- Create officiant teams - Invite people to join an officiant team that is responsible for one day each week. The teams may range from two to four people. Ask people to sign up on the assumption that the whole team is present on that day. It makes it a more pleasurable activity.
- Involve people – Invite people to offer themselves as officiants on one day of the week.

171

- Connect - On occasion invite people to have coffee in the parish kitchen after Morning Prayer or go out to a bar together after Evening Prayer.
- Make it reliable - Work at making the flow and rhythm of the Office much the same day by day. Provide a customary, training and coaching to those willing to officiate; this shows that it is valued and worth doing well. Make it the same time every day, e.g., Evening Prayer at 5:30 p.m. Do it only if you can sustain in at least four days each week. It needs to be "daily" enough to be the Daily Office. Don't turn it into an occasional service that may undermine the role of the Office in people's spiritual life.
- Work with, and teach, the prayer book pattern - Sunday Eucharist, daily office (or almost daily), and personal devotions according to gift and inclination. Offer this as part of what makes for a balanced spiritual diet. Avoid things that will confuse people about the pattern (e.g., using Morning or Evening Prayer once a week, having a daily Mass but no Office, using forms of personal devotions as a corporate prayer in place of the Office.)
- Clergy participate - Parish clergy, even those with very part time positions, need to participate frequently.

Other ways to support to the saying of the Office by individuals and/or on the parish schedule
- Create a card based on the Daily Office and made it available to all members; introduced it by first asking members of the vestry and other key groups to experiment with the card and reflect on its use
- Say an Office at the beginning or end of all meetings and gatherings in the parish; use a form that in length is between the two offered by the prayer book; the BCP's short form seems skimpy and the full Office is usually longer than seems appropriate to people in this setting.
- Have the parish web site link to the Daily Office on the web.

PR for the Office

Here are a few ideas about helping people consider participation in the parish's saying of the Office.

1. Have the times posted on the web site and in the Sunday bulletin

2. In a core foundations course – during one module make the Office a significant element (e.g., have people explore options, try it out during the program and debrief the experience of saying the office at least once); and bring it up in other models dealing with the spiritual life and the use of the Bible.

3. In spiritual guidance with an individual have the person practice the use of the Office in some form; reflect on the experience, and offer coaching.

4. During Advent and Lent call special attention to the saying of the Office. Invite people to consider experimenting with it during that season. Some parishes have used these seasons as time to introduce the parish to saying the Office.

5. At some point ask those in the parish who say the Office to share what it means for them. Rebecca Riviere of St. Stephen's in Huntsville, Alabama wrote, "We who regularly participate in the Daily Office find that we are surrounded by a Great Cloud of Witnesses and are deeply connected with the praying Church throughout the world who give Glory to God daily and intercede for the needs of others continually." In the earlier comments there is a mix of theologically, poetry, and practical insight – "All the hosts are gathered round"; "a way for me

to slow down"; "engages my mind and forms my heart"; "pry me out of my own agenda"; "I love that it can be done anywhere"; "that I can show up as I am".

6. Include a form of promotion in the Sunday bulletin, on the parish e-list, in blogs, and as posted notices around the parish. For example:

a. Post attractive flyers around the parish
b. If the parish has a second reading that is consistently from a certain Christian writer on a given day; call attention to that practice.
 c. Have a description of what happens at MP/EP posted (so people have an idea of what it will feel like.
d. Interview people who attend regularly, publish their comments in the parish newsletter
e. Run a series of quotes about the spirituality of the Office. Place the quote in a context, such as:

The Daily Office: *This parish participates in the church's daily offering of praise as individuals at home and as a community at 5:30 p.m. Evening Prayer.*

If you would like some guidance in how to say the Office speak with one of the clergy and/or attend a related Foundations Course.

Examples of quotes:

The real significance of the Divine Office is that in its recitation the individual or group enters the ancient cycle of prayer, by which day by day and hour by hour the church in the name of all creation adores and implores the eternal God. -Evelyn Underhill, quoted in John MacQuarrie's *Paths in Spiritualty*

Daily prayer in the prayer book tradition embodies a spiritual practice that is practical, ordered, and not dependent on feelings that are subject to change. The daily offices of the prayer book are intended to be familiar, regular, and participatory, leading to what one author calls a "divine monotony." Indeed, the word "office" is derived from the Latin officium, meaning the performance of a task or duty. The offices have a corporate familiarity that leads us deeper into the regular rhythms of the day and of our life with God From - *Opening the Prayer Book*, Jeffrey Lee 1999

The value of the Office is its objectivity. It is a means by which we pray with the whole church, uniting our prayer with that of millions of other Christians living and dead. This is true whether one is alone or in a group, for the Office is essentially a corporate act. It is objective too in that it does not depend on our feelings, but gives our prayer life a regularity and a disciplined framework. -Kenneth Leech, *True Prayer*

The Office holds up in a public way the fact that the journey with and to God is central - God is all in all. It enables a connecting-up process where individual and community are held in contact with God. In a very particular way it builds community, providing bricks and mortar wherewith God's community is continually brought to be. It releases love, not simply for the community, or even perhaps not at all for the community sometimes, as far as they can perceive it. It feeds into the invisible economy of Grace, God's hidden plumbing, for the good of the world. From - *What shall we say about the Daily Office?* Father George Guiver CR

I lost fear in the black belt when I began to know in my bones and sinews that I had been truly baptized into the Lord's death and Resurrection, that in the only sense that really matters I am already dead, and my life is hid with Christ in God. I began to lose self-righteousness when I discovered the extent to which my behavior was motivated by worldly desires and by the self-seeking messianism of Yankee deliverance! The point is simply, of course, that one's motives are usually mixed, and one had better know it. As Judy and I said the daily offices day by day, we became more and more aware of the living reality of the invisible "communion of saints"--of the beloved community in Cambridge who were saying the offices too, of the ones gathered around a near-distant throne in heaven--who blend with theirs our faltering songs of prayer and praise. With them, with black men and white men, with all of life, in Him Whose Name is above all the names that the races and nations shout, whose Name is Itself the Song Which fulfils and "ends" all songs, we are indelibly, unspeakably ONE. - Jonathan Daniels on the Daily Office

...a way by which we keep ourselves in constant awareness of the divine order; an order of love and justice which embraces and underlies all order .... "The cantus firmus *is the recurring rhythmic pattern which serves as the basis for the music, giving it a unity and consistency. ...it is the recurring cycle of prayer and communing with God which gives, as it were, the dominant 'set' to life. But over that cantus firmus all kinds of distinct melodies may be heard interweaving in a complex texture"* .... *"...the offices keep us in touch with the whole church. They do not impede the individual's spiritual growth, but both nourish it and supply a standard by which it is to be judged"* .... *"..we need immersion too in Christian truth if we are rightly to interpret life and culture* -John MacQuarrie , *Paths in Spirituality*

The Stories of Parishes Saying the Daily Office

Saint Philip's Church, Durham

From Scott Benhase, former rector, now at Saint Alban's, D.C. We have the daily office here Monday through Friday at noon (with mass on Saints' days). We chose noonday because we are downtown and many folk are dealing with a carpool and getting to work at the beginning and ending of the day. At noon, however, they can participate as part of their lunch hour.

The parish always keeps the 12 noon to 12:30 p.m. time slot free of all other meetings, so people know that we stop what we are doing and go pray at noon. We've done this now for ten years. When it is Eucharist one of the parish priests presides. For noonday prayer, different lay folk are assigned a day of the week, some of them are staff and some are not.

We average between 5-10 people each day in our side chapel. Most are parishioners, but regularly there are homeless folk off the street or clients from the county mental center across the street. There are also parishioners who come from other Episcopal churches. They work downtown so it is convenient for them.

A significant part of the liturgy (whether it is Eucharist or the office) are the prayers of the people. The officiant/celebrant prays for each person on our parish prayer list and invites other names. We pray for the city and its leaders by name. We have members in jail and we pray for them by name. We have members in Iraq and we pray for them by name. The importance of this for our common life is that people know that whether they are present at noon or not, we as a parish are interceding daily for God's world and our particular part in it.

St. Gregory of Nyssa Church, San Francisco

From Sara Miles. I've been leading a sung morning prayer service every weekday for about 3 years. I put together the liturgy with another lay person, using the BCP but adapting it, looking for a service that would be:

- sung as much as possible;
- flexible, changing music with the seasons;
- workable with 2 or 3 people, or with 30
- half an hour.

St. Gregory's is a parish with about 180 members; three Eucharists on Sunday; highly participatory, mostly sung liturgies (no organ, all *a capella*) with some congregational dancing; a mix of ages; strong tradition of lay leadership and congregational participation in liturgy. Many of the scripts and liturgical materials are on our Web site, as is much of the music we use. Below you'll see songs referenced from our book, Music for Liturgy (MFL) that you can find there, or order in a print version.

Morning prayer right now has a regular core of three people (including one Lutheran who doesn't attend the church)—and several others who've had long regular stretches. We have many drop-in visitors (we are located near offices, and have many regular visitors) several times a week. It's very easy for visitors to pick up; informal and contemplative in tone.

We use a 15-week psalm cycle of about 3-4 psalms daily (from the ICEL translation) that our rector, Rick Fabian, put together; we move through those psalms and change the canticles and hymns in for Advent/Epiphany; Lent/Easter; Pentecost. We add the O Antiphons in Advent (7 weeks of them) and use Easter Troparia during Eastertide to open; after the Lord's Prayer and at the font.

We sit facing one another across a solea; at the end of the service we walk together outdoors to our baptismal font. I mark silences by striking a large Tibetan bell, then ending the silence with a handbell. No other instruments—I usually start out each song offering a pitch, and people follow it by ear. I improvise a chant tone for the opening versicle; use a very simple tone for the psalms (people improvise harmonies on the Hallel); use a Russian chant tone for the closing prayer. Whoever sings the Gospel for the day improvises a tune or chant.

The order is:

- Someone rings church bells; Officiant lights candle, sprinkles incense, everyone stands.
- Officiant: (chanting) Send out your light and your truth, that they may guide us and lead us to your holy hill and to your dwelling.
- All: (chanting) Open my lips O Lord, that my mouth might sing your praise. Glory to the Father, and to the Son, and to the Holy Spirit, as it was in the beginning, is now and shall be forever, AMEN.
- Officiant leads Trisagion, or "Come Heavenly Comforter" or the Sh'ma (all in MFL.)
- All sit; officiant leads psalm-singing.
- Officiant strikes bell; 4 minutes silence.
- Handbell; all stand; officiant leads chanted canticle from Hebrew Bible ("Arise, Shine; Pour Down You Heavens, etc.—all in MFL; during Advent often the Magnificat.)
- Someone chants Gospel reading appointed for the day.

- All sit; officiant asks people to share a word or a phrase from the Gospel or the songs. People speak their word or phrase aloud; officiant strikes bell; 5-6 minutes silence.
- Handbell; all stand; officiant leads Lords Prayer (usually plainchant version in MFL.) All offer their own prayers and petitions aloud in the center of the prayer; officiant concludes with prayer for the dead and collect from the BCP morning prayer selection.
- All walk out to the font, following the officiant with cross, singing a hymn ("Not here for High and Holy Things;" "Love Divine"....any hymn that's rhythmic and easy to walk to in time.)
- At font, officiant chants the prayer of St. John Chrystomson ("Almighty God, you have given us grace at this time with one accord...."). Concludes: Let us bless the Lord! All bless one another with water from the font and exchange the sign of peace.

Morning prayer has been a wonderful centering practice, and it gets the church open and used and sung in first thing each day.

Saint Paul's Church, Seattle

This is my own view of what was done at Saint Paul's when I served as a priest associate, saying the Eucharist during the week and helping to coordinate the Evening Prayer Teams. Saint Paul's had Evening Prayer from Tuesday through Sunday at 5:30. During the weeks I was writing this section of the book the weekly attendance varied from thirty eight to forty eight. That involved 30- 41 individuals, which was about a fourth of the Sunday Eucharist average attendance. Some weeks were lower, others higher. There are others who rarely attend Evening Prayer at the church who do it at home. The climate is contemplative with a good bit of silence. There is a careful rhythm that includes the times of silence; saying the psalm by alternating sides of the chapel by whole verses with a pause at the asterisk (see BCP 582 – 583); and following the tradition of bowing at the Gloria Patri.

Here's how St. Paul's has organized the offering of the Daily Office:

- A focus on Evening Prayer, rather than Morning Prayer, when more lay members are able to attend.
- The EP focus is also about maintaining the community's energy. Earlier attempts to also do Morning Prayer had spread out the numbers and created a sense of burden for some.
- Teams took responsibility for one night of the week. There were a total of twenty people involved in the teams; two were priests, the rest laity. The teams ranged in size from two to six. There were opportunities to sign up for a team every few months.
- To emphasize the communal nature of the Office the agreement is that the entire team will be present on its assigned evening. The team shares roles of officiant, lectors, and helping arrange the space. The person officiating wears a black cassock (with surplice for Evensong).
- The order is somewhat simplified: one psalm, the appointed reading from the Gospels, a reading from an Anglican writer on spiritual life, a couple of collects, a hymn, time for intercessions and thanksgiving. There is a minute or two of silence before beginning and after each reading.
- A customary, coaching, and order-of-service card are provided to facilitate quality and a degree of uniformity. The parish gathered information in 2005 that suggested that some people were not coming to EP because they had difficulty participating. That turned around after the creation of a customary, the card for everyone, the use of the Prayer Book rather than some alternative book, and coaching Officiants.

- The rector attends most nights and serves on one of the teams.
- A small chapel is used.
- On occasion some of those who have gathered for the Office go around the corner for a drink or dinner together.
- On Sunday evening a team conducts Evensong.
- Once a month the parish has "Last Fridays" – an Evensong followed by a social time with wine, cheese, and other beverages and snacks.
- The parish says Compline at the end of evening meetings and programs. In the core foundations course members are trained how to use the office at home.

How is it that so many people are part of Evening Prayer in this parish?

1. There was a readiness. Over time the parish developed a culture of deep and rich spirituality. Many people understood the place of the Office in the spiritual life.
2. The Office had been said as a public service for many years. Attendance had been limited to clergy and a few lay officiants. This was another aspect of the parish's readiness.
3. People were invited to offer Evening Prayer in teams. Fourteen initially agreed to serve. The positive response to the invitation was rooted in #1 and 2. People seemed to develop a commitment to their team and its ministry.
4. The rector participates on most evenings. People notice what leaders give time to

Trinity Church, Seattle

In 2007 a member asked if she might offer Evening Prayer every weeknight during Advent. The rector agreed. She asked several people if they would agree to officiate or read on a set night each week. She committed herself to be present every night to provide general oversight. Attendance was between 2 and 8.

As Lent approached in 2008 a members of the vestry raised the possibility of having Evening Prayer during that season. They had been struck by how the Advent experience worked. The woman who initiated the Office during Advent and another long-term parishioner were asked to coordinate.

The parish already had a tradition that included daily Morning Prayer. There is one layperson that sees it as part of his rule and vocation to offer it.

The establishing of daily Evening Prayer during Advent and Lent may take on a life and continue or not. It will be interesting to see what happens in Advent 2008 and beyond. The process of initiating the effort is an example of making a small intervention that grew.

Amy B. Hunter wrote a poem on the Office that she shared with CDI participants.

daily office

three days on the Cape
sharing the sacrament of coffee
doing morning prayer on a porch
from which I could see the ocean
the morning office spoken and laughed
as we read one another's lines
or added comments to the Scripture
until my husband said from the other room
"that was lovely
but I've never heard it done as stand-up before"
and you said
"we've been doing this a long time"

and now I've fallen among monks
five days retreat where I could see a river
were I to walk that far
we pray five times a day
and here no one laughs at the mis-said lines
when guest or brother misses a cue
reads loudly into the silence
then fades—embarrassed perhaps
smiling I hope
and no one begins the reading
"now here's a surprise—
the people did what was evil
in the sight of the Lord"
and no one slurps coffee
in the midst of confession

yet both catch me and hold
because these prayers are not woven by angels
but are built
           every day every office anew
by human voice and hunger
the work of a people
who have been doing this
a long time

~abh~
Transfiguration 2002
Emery House
        for Tom Barrington
        for the Brothers at Emery House
(Printed with permission Amy B. Hunter)

178

Shaping Your Spiritual Discipline

A Renewal Pathway

Our pathway is in response to, and in cooperation with, God's love and presence. God loves us and would bring us into the very life of God.

Spiritual discipline is directed toward full and real human growth. The end is a human being fully alive. It's not about becoming "religious", it's about becoming human. God isn't particularly interested in us becoming a religious person, but in us becoming a whole person. The way to that life, to our own selves, is by participation in God's life—which is to say by prayer and in community with others.

Another way of stating the objective is that we seek to live in Christ and for Christ to live in us. It's what has been called holy worldliness and habitual recollection. We seek maturity in Christ, to live as mature Christians in daily life.

Maturity is marked by an increased consistency of personality in which the person is brought into harmony with self, others and God. There are three aspects of this harmony I'd highlight – 1) Remembering who we are in Christ. We are baptized members of the Body of Christ; we are instruments of God's love, 2) Emotional stability and intelligence, and 3) Being the unique, odd person we are.

Maturity in Christ is not a state of being that once arrived at just continues on; but a state of being requiring the humility of living within the Body of Christ with a dependence on life in community. The Renewal – Apostolate Cycle continues at all stages of Christian maturity.

This maturity is the result of living within the Body of Christ; living in its rhythms, being fed by its sacraments and the organic life of the Body. Christian maturity is the product of persistence in living a disciplined response to God's love. Two patterns of thought that have confused many people in their journey are a negative stance toward creation and an excessive spiritualizing of the journey. The one leads to a faith that is largely about rules and judgment, the other to a faith that is disconnected from real life.

The pathway into maturity will be shaped as we take into account:
- The tradition of the church – what we as the People of God have learned about the process of sanctification
- Differences in personality – while all may need certain common foods to nurture us, we will also be fed by taking into account our own particular needs
- The culture and age we live in – Some ages or cultures carry us more than others; some require more self-consciousness, responsibility and discipline.

A Pattern

I believe that we live in an age in which the Christian life is not automatically reinforced by our culture. Some Christians have found that freeing, others see it as a loss.

It does place the responsibility for personal development on the individual. Episcopal spirituality would seem especially appropriate for such a time. Our emphasis on adult and responsible faith is a good match for the times.

A useful pattern of spiritual discipline might look something like this.

1. **Eucharist and Daily Office**
   This is the source of our frequent and regular participation in the rhythms of the Body of Christ – Eucharist once per week. Daily Office with psalm, reading and the prayers on 3 or 4 days of the week; some more limited participation in the Office on the other days.

2. **Disciplined ways of reflecting**
   We need ways of reflecting that allow us: a) to see our experience in relationship to who we are as baptized members of the Body; b) to learn what advances and what hinders our development; c) to draw learnings from our reflection on experience; and d) to act on those learnings with the behaviors of new life.

   Three specific disciplines that may help are:
   - Prayer that brings the stuff of our life into conscious relationship with Jesus Christ, in a manner that allows us to be reflective about our life, e.g., meditation, *lectio divina*
   - Spiritual guidance from other Christians. That can be accomplished in a variety of ways – a formal spiritual director relationship, working with another person in a peer spiritual friendship; it might be one-on-one or in a group; it could be a meeting of one hour or yearly retreat at a monastic house.
   - Prayer that develops our capacity for stillness and silence. If we are to become more reflective about our experience we need to increase our ability to listen to God, others, and ourselves.

3. **Other disciplines useful for you**
   It may be that nothing else is needed beyond the core pattern of Eucharist, Office and disciplined, reflective prayer.

   There are all sorts of devotions that might enhance and supplement the core.

Experiment

Experimentation is the way to find the pattern that best serves you at this time in your life, in you current state of maturity. The process can be described as – experiment, reflect on, and learn. A resource for increasing our ability to learn from experience is experiential training with groups such as Leadership Training Institute and National Training Labs.

For some of us it is a new idea that we are responsible for our own spiritual life; especially with the thought that we actually may need to change our behavior and values as part of that responsibility. On the journey into maturity we will find ourselves needing different things at different times --- at one point spiritual guidance that is more a form of direction and coaching, at another time guidance that is more suggestion and encouragement; there may be times of affective forms of prayer and times that are more meditative; and there are likely to be times of acceptance more than challenge and others of confrontation more than support.

Creating Your Spiritual Discipline Worksheet

Current Practices

The Anglican tradition assumes that adults are responsible for their own spiritual life; for shaping their own rule-of-life. This is grounded in the state of being that exists by having been baptized into the Body of Christ. We develop our rule by accepting responsibility and drawing on the resources and tradition of the wider church. So, we take into account the church's threefold rule of prayer and ways in which we may best receive spiritual guidance.

You are invited to make use of these two worksheets in reflecting on your spiritual discipline. This first worksheet is about the ways in which you currently are renewed.

Current Practices

How I am renewed emotionally & physically	
Participation in the Holy Eucharist	
Participation in the Daily Office	
Personal Devotions	
Study of Scripture, spiritual life, theology, etc.	
Being equipped for Christian action	
Other	

Creating Your Spiritual Discipline Worksheet

Practices to Explore and Try Out

This second worksheet is to help you in identifying revisions to your practice; ways in which you may want to experiment. Make notes in each area. If possible share what you are thinking with your spiritual director or others whose counsel you value.

Practices to Explore & Try Out

How I am renewed emotionally & physically	
Participation in the Holy Eucharist	
Participation in the Daily Office	
Personal Devotions	
Study of Scripture, spiritual life, theology, etc.	
Being equipped for Christian action	
Other	

© Robert A. Gallagher, 2001, 2005

182

Foundations Courses

A Foundations Course is an adult formation program. It's a resource for:

- People exploring faith and spiritual life
- People joining the parish and/or the Episcopal Church
- Existing members who have not engaged these issues in recent years
- Adults preparing for baptism, confirmation, reception, or reaffirmation
- New comers who want to connect to the parish and meet other people

The course is a tool in creating a "critical mass" of members who have some competence for living the life. So, it's very important that it be experiential and include skill training along with presentations and group discussion.

Most parishes can make good use of an adult foundations program. A Foundations Course is a substantial educational offering that grounds people in the thinking and practices of the Christian faith as lived in the Episcopal Church. It can serve multiple purposes. Use it in place of all "inquirers" classes or adult baptismal or confirmation instruction.

A foundations course is a resource for setting loose an energy in individuals and the parish that can stir new thinking and behavior and may help move some people into a more Apostolic expression of faith and practice. There needs to be enough substance to it that it has the potential of taking participants to a new place in their spiritual life. Some parishes have nine or ten sessions. Others have modules that extend over three years. Below is an example of each.

Foundations of Christian Spirituality and Life

Foundations is offered in modules of three or four sessions at a time. The usual practice is to offer a module each in the fall, winter, and spring. Sessions are a mix of presentation, discussion and experiential activities. Participants are usually asked to do some reading or experiment with some form of spiritual discipline or study in between sessions. There is often a small materials fee attached to a module. If the fee makes it difficult for someone to participate the parish could cover the cost.

Those preparing for baptism, confirmation, reception, or reaffirmation are usually expected to complete at least three of the modules before being presented.

The Modules
Below are examples of the kind of models a parish can offer. I have fleshed out some more than others.

Anglican Spirituality
This is a broad overview and introduction. Other modules will provide fuller work in some areas.
The Threefold Rule of Prayer: Eucharist, Daily Office, Personal Devotions. How these three forms of prayer relate to one another in the spiritual life. Experiment with, and reflect on, several methods during the program.
Spirituality in relationship to the whole of life: Ways of understanding the relationship; an exploration of how this works in your own life.

Episcopal Spirituality

The Episcopal Church has a particular culture of spirituality that shapes its worship, thinking and action. It is a way of being & doing that rises out of several core values and assumptions about our existence as people and Christians. Explore how it works in this parish and in your own life.

Personality & Spirituality

The relationship between our uniqueness and spiritual practices that best serve our particular personality.

Use Type theory: Make use of Type theory and the MBTI if available.
Relationship with the Threefold Rule of Prayer: Explore how personality type may relate this pattern of prayer. In theory how are different personalities nurtured by each element? How might we be stretched and grow in relationship to those we have more difficulty with?
Other ways of looking at spirituality: Explore other ways in which personality type and spiritual life have been discussed.
Experiment: Have people experiment with forms of prayer and spiritual practice in sessions and in between sessions.
Disciplined reflection on the experience: Have a specific process in which people reflect on the experience and then state what they have learned.

Shaping Your Spiritual Life

Assessing your spiritual life and discipline: Operate on the assumption that everyone has a spiritual discipline of some sort (from very mature to much less so). Use worksheets and peer interviews to assist reflection.
Options for growth: Look at various forms of spiritual discipline and ways of shaping your - spiritual life. Explore resources such as -- spiritual guidance, sacramental confession, rule of life, retreats, association with a religious order.
Create a rule of life: Participants each shape a rule of life, share it and receive feedback at a level appropriate to the group's ability.

Understanding & Using Scriptures

Praying with the Scriptures: *Lectio divina*; The Story of the People of God: An Overview of the Biblical Drama; how the church uses the scriptures in decision making and prayer; Modern scholarship; relationship of Scriptures to tradition, reason and experience.

The Christian Moral Vision

The formation of Christian character, relate to emotional intelligence and maturity; the views of various Christian communities on social issues.

Eucharistic Spirituality & Living

Rooting our life in the mystery of the Holy Eucharist. Ways of deepening our participation in the Mass.

Baptismal Living

Exploring the cycle of renewal & apostolate; of reflection & engagement. Discernment and decision making.

Engaging the gifts of "an inquiring and discerning heart, the courage to will and to persevere, a spirit to know and to love you, and the gift of joy and wonder in all your works."

Apostolate in Daily Life: being instruments of God's love in workplace, with family & friends, in civic life

Daily Prayer

Learning and experimenting with various forms of prayer and spiritual activity, e.g., intercession, praying with icons, *Lectio divina*; contemplation, centering, meditation, etc. Also, the Daily Office.

Benedictine Listening: Participation & Decision Making in Community

- Skill training in listening, communication and negotiation methods – paraphrase and itemized response, active listening, feedback, offering proposals, the parish as a school of love (Aelred's thinking about the role of the community)
- Each session includes a brief presentation on some aspect of Benedictine thought related to the topic – listening & obedience, grumbling & consultative processes
- Group methods for communication, listening,
- The parish as a learning community ways in which the parish can be helped to learn from its experience.

Christian Thinking

- The relationship between Christian sources of authority and our decision making. The relationship of Scripture, Tradition and Reason with one another and with our life experience.
- The development of Christian thinking. Offer (briefly) several ways of understanding the development of doctrine and moral vision in the church's life. Have a way for participants to explore the development of their own thinking about doctrine and moral living.
- Resources: *A Church that Can and Cannot Change: The Development of Catholic Moral Teaching*, John T. Noonan, Jr., University of Notre Dame Press, 2005; *The Christian Tradition: A History of the Development of Doctrine,* Jaroslav Pelikan, University of Chicago.
- Differences and similarities in Christian communions. Look at the views of several denominations on the same moral or doctrinal issue, e.g., abortion, the rights of labor, the Eucharist, etc. Also, have participants examine what they understand to be the differences/similarities between the Episcopal Church and any other denomination they have been part of or considered joining.
- Prayer and thinking. Practice an approach to prayer that is strongly rooted in thinking

Parish Tradition of Spirituality

An exploration of the parish's roots in a traditional spirituality within the Episcopal Church, e.g., Prayer Book Catholic, Anglo-Catholic, Evangelical, Liberal/Broad, etc. Here's a sample outline for the Anglo-Catholic tradition.

Anglo-Catholic

- A connecting exercise each evening based on participants researching material on the web. One evening on Anglo-Catholic historical figures, another on Anglo-Catholic parishes, one on religious orders and Christian communities. Each would be used at the very beginning of a session to help participants get connected with one another, build a sense of community and begin to be present to the group and the work
- Background readings, most to be completed by the last session when the readings are the center of the group's work.
- Session 1 – The place and role of Anglo-Catholicism in the church. Exploring ways of understanding the various tendencies in the church? A timeline and a look at sub groups within Anglo-Catholicism.
- Session 2 – Practices during Mass. An experiential segment in which people physically engage the "dance" of the liturgy, crossing themselves, genuflecting and bows. A second segment on the Anglo-Catholic inner city experience.
- Session 3 – This and other Anglo-Catholic parishes. A session based on some participants having interviewed leaders in other Anglo-Catholic parishes that are somewhat like our own (to give us the most potential for learning.
- Session 4 – This is based on readings done by the participants.

Outline of an Adult Foundations Course in Faith & Practice

The Objective: Enfolding people into Christian Faith & Practice as lived in the Episcopal Church

A few suggestions:
1. Use a mix of experiential, group discussion, and presentation
2. Present the course at least once a year. More often in a large parish.
3. Allow people to do part of it one year and complete it the next
4. Acknowledge those who complete the whole course
5. See it as part of building the *Shape of the Parish*

Session 1:

The Christian Life
Your relationship with God & the Church

The Story of the People of God
The People of Israel

Session 2:

The Christian Life
The development of Christian character

The Story of the People of God
Jesus Christ: His Life & Work

Session 3:

The Christian Life
Sharing the priesthood of Christ: Baptismal Life

The Story of the People of God
The Holy Catholic Church: the nature of the church

Session 4:

The Christian Life
The Christian Moral Vision

The Story of the People of God
The Church" Renewal & Reform

Session 5:

Spiritual Life & Development
The Threefold Rule of Prayer: The Eucharist

The Story of the People of God
The Mission of the Church: Holy Unity

Session 6:

Spiritual Life & Development
The Threefold Rule of Prayer: Personal Devotions & Daily Office

The Story of the People of God
The Anglican Communion & the Episcopal Church

Session 7:

Spiritual Life & Development
Sacrament of Reconciliation; Rule of Life

The Bible
How the Bible came to be; how to use and understand the Bible

Session 8:

Christian Action
Stewardship, Evangelization; Service

Christian Believing
Sources of authority; God & Humanity

Session 9:

Christian Action
Responsibility & Freedom: Choice & Faith

Christian Believing
Evil, sin and forgiveness; hope

© Robert A. Gallagher, 1976, 1983

Offering Spiritual Guidance in the Parish

Most parishes have the capacity to offer some form of spiritual guidance for members. Here's one model for doing that. Most priests, and some laity, are able to design and conduct at least the first four programs. Those doing so will need to have some group process awareness and skills for designing participatory educational events. Obviously those leading such events need to have significant experience in living with a Rule of Life.

Developing a Spiritual Discipline (For the First Time)

The group will go through a process of looking at the elements of current spiritual life, considering traditional elements, and drafting a Rule of Life to experiment with. This is for those who have never really had a formal Rule of Life or those who have had some false starts. This is a one session, two-hour program that begins with an Office or Mass on the parish schedule. Session to last around two hours including the worship. Offered once/year or as needed.

Revising your Spiritual Discipline (for Those with a Working Rule of Life)

The group will go through a process of reflecting on our existing spiritual disciplines, exploring possible revisions, and drafting a revised Rule to experiment with. This is for those who have an effective Rule of Life and would like to explore possible changes. This is a one session, 2 – 2 ½ hour program that begins with an Office or Eucharist on the parish schedule. Offered once/year or as needed.

Readings in Spiritual Life and Direction

A book discussion group. Sometimes used as an introduction to the idea of spiritual guidance; others times as a more advanced exploration.

Mutual Spiritual Guidance (an Intermediate Program)

For people with a fairly effective, settled spiritual disciple (Rule of Life). This is done in small groups of five. The groups are guided through a process that allows the participants to reflect on various issues in our spiritual life. If there is more than one group – we stay with the same people through all the sessions. This is an opportunity explore your spiritual life with others. On occasion spiritual friendships may emerge for some in the group that continue on beyond the program. This program has four sessions of 2 – 2 ½ hours each. It is offered as a module of the Adult Foundations Program (and may be offered a bit more frequently that other Foundations modules).

Mutual Spiritual Guidance (an Advanced Program)

For people with effective, settled spiritual disciples (Rule of Life). Participation is limited to four people plus the leader. Those participating need to already have a good bit of spiritual maturity. Admission to the group is based on your self-assessment (an assessment from will be provided) and that of the group leader. This is an opportunity to do spiritual guidance in a truly mutual manner. The group meets for sessions of 3 – 3 ½ hours and includes a meal together. As part of its life the group will decide to make use of an Office or Eucharist on the parish schedule, or say an office on its own, or make use of a more contemplative form of prayer. The leader will function more as a facilitator than as a spiritual director. On occasion spiritual friendships may emerge for some in the group that continue on beyond the program. Another possibility is that a small group might decide to continue meeting a few times each year or go on several days of retreat together.

Spiritual Friendships

An informal relationship between two Christians who agree to meet on a regular basis to discuss what is happening in each person's relationship with God, others and self. It is usually best to agree in advance on a specific number of times to meet. You can extend that agreement if both parties wish. The parish plays no formal role in this.

Individual Spiritual Direction

For people who are interested in one-on-one spiritual direction. May obtain expertise outside the parish. Will typically involve the payment of a fee.

Occasional Events

Programs that fit a season or special opportunity.

Example - Exploring your Lenten Discipline – An opportunity to share with a few others what you are considering as your way of entering into this time of mystery and the inner life. Begin with an Office or Mass on the parish schedule.

The Entry Process of Newcomers (and the Parish's Orientation Process)

Orienting people to the parish includes multiple elements: There's getting to know other people; there's engaging the best of the Episcopal Church's and parish's culture; there's offering pathways for involvement in the parish's life for those who are ready; and there's making a connection in such a manner that it has within it the possibility of new life.

Ideally we want to have an orientation process that spans the first six to eight months of a person's entry. For many newcomers the first month is a time of hesitation and testing. Many will not attend any organized newcomer event yet. Others will jump right into anything offered.

Possibly the most significant thing parish leaders can understand about the orientation process is that newcomers have their own energy around entry. There are two expressions of that. First, there is a self-generating motivation; the person will enter because they have their own reasons to do so. Second, the energy of people differs. Extroverts and introverts will enter in different ways. Some need to connect with other people; others with an intellectual understanding of why it makes sense to be part of any church and this parish in particular.

The parallel understanding for leaders to grasp is that the parish has its own energy. It assimilates people at a certain speed. It is more introverted or more extroverted; it is more about relationships among members or more about relationship with the ideas of the faith tradition. The parish needs to offer an orientation process that builds on its strengths while attending to its blindside in some manner. What that means is that the parish is likely to most effectively attract and incorporate new members who fit the existing culture while offering space for those who may find themselves challenged by the parish's ways of doing and being.

What I'm offering below can be used as a starting place for parish leaders in designing an orienting process that is appropriate to the parish's size and energy. You want to design something that is manageable and sustainable.

First Visits

Most newcomers are likely to arrive for a Sunday Eucharist. Parishes with strong mid-week schedules of the Daily Office or the Eucharist find that those events become a significant entry point for people; especially people who may be more introverted or may be going through a difficult emotional time.

The key is for someone to make connection with the visitor. Find out a bit about them; ask for contact information, and suggest that they come to coffee hour, or if it is during the week invite them to join you for coffee right then.

Coffee with the Rector

The rector needs to make contact within a week after the visitor's appearance in the parish. That can be a brief e-mail, phone call, or note. Beyond that the rector needs find a way to sit down with the person over coffee (or tea or beer). With some visitors that will happen easily; others may not be ready to do it for three months. For many people this will seem most comfortable at a local diner or coffee shop; others may need a more private space.

This isn't something to delegate to a lay leader or assisting priest. Having the rector take the time to be with the newcomer is deeply appreciated by most and may help establish an early connection that may serve the person's deeper incorporation process. This time together is appropriately social. The rector needs to ask about the person's life and work, about their experience with the church, show interest and ask follow up questions. That usually needs to be most of the conversation. The rector may also want to offer some information about her life (e.g., "Let me tell you a few things about me."). You don't want the rector to be the mystery person.

This encounter has the potential to bring the person into parish's life in a manner that gets them relating to the church around new life in Christ and the task of shaping a Renewal – Apostolate Cycle that is effective for them. So, bring up something that is directly related to that cycle. Listen for an opening in what the person is saying about himself or herself. If the person talks about how they are touched by liturgy, expresses difficulties they have had with church teachings, or shares something about the pleasures or pain of work or family life – invite them to say more if they seem ready. Say something in response that offers connection (e.g., "It sounds as though you have struggled with your prayer life, maybe that's something you could address in your time at Saint Mary's" or "I'm glad you are so drawn to worship; it's a way in which God shares life with us."). If they don't touch on anything that provides an opening create your own with a question – "How has participation in other parishes renewed you? Have you found yourself more renewed by worship, learning or some form of service?"

Clergy who avoid this kind of work with excuses about being too busy, or too introverted, or not being socially skilled enough, need to take the matter up with a spiritual director and/or do a few workshops in human interaction skills or emotional intelligence. As clergy we need to do "the job" and watch out for the temptation to excessively indulge ourselves; otherwise known as sloth. For some clergy this aspect of ministry is an opportunity to grow, to become more disciplined and open.

Events

1. A social evening at the rector's home.

This is, in a sense, an orienting of people to the rector as a person and to the other newcomers. Let most of it be purely social. About 40 minutes into the evening gather people. Have them go in a circle and introduce themselves. You might ask "what drew you to the parish?" Then you might say a few words about one topic. You could offer a handout on Episcopal Spirituality and briefly mention one or two elements that the parish is especially noted for or that people mentioned in some fashion when they went around the circle. Then let people return to their own conversations.

2. An evening primarily orienting people to the parish and the Episcopal Church.

This could be held at the rector's home or at the parish. Look at the "Newcomers Gathering" below for a possible design of the evening.

3. A tour of the church.

This might be done spontaneously from time to time or scheduled every five months. It needs to be a tour that connects people to the spirituality of the place. Stand around the altar, the font and the lectern. Talk about what happens at each, how they are three of the four primary focal points of the liturgical space (the forth being the People of God, the Eucharistic community). Then stand near a few other sites. For example, at Saint John's in the Village, NYC, there's a beautiful set of Stations of the Cross done in an icon style. They are part of what makes it a special space. Use quotations and poetry. Pray at a few points. At all costs avoid complaining about building problems or talking in terms of who gave what as a memorial.

Newcomers Gathering

Objectives

Creating connection between the newcomer and:
- The rector
- A few other people who might establish a parish based friendship -- other new people, possibly someone who is likely to connect with these particular people.
- The parish and the Episcopal Church -- as institutions and communities

Creating a pathway toward membership
- Providing information that would allow the new person to make a decision to join the parish (or establish a "Friends of St. _____ " relationship)
- Offers some specific next step, e.g., the next Foundations Course offering

Schedule
1. Newcomers gathering held every quarter
2. On an evening or Saturday morning with a defined beginning and ending time
3. Allow 2 ½ hours

Rationale: We need a sense of stability about offering the event. Done even if there is only one new person. The newcomers need to know how much time it will take and have some idea of what will happen. We don't want them seeing it as primarily a social event. There needs to be enough time to accomplish the objectives.

Participating from the Parish
Just a few people (no more than 3 or 4 from the parish even when it is a large group, fewer when less newcomers)
- The rector/vicar
- Another member or two who's willing to assist with the logistics and is good and connecting with people. If there are other clergy in the parish rotate them; one at each event.
- Someone involved in leading the upcoming Foundations Course (person can say a few words about the program; pass out information and a way to register).

Rationale: The room needs to feel like the newcomers are the center of things. They need to be the majority of those present. Those present from the parish need to be those most directly related to the objectives. It is fine for this to have a social dimension but it needs to serve parish growth objectives. If it ends up primarily social then it can only work if the parishioners present are very much like the newcomers. While as a person continues to participate in the life of the parish we would hope they would end up connected to a wide range of people; in the first few months we need to pay attention to inclusion 101 – that means focusing on what they might gain from joining the parish and meeting people they are easily comfortable with.

Format (an example)

Activity	Time

1. Getting connected to one another
    ▪ Welcome and overview of the session
    ▪ A connecting exercise
	15 – 20 min

2. Pass out cards with "questions people often ask about the parish and the Episcopal Church" – people can check off up to three they have interest in and/or write down questions of their own	45 min
3. Food and social time (informal time)	40 min
4. Gather as a whole group – pass out packets, say something about becoming a member/friend of; etc.	15 min
5. Close with Compline or noon day prayers. Use cards. Have a hymn on the card (use if there are enough people)	10 min.

Materials   A newcomers packet that is only given out at this gathering (there might be something shorter provided when the person first appears) Copyright Robert A. Gallagher, 2003, 2006

ASSESSMENT OF PARISH LIFE AND MINISTRY
The Christian Life Model

Christ comes to us and we seek Christ in worship, doctrine and action. Each is a pathway into a transformation of life, our growth into our own uniqueness, and our union with the heart, mind and work of Christ

1. *Overall satisfaction* with Parish Life and Ministry

I am very dissatisfied	1	2	3	4	5	6	I am very satisfied

2. *Worship* - How well we worship as a community in Sunday's primary Eucharist and other public worship. In liturgy clergy, servers and lectors function with dignity, grace and competence. There is participation as a congregation rather than as an audience requiring prompting. There is adequate teaching, coaching, and resources to assist the congregation develop liturgical competence and fully participate. Guidance and resources are available for members to grow in their prayer life.
A use of the Holy Eucharist and Daily Office that is appropriate to the parish's context and capacity.

    a. *Overall satisfaction*

I am very dissatisfied	1	2	3	4	5	6	I am very satisfied

    b. *Weaknesses*

    c. *Strengths*

3. *Doctrine* - The parish's awareness of, and ability to use, the sources of authority in the Christian Life – Scripture, Tradition and Reason. Competence in relating those sources of authority to decision-making. Allowing them to influence and shape us on a regular and frequent basis. Being open to the views of people who think and feel differently from ourselves.

    a. *Overall satisfaction*

I am very dissatisfied	1	2	3	4	5	6	I am very satisfied

    b. *Weaknesses*

    c. *Strengths*

4. *Action* – Parish corporate action of service, evangelization, stewardship that is congruent with the parish's ethos, gifts and resources. Members' awareness of their apostolate in family and friendships, in the workplace, civic life, and church. Parish's dealing with the tension between the parish's corporate ministries and the individual's apostolate in daily life.

    a.   *Overall satisfaction*

I am very dissatisfied	1	2	3	4	5	6	I am very satisfied

    b. *Weaknesses*

    c. *Strengths*

5. *Oversight* - Competence and commitment of lay and clergy leaders for leadership and management; building community; and deepening the congregation's spiritual life. Leaders serving, guiding, leading and managing the parish into an appropriate and full living of the Christian Life: bringing and preserving a proper order/shape in the parish's life; methods for reflecting, discerning and planning in parish life; lay-clergy relationships; sense of identity and direction.

    a.   *Overall satisfaction*

I am very dissatisfied	1	2	3	4	5	6	I am very satisfied

    b. *Weaknesses*

    c. *Strengths*

6.   *Other Comments*

CLERGY ASSESSMENT

The purpose of a clergy assessment is to provide the priest with information that he or she can use to improve his or her functioning. For that to happen it's important that the priest take the lead in shaping the feedback process.

A. Possible Steps
1. For use after an overall parish assessment based on the same model.
2. Members of vestry complete the assessment form. The priest fills out the form as a self-assessment.
3. All forms are returned to the Rector or Vicar for review and reflection. If the priest desires it the reflection could be done with the Wardens or a few other trusted leaders.
4. Within a week or two after the vestry's filling out the assessment the rector offers a response to the Vestry, i.e., "You seem pleased with…" "Some concern was expressed about…" "I see myself giving special attention to…"
   Or "I've learned …" "I'm challenged by …" "My next steps are …"

B.   Please write comments in each of the following areas

	Like about your ministry in this parish	Concerns I have	Things I wish you would consider doing differently
Worship			
Doctrine			
Action			
Oversight			

C. Other Comments

Copyright Robert A. Gallagher, 1994, 2007

Categories are based on a framework in Robert A. Gallagher's, *Fill All Things: The Dynamics of Spirituality in the Parish Church*, Ascension Press, 2007, and in *Power from on High*, 1982

Parish Oversight Assessment

Using the Form

This form is a *tool to stimulate discussion* about parish oversight and to help identify areas in which objectives might be set for enabling the parish in more faithful and effective oversight. A rector and vestry or a rector and the wardens might use it in a exploration of mutual ministry. It should only be used in situations where those involved respect and have some trust in one another. It is an inappropriate tool if the parish is in conflict or if there are several vestry members who are angry with the rector.

A professional consultant might be asked to facilitate the process.

Five steps are recommended:
1. All participants fill out the form.
2. The ratings are collected on newsprint or a white board for the group to see.
3. Discuss the responses in small groups.
4. If desired, each small group may make a brief report.
5. If desired, a sub-group that includes the Rector may be appointed to draft objectives based on the conversation. These would be submitted to the Rector and Vestry for follow-up work.

A. Overall satisfaction with parish oversight - The competence and commitment of clergy and lay leaders for leadership and management; community building and deepening the congregation's spiritual life.

I am very dissatisfied	1	2	3	4	5	6	I am very satisfied

B. Spirituality -Shaping a healthy corporate spirituality; enabling a pattern and climate that focuses the parish on Christ; that encourages people to discover the claim Christ has on them; that helps people to trust and rest in God; that calls the parish to contemplation, surrender and transcendence. Knowing ways to understand and guide the parish's spiritual life. A strong parish prayer life.

1. Rector/Vicar: comfort with, skills and knowledge for parish spiritual direction

I am very dissatisfied	1	2	3	4	5	6	I am very satisfied

Weaknesses   Strengths

2. Lay leaders: comfort with, skills and knowledge for parish spiritual direction

I am very dissatisfied	1	2	3	4	5	6	I am very satisfied

Weaknesses   Strengths

C. Community - Enabling an awareness that the parish is a local expression of the one, holy, catholic and apostolic Church; that it is the Body of Christ; that it has a mission given by God. Focusing the parish and each group in the parish on the mission of the Church (restoring all to unity) and the parish's primary task (facilitating a cycle of renewal in baptismal identity & purpose and an apostolate in family, work, and civic life). Enabling a way of parish life in which people may be transformed more and more into the likeness of Christ. Being a community in which there is both acceptance and challenge. Being a caring community - bearing each other's burdens and celebrating each other's joys. Clearly presenting the Church's expectations and standards regarding membership, sacraments, and the duties of Christians in a manner appropriate to the parish context. Having opportunities for a common social life.

1. Rector/Vicar: comfort with, skills and knowledge for enabling the parish as a transforming community

I am very dissatisfied	1	2	3	4	5	6	I am very satisfied

Weaknesses   Strengths

2. Lay leaders: comfort with, skills and knowledge for enabling the parish as a transforming community

I am very dissatisfied	1	2	3	4	5	6	I am very satisfied

Weaknesses   Strengths

D. Leadership - Use of the knowledge and methods of management and organization development. Has a clear direction and the skills for guiding the parish in that direction - a yearly assessment and exploration of parish life and ministry. Development of an informed, self-disciplined, faithful lay leadership. Clear decision-making and discernment processes. Effective financial, property, office management. Clear and appropriate use of authority. Conforms to the standards of the Church in regard to business methods.

1. Rector/Vicar: comfort with, skills and knowledge for leadership management and administration of the faith community and organizational life

I am very dissatisfied	1	2	3	4	5	6	I am very satisfied

    Weaknesses   Strengths

2. Lay leaders: comfort with, skills and knowledge for leadership management and administration of the faith community and organizational life

I am very dissatisfied	1	2	3	4	5	6	I am very satisfied

    Weaknesses   Strengths

Categories are based on a framework in Robert A. Gallagher's, *Fill All Things: The Dynamics of Spirituality in the Parish Church*, Ascension Press, 2007, and in *Power from on High*, 1982

The Church: Analogies and Images

IMAGE	MISSION/ PURPOSE	ROLE OF PRIEST	EVANGELIZATION	STEWARDSHIP	WHAT HOLDS IT TOGETHER?
CLUB					
FAMILY					
CORPORATION					
SOCIAL CHANGE MOVEMENT					
SOCIAL WELFARE AGENCY					
MENTAL HEALTH CENTER					
PEOPLE OF GOD					
BODY OF CHRIST					

People naturally make the analogy between the Church and other groups with which they are familiar: clubs, corporations, families and so on. References to "organized religion" or "institutionalized religion" reveal the assumption that the Church is just one more form of human organization. While the process of making analogies with the club, corporation, etc., is inevitable, it also creates a problem. "People come to the conclusion that the Church is a "society created by human enterprise and designed to serve particular human ends," that it is created by the "agreement of a number of individual persons who presumably define the terms of their association and its goals." ... "Church means, not corporation and not club, but a collection of people who have been called out together by a voice or a word or a summons which comes to them from outside." (Richard Norris, *Understanding the Faith of the Church*, Seabury Press, NY, 1979)

Possible Process to Use
1. Pass out the above chart as a handout. You may also want to have it on a newsprint pad in front of the group.
2. Present the idea of how images and analogies influence our thinking about the church. Walk through one of the first few and one of the last two images.
3. Have small groups explore one of two images each.
4. Report back to the whole group.

If the group seems to have the willingness and capacity to go deeper
Explore which of the images has the biggest impact on this parish.

Distorting tendencies

There are several ways in which the parish can cut across (i.e., sabotage, distort, block, become a barrier to) people's Renewal-Apostolate Cycle? There is not any way for a parish to avoid having some of these tendencies present in its life. They are part of the larger social and religious culture. We absorb them. Our awareness of those that are most strongly present in our own parish allows us to better understand parish dynamics and take constructive action.

Assess your own inclination and your parish's – 3 is high, I is low

Distorting tendency	**My parish**	**Self** – I have some inclination towards it
1. The parish gives the impression, that the world doesn't matter. There may be a protective or sentimental piety involved. It's as though we are stuck on the renewal side of the cycle.		
2. The parish has a fearful spirit. The fears generated by daily life have an emotional upper hand. The irrational reactivity of the world has a grip on people, e.g., feeling safe by getting SUV's that are big but role over, intincting at communion to avoid illness when we know that to be the most dangerous practice, etc. The parish may facilitate a form of unproductive dependency.		
3. The parish seems to imply that our task is to force the society to conform to "Christian" views. The language of the parish may have an over-and-against quality; sermons and newsletter articles attack the "secular" culture and there is an angry undercurrent.		
4. The parish functions as a place to reinforce and support already established and safe religious views. There is little challenge to the culture or conventional religious views.		
5. The parish operates as a reinforcer of secularism; gives the impression that this world is all there is, that there is really no need for renewal beyond oneself. The focus is on achievement in this life, here and now. It may take on an activist stance for many good works of service and justice. It may have a stance that is wrapped around a desire for financial success or social status.		
6. The parish becomes just another demand upon people for their energy, money and time. Parish life seems hectic and overly busy. There is pressure on people to take part in parish activities; e.g., to serve on the vestry, attend the pot luck dinner. There may be a weak sense of the centrality of participation in the Sunday Eucharist, i.e., a productive message might be "It is okay to come to the 7:30 Eucharist, participate in the daily prayer of the church, give financially according to your means, participate in an occasional parish town meeting; and to never serve on a vestry, teach church school, come to social events, or be on a committee.		
7. The parish has a climate that helps people avoid their deeper and broader self.		
8. The parish doesn't challenge people's being captured by the demands and expectations of workplace, family and civic life. It may even encourage them, e.g., a workaholic behavior, or an idolizing of the family, or a restless activism about social justice.		

9. Gives the impression that the apostolate in the parish is of more value than the apostolate in the world, e.g., on the parish web site there is a lot of mention of activities and people that serve the parish's life and there is little or no mention of the apostolate in the daily life of the laity at work, in civic activities, and with family and friends. This may reflect a condition in which people don't fully enter into the renewal end of the cycle.

Three Interview Process

This process has been used by hundreds of participants in the Church Development Institute as part of their work on interviewing skills and deepening the spiritual life of the parish.

While CDI requires participants to interview three parishioners the process has also been used as a major intervention in parishes as away of:

1. Helping leaders better understand the congregation
2. Strengthen the relationship of spiritual guidance and support among members
3. Getting the spiritual life onto the parish's agenda and into the minds of many members
4. Providing a starting point for further work in assisting people establish a rule of life, or spiritual discipline

Interviews are not only a data gathering process but are also system interventions. They are not neutral; they affect the people being interviewed and those doing the interviewing. Interviewers need to have an adequate degree of emotional maturity to be able to listen without judgment, or turning the interview into an opportunity to teach, or making it about themselves.

The same basic tool may be used as a congregational development intervention, in an expanded process, involving a significant potion of a congregation's members. Such a process might open up issues regarding a congregation's living of the renewal-apostolate cycle -- helping a community both come to appreciate what is done well and to improve.

The Process for Use in a Learning Setting

1. Interview three members of the congregation -- two who are regular and frequent participants in the Eucharist and one who is regular but not frequent. Your task is to listen deeply, with an appreciative ear, and record their responses to the questions. Please do not allow yourself to take on a teaching or explaining role in relation to the issues that emerge. If that seems called for ask if the person would like to do that in a second session. If a person is confused by a question or doesn't like the question, move on. While you want to complete the interview in a timely manner, you may also want to enter into the process with follow up questions. Please avoid any judgment on what the person is sharing.

2. A good preparation for interviewing is to have someone else interview you asking the same questions or to fill out the sheet on yourself.

Interview Questions

1. What are the major sources of pressures, demands and expectations in your life? How do you see them as helpful or stressful?

2. How do you work at "balancing" these expectations, demands and pressures?

3. How do you renew yourself emotionally and physically?

4. How do you renew yourself spiritually?

5. How does your practice of Christian faith and/or the congregation's life help or hinder each of the areas noted above?

      a. Expectations/demands/pressures

      b. Emotional/physical renewal

      c. Spiritual renewal

6. How does your practice of Christian faith and/or the congregation's life relate to your work, family and civic life?

© Robert A. Gallagher, 1996

CONGREGATIONAL DEVELOPMENT STRATEGY: SOME HINTS

The congregational development practitioner may be a parish leader, a consultant, a diocesan staff person or a parishioner who has some change agent awareness and skill. The task is the same -- the shaping of a healthier, more faithful parish. Here are a few hints about that task.

1. Nurture a "common language" of skills, knowledge, attitudes and values for congregational development in the parish.
This includes skills, knowledge, attitudes and values related to:

a. Developing the community of faith with its unique identity, purpose and dynamics. Living the Christian life as a baptismal and Eucharistic community in the Anglican tradition. Shaping a congregational spirituality that facilitates a healthy community life and healthy people.
b. Developing the congregation as an organization that has an ability to manage its life, solve problems, learn from experience, adapt to new conditions, and attend to its long-term development and renewal.
c. The "common language" of a system, in a pluralistic society and a global economy, is less and less a national language (e.g., English) and more about common values, skills, etc. This glue, that holds a system together, will change as the environment of the system changes. The glue needs to help the system define itself at its best.

2. Develop a critical mass of people that share that "common language".
This will take the shape of a series of circles, one within the other. Those at the center will share more of the "common language" of skills, knowledge, attitudes and values. They will in effect carry it on behalf of the whole parish. There will be a second ring of people with less, yet some of the "common language"; possibly glad to be part of the venture but not as fully invested. A third ring may consist of those who are in practical terms "just going along" with the dominate culture of the parish.

3. Create a Sunday morning experience that is focused on the gathering of the Eucharistic community.
An event that is centering and renewing for people rather than simply another experience of demands and pressures for their time, money, and energy. A community that is competent for Eucharistic worship, spirituality and living.

4. The presiding priest of the community needs to establish habits and skills that help her/him be a centered and healthy presence as leader of the community in its life and worship.
This means being part of the leadership of those who share the "common language". It also means accepting oneself as a person on a journey to wholeness and holiness. This might include:

a. Becoming a person of stability, conversion of life and obedience -- giving oneself to a spiritual discipline (a rule of life), learning to listen, being collegial and collaborative, learning how to be "grounded" when presiding in the liturgy and in the community's life, committing to one's own maturity, etc.
b. Rejecting the stances of over functioning/under functioning, enmeshment/disengagement, cynic, victim or bystander.

c. Giving oneself to a stance of engaged detachment.
- Learning to define and present their own vision and values
- Being in touch with the needs and views of the congregation
- Being as collaborative as the commitment and competence of members allows
- Learning to cope with one's own tendency toward excessive control/passivity,
- Knowing how to cope with dependent personalities

d. Learning the skills and knowledge for congregational development leadership

5. Nurture and shape the congregation's life and ministry

a. Have a vision of what a more faithful, healthier congregation looks like.

b. Attend to the many small "habits" (practices, disciplines, skilled behaviors, etc.) that make up the culture of a congregation. Teach, train, coach.

c. Start in places that are both strategic and "easy", e.g., work with groups of mostly people of apostolic faith in mutual spiritual guidance and exploring their vocation in the family, workplace and civic life; begin and maintain an adult foundations course; train the congregation for participation in the Eucharist; begin using the Daily Office during the week, etc.

6. Think about the development of the congregation in terms of at least three to five years

a. It will take three to five years to significantly improve the community and organizational life of the congregation so it is "owned" and sustainable. Watch out for attempts at a quick fix.

b. Seven or more if it is in serious decline.

7. Think of your work as moving from one congregational development project to another toward a vision

8. Other Hints -- start where the system is, not where you wish it were; strive for maximum ownership by key people and the overall system (those in the system with power are the ones who will make any changes, those in the system with health will make the change worthy of the effort); use an external consultant to give additional competence to the effort and to create an additional "demand system" for improvement; let the data speak; work with promising areas, begin in the places of health, strength and success; leaders need to resource themselves as needed with training, spiritual guidance, a learning-application team to provide peer support, therapy; influence your larger institutional context, e.g., diocese, toward an increased competence and commitment in congregational development.